# The Bedside
# Guardian 2008

# The Bedside Guardian 2008

EDITED BY MARTIN KETTLE

**guardianbooks**

First published in 2008 by
Guardian Books, 119 Farringdon Road, London EC1R 3ER
www.guardianbooks.co.uk

Copyright © Guardian News and Media Ltd 2008

Martin Kettle has asserted his right under the Copyright,
Designs and Patents Act 1988 to be identified as the editor of this work

2 4 6 8 10 9 7 5 3 1

A CIP catalogue record for this book is available from the British Library

ISBN 978-0-85265-111-7

Designed by Two Associates
Typeset by seagulls.net

Printed and bound in Great Britain by TJ International, Padstow, Cornwall

#### ACKNOWLEDGMENTS

Thanks to Alan Rusbridger, the *Guardian* editor, for choosing me to edit this year's
collection. Thanks also to Lisa Darnell, publisher of Guardian Books, who saw me
through the various stages of what, because of her, was never an ordeal. Helen Brooks,
Lisa's managing editor, was unfailingly helpful at the business end of the production
process. Ben Clissitt gave me many helpful tips from his editorship in 2007 as well as
thoughts for this year's. Several other colleagues at the *Guardian*, past and present, also
helped with ideas and suggestions and with answers to questions: among these were
Polly Curtis, Suzanne Goldenberg, Luke Harding, Victor Keegan, Ewen MacAskill, David
McKie and Robert White. Both Julian Glover and Georgina Henry were very
understanding when I sometimes pleaded *Bedside* obligations when they asked me to
write for their sections of the paper and website. Richard Nelsson and the *Guardian*
research department patiently answered many requests for help. Roger Tooth, the
*Guardian* picture editor, deserves special gratitude for selecting the pictures — which
are all by *Guardian* staff photographers. Finally, thank you to Cherie Blair, who
characteristically belied what is too often written about her by instantly
agreeing to write a foreword without a fee.

# Contents

CHERIE BLAIR Foreword                                                    1

MARTIN KETTLE Introduction                                               5


AUTUMN

POLLY TOYNBEE Whatever that strange spasm of public                     13
    anguish was 10 years ago, it ended here

PATRICK BARKHAM 205mph but still three minutes late                     16

JESS CARTNER-MORLEY Lauren still a class act, 40 years on               19

LAWRENCE DONEGAN Le Saux's honesty can help bring pride                 22
    to English game

MICHAEL WHITE Fuchsia is the colour, politics is the game              24

MICHAEL HANN In praise of the humble pork pie                           27

TIMOTHY GARTON ASH Only Burma's neighbours can stop its                 28
    dictators beating up the Buddha

ANDREW CLEMENTS Review: *Carmen*                                        32

PATRICK WINTOUR An election? Bring in on now                            34

ALEXIS PETRIDIS A triumph of wit, romance and neurosis                  37

ED PILKINGTON Al Gore wins Nobel peace prize. And this                  39
    time, no one can take it away from him

SIMON HOGGART End of the Ming dynasty                                   42

DECLAN WALSH Before the tragedy, an emotional                           44
    homecoming

JULIAN GLOVER Riven by class and no social mobility –                   46
    Britain in 2007

SIMON HOGGART Light on dogma, generous with laughs                     48

TONY GREENBANK Country Diary: Lake District                            50

STEPHEN FRY Not sensible, but, oh, the joy of it!                       51

MARTIN WAINWRIGHT No need for cold feet over Leeds, Chelsy             53

LEADER In praise of ... Gérard Errera                                   55

## WINTER

JILL TREANOR Bankers party even as fears grow for City        59
    bonuses and jobs

MAEV KENNEDY Hotel checks out: Last day of cucumber        60
    sandwiches before Savoy closes its doors

JULIE BURCHILL Why I love supermarkets: (and why people who        63
    don't should get a life)

MARTIN KETTLE Gout is no joke. This I know from painful        67
    experience

JOHN FORDHAM Obituary: Oscar Peterson        71

EWEN MacASKILL Straight talking and war stories help make        75
    McCain the oldest Comeback Kid in town

JIM PERRIN Obituary: Sir Edmund Hillary        79

PETER BRADSHAW Review: *No Country for Old Men*        85

KATE PULLINGER The city is mine        88

RICHARD WILLIAMS Munich 58: presses stopped in        93
    Manchester as *Guardian* man confirmed dead

MICHAEL TOMASKY Super Tuesday: there's been no contest        97
    like it. Not since never

JUDITH MACKRELL Review: Pina Bausch – Tanztheater Wuppertal 104

STEPHEN BATES They're all guilty? 'Definitely'        106

ALAN RUSBRIDGER Review: Daniel Barenboim        109

TIM HAYWARD The future's orange        111

MATTHEW FORT Shaun Hill, the thinking diner's favourite cook        114

PETER PRESTON The kindness of strangers        116

LEADER In praise of … Lincolnshire        119

## SPRING

STEPHEN MOSS The thrill of the chase        123

JONATHAN WATTS Mountain roads are a greater risk than        130
    the police

TIM HAYWARD In pursuit of the 'God shot'        133

GARY YOUNGE A sore that still festers        136

ANGELIQUE CHRISAFIS 'Look at me! I'm at the castle!'        138

DAVID McKIE Bliss of the bus-crawl        141

JACKIE ASHLEY Clarkson for prime minister?        144

LYN GARDNER Review: *Peter Pan el Musical*                                    147

SIMON JENKINS Here's to the mob, for its humiliation of                        149
     dictators and hypocrites alike

ADITYA CHAKRABORTTY Fields of gold                                             153

PHIL GATES Country Diary: Yorkshire Dales                                      157

IAN JACK If Boris Johnson wins next week ... it might be time                  158
     to leave England and move north

MAX HASTINGS We should stop fooling ourselves. Our armed
     forces are no longer world class                                         164

LIBBY BROOKS Forget shoes and men – this show nailed our                      168
     friendships

JONATHAN FREEDLAND Eleven years after it promised a new                       171
     dawn, Labour's dusk has arrived

LEADER Plus ça change: Russia's new president                                 175

MARCEL BERLINS When their number is up                                        177

LUKE DODD Obituary: Nuala O'Faolain                                           178

TANIA BRANIGAN The last photo of Zhou Yao                                     182

LUKE HARDING Hangover, what hangover?                                         184

NANCY BANKS-SMITH TV review: *Filth: The Mary Whitehouse Story*               187

JONATHAN JONES Review: *The Lure of the East: British Orientalist*            190
     *Painting*

## SUMMER

SUZANNE GOLDENBERG A milestone of sorts as Clinton cracks,                     195
     but doesn't break, the glass ceiling

PETER WILBY Stream the pupils – and stream the teachers too                   198

SAM WOLLASTON TV review: *Lost World*                                         204

JON HENLEY 'I'm waiting for riots in the streets'                             206

CHRIS McGREAL Ink-stained finger voters hope will keep                        214
     them alive

MARTIN KELNER Can Laura avoid the path to celebrity                           220
     wrestling?

CHARLIE BROOKER So, you believe in conspiracy theories,                       223
     do you?

AUDREY GILLAN For hard-up voters, it's about local issues –                   226
     if they vote at all

DAVID MILIBAND Against the odds we can still win, on a 232
platform of change

LETTERS AND EMAILS Miliband's sink or swim challenge to 236
Labour

SIMON TISDALL Once again, modern Turkey has hauled itself 236
back from the brink

LEADER Faith 1, Charity 0 238

MICHAEL BILLINGTON Review: *Hamlet* 240

ALEXANDER CHANCELLOR I can't prove it, but I'm sure that it 242
was the notorious Johnson clan who burgled my uncle's
house – twice

IAN TRAYNOR It's not just war – it's personal 245

CHARLOTTE HIGGINS Hare's satire crucifies New Labour 248

RICHARD WILLIAMS China makes its point with greatest show 251

LUKE HARDING Amid promise of peace, Georgians live in 254
terror

MARINA HYDE It's WrestleMania: Swede gets his mankini in 256
a knot and throws back bronze medal

MICHAEL PHILIPS Just how fast will Bolt go when he really 259
puts his mind to it?

STEPHEN MOSS, KIRA COCHRANE AND SIMON BURNTON Baffled by 262
Beijing?: Britain's brilliant Olympic weekend has
provoked intriguing questions

RICHARD WILLIAMS The Great British Games 264

MARINA HYDE The torch is passed, from Beijing epic to 268
London bus queue

JONATHAN FREEDLAND Clinton dazzles while Biden stirs 271

LEADER Barack Obama: American promise 273

DECCA AITKENHEAD Storm warning 275

LARRY ELLIOTT This may help Brown. It will not help home 286
buyers

MICAHEL TOMASKY Who came out on top in the convention 288
battle?

POLLY TOYNBEE Unseating Gordon Brown may be Labour's 290
last chance

PAUL LEWIS Muddy end to season in which some thrived but 294
others went to the wall

# Foreword

CHERIE BLAIR

I have been a *Guardian* reader for nearly four decades. Not a daily reader, and certainly not always an uncritical one, but one who enjoys the *Guardian* for all that it stands for and which is so clearly demonstrated in this selection of extracts from the newspaper and website from the last year. And this year represents a personal milestone for me since, yes, for the first time ever I had a letter printed in the *Guardian*. Sadly it did not make it into this year's selection.

The *Guardian* is not only distinctive in its journalism but in its structure. There is no other paper in the UK which is owned by a trust dedicated to promoting a national newspaper without party bias and to promoting the cause of freedom of the press and liberal journalism. It was a visionary idea in 1936 when the Scott Trust was first set up and, with its twin purposes of making the paper both profitable and principled, it can be said to be a very early example of the 'social enterprise' model which is becoming more prevalent and successful in the early 21st century and which often features in the pages of the *Society Guardian*. This year's edition of *The Bedside Guardian* clearly demonstrates that all that CP Scott and his family held so dear is alive and well in Farringdon Road – and now King's Place.

For an early convert to the joys of the world wide web like me, one of the fun aspects of this book has been to see articles which were previously available only on the web take their rightful place side by side with articles written for the paper version. When I am overseas, I always turn first to guardian.co.uk which not only provides you with instantaneous news and comment which you would expect from a newspaper but also with an ability to participate in a global community where your own reaction to an article can be tested against the expression of opinions of others, some of whom you start to recognise as regular contributors. The web too offers you the chance to view the wonderful photo journalism of Dan Chung, who has surely taken the genre to a new art form, and to catch up with stories not only in writing but in video. And through this book those who are less familiar with Guardian Unlimited can get a glimpse of what it has to offer.

So what does the last year in the UK look like when viewed through the prism of 'liberal journalism'? Looking back I detect a distinct darkening of tone as the early optimism about Britain and the world, reflected in the extracts in the autumn section, fades under the harsh glare of global uncertainties and a questioning of what it means to be 'liberal' in its broadest sense in a world turned fearful by the economic downturn.

I find it sobering to remind myself how quickly we forget issues which at one time were so prominent — like Burma — but which now seem to have slipped once again into a backwater where they do not progress but fester, neglected by all but a small group of committed activists. One such issue I would have liked to see covered was the continuing attempts to oppress women in Afghanistan. This came to the fore again at the end of September with the murder of Malalai Kakar,

Afghanistan's most famous policewomen. One of the strengths of the *Guardian* must surely be its commitment not merely to comment on world affairs but to solid and hard hitting reporting through its network of experienced correspondents who write so authoritatively in this volume on China, Russia, Georgia and Zimbabwe simply because they have the space and talent really to understand the country.

As someone who studiously avoids the sports pages (except in relation to the Olympics) but whose grandfather devoted hours to following horse racing in my childhood, I was fascinated by Stephen Moss's description of the Cheltenham Gold Cup. It made me realise that I was missing some fantastic writing by ignoring the sports pages. I am also glad the broad sweep of culture is there too, with a reminder that in its quest for the truth the *Guardian* can be piercingly critical as those who had the bright idea of turning Peter Pan into a Spanish musical found to their cost in Lyn Gardner's review.

For me one of the greatest strengths of the *Guardian* is its writing about women. I laughed out loud at Julie Burchills' glorious attack on Jeanette Winterson's elitist dislike of supermarkets. As someone who relies on online shopping to keep my family going, I too appreciate the convenience and choice that was not available to my mother and grandmother when I was a child. But is this article a straw in the wind? Are we now seeing a backlash against the working wife and mother, where the domestic goddess once again reigns supreme? Certainly Suzanne Goldenberg's wonderful epitaph to Hillary Clinton's campaign reminds me that I had tears in my eyes when I watched Hillary deliver that speech, but I remain convinced that the door to women's equal participation in public life cannot now be closed even though the battle is never over. I believe that on the day that a woman takes the oath of office as president of the USA she will link her achievement to all of those who helped put the 18 million cracks in that glass ceiling. And when we can morph from a review of *Sex and the City* to an obituary of Nuala O'Faolain, you can rest assured that women in all their diversity are alive and kicking in the *Guardian*.

Something for everyone? Well not quite. After all, this is 'liberal journalism'. So here it is, in all its eclectic glory, the year 2007/8 as seen through the astonishingly typo free *The Bedside Guardian*.

# Introduction

## MARTIN KETTLE

About a year ago, I asked the *Guardian*'s editor, Alan Rusbridger, in an unconvincingly casual manner that I hoped would embarrass neither of us, whether one applied to edit *The Bedside Guardian* or whether it just happened. Be careful what you wish for, he replied darkly, immediately seeing through my pathetic attempt at insouciance. Nothing more was said about my inquiry, much time passed and I can truthfully say that the subject receded to the further reaches of my mind. Then, shortly after the turn of this year, I chanced to pass the *Guardian*'s book publisher, Lisa Darnell on the stairs. 'Alan tells me you are editing this year's *Bedside*,' she said with a smile. 'We'd better sit down and go through the timetable.'

We duly did so – and this book is the result. I don't know whether any of this clarifies the mysteries of the annual editorial appointment process for you, but it was certainly a pleasure and an honour to get the nod and I have enjoyed myself no end. Most of all, though, I hope you enjoy reading and dipping into it. In addition to thanking Alan Rusbridger for the opportunity, however, I owe a debt of gratitude to Ben Clissitt, my immediate predecessor, for his advice and time, and also for having paved the way last year by reinstating the volume's original and, I believe, best title. I also want to mention the shining example of Bill Webb, who edited the *Bedside* for many years when I first joined the *Guardian* and who regularly conjured a beautifully balanced (and always subtly subversive) collection for so many years. One of the many things you could read in the *Guardian* during 2008 was that Bill turned 80 this year. I hope Bill enjoys this imperfect attempt to emulate one of his many *Guardian* achievements.

If applying to edit the *Bedside* proved to be the easy bit, the editing itself was another matter. Like every one of my predecessors, I have discovered afresh that there are two major challenges in putting together this annual collection of *Guardian* writing. The first is simple enough. It is the challenge of trying to keep abreast of what the *Guardian* is publishing. I daresay that was hard enough back in 1952, when Ivor Brown edited the first of these annual volumes. Yet it is certainly many times harder 56 years later, when the annual output of the paper, its web news site, its video and audio, its blogs and other sites, including Comment Is Free, runs to dozens of millions of words. It is an immense task to read everything the paper produces on a single day – equivalent to the average length novel – and I assure you that I did try intermittently to do so. But it is even more daunting to read it all every day of the year – which I freely confess I did not.

Having accepted the limitations of my ability to cover it all, the second challenge was deciding what to include and what to leave out. Early on, I made several lists of themes and topics of the year that I wanted to be touched on, writers I needed to include, and innovations I hoped to attempt. In the end most of this proved a hopeless task. For a long time, I was determined to try to ration every writer to a single appearance. I know from my own experience the pleasure and pride that comes from having one's own work selected for the *Bedside*, even if you have doubts about the *Bedside* editor's choice. And I suspect, as the *Guardian*'s staff grows, that there are many colleagues whose first action when they encounter a copy is a discreet scanning of the contents in the hope of finding themselves included. So I have indeed tried to cast the net wide, giving as many people as possible the chance of having their work included. Yet in the end, this is a collection for readers, not writers. As with a newspaper itself, events dictate what goes in and what does not. Some writers are simply in the right place at a number of right times, so this collection properly reflects that fact.

It was predictable from early on that the American presidential election and the Olympic games would generate important moments in this collection. It was less obvious, at the outset, that 2008 would also be a year dominated by lurching economic downturn and simultaneously by the nosedive in the standing of Gordon Brown, who only 12 months ago seemed a man whose moment had at last come. Neither of these two resonant declines has fully played itself out as I write, in September 2008, but some of the paper's best journalism of the year has tracked their respective slides and will continue to do so in 2009.

The US election and the Olympics are more finite dramas. But I doubt if many of us could have predicted precisely how gripped the nation would become by both of them this year. At one stage in the year, British enthusiasm for the Olympics seemed in distinctly short supply – a combination, perhaps, of widespread political and moral unease about the choice of Beijing and considerable homegrown ambivalence about the award of the 2012 games to London. In the end, though, the Beijing games finished solidly on the plus side of the ledger – and were marked by some great sports and political reporting by the *Guardian*'s Beijing team, a selection of which chose itself for this year's collection.

By any standards too, the US contest has been one of the most theatrical and exciting democratic exercises of modern times. There hasn't been a fight for the Democratic nomination to compare with the Barack Obama-Hillary Clinton scrap since at least 1968. And there hasn't been such a longshot winner of the Republican nomination as John McCain since about the same time. By the time you read this essay, you will know whether Obama or McCain is to succeed George Bush. It was my hope that we could hold the final deadline for this collection until that result was known – but it was not possible. Whether my selection now seems appropriate in the light of what you already know and I can only guess at, is hard for me to say. But I know the paper's reporters and commentators who were fortunate enough to take part in it will never forget the journalistic excitement of this remarkable election. I hope this shines through, whatever the outcome, though I passionately hope Obama wins.

In the end, a collection of this kind can only reflect one person's attempt to fit several dozen gallons into the usual pint pot. There is a vast amount of spillage in this process and, even if each editor says this every time, it nevertheless remains true that the material that has been discarded at the final cut would make an entirely satisfactory *Bedside* volume all on its own. The collection that survives reflects my own priorities and my own prejudices, as well as the necessary chronicling of the high and low lights of the year.

I started to write this introduction in Denver, sitting in a media marquee during the Democratic convention. Eight years ago, when I was the *Guardian*'s Washington correspondent, three of us covered the equivalent event in Los Angeles, where Al Gore was nominated, in the old way – main news story, second news story, sketch and background feature – which Alastair Cooke would have recognised. This year, in 2008, the *Guardian* sent 12 journalists to Denver, who reported, commented, videoed, recorded, blogged and – in the case of Steve Bell – drew the proceedings almost without pause for a week. By the time we got back to our hotel at the end of the day, our work was already up on the guardian.co.uk website.

I am finishing writing this introduction in London at my desk in 119 Farringdon Road, the *Guardian*'s home for more than 30 years. By the turn of the year, this building will be a hulk and the *Guardian*, the *Observer* and the website will all have moved to a brand new home, Kings Place, a mile up the road. When the *Guardian* bought Farringdon Road it seemed to offer the chance to do everything (save printing) that a modern daily newspaper could dream of doing. By 2008, Farringdon Road had become inadequate in almost every way for the production of a modern web and print 24/7 news centre.

Nothing in journalism stays the same for long, and rightly so. The *Guardian* must always change to survive and succeed. The *Bedside*, perhaps, is one of the exceptions – an annual, bound collection of some of the best writing of which the paper has been capable over the previous 12 months. Long may it prosper – and I hope you enjoy reading it as much as I have enjoyed compiling it.

*September 2008*

# Autumn

# Whatever that strange spasm of public anguish was 10 years ago, it ended here

### POLLY TOYNBEE

'Let it end here,' intoned the Bishop of London, weighting these words in his address with sonorous emphasis. How this great assemblage of 30 Windsors on their knees must have prayed fervently, sincerely, deeply for just that. 'Let this service mark the point at which we let her rest in peace,' said the bishop. And lo, miraculously, their prayers were answered. The nation did just that.

For outside the chapel, where police with barriers expected multitudes, there were barely more watchers than at an ordinary August changing of the guard. An outraged *Daily Telegraph* had called for 10 giant screens to satisfy the expected throng. But journalists and camera crews from around the world almost outnumbered royalists, with a shortage of Diana worshippers to film. Most who thinly lined the rails were curious tourists, few were British. Whatever that strange, wailing, teddy-bear-hugging spasm of public anguish was 10 years ago, it ended here yesterday.

What remained that was best of Diana was there in her son Harry's touching, feeling, unWindsorly tribute with his memory of her death as 'indescribably shocking and sad' and his simple 12-year-old's description of her life: 'She made us and so many other people happy.' He had written it himself and polished it with others, they said. It takes a certain skill to write with such word-perfect innocence.

Did Diana change the nation's relationship with its monarchy? Perhaps not as much as Helen Mirren did in her Oscar-winning transformation of the Queen into a woman filled with tender, private, emotional dignity. Yesterday the real Queen, her consort and her heir wore lemon-sucking expressions, looking as if they were doing a wretched penance. Who knows what they feel, but how they must hope the ghost of Diana and her cult is at last at rest.

As many predicted at the time, Diana dead was far harder for the monarchy to cope with than Diana living. Ten years ago the crown wobbled in that sea of decomposing flowers, candles, poems and queen of hearts cards. Yet even at the time, reporting on the crowds in Green Park the night before Diana's funeral, I found mainly cheerful trippers there for the spectacle, come to stare at others weeping, bringing their children so they could tell their grandchildren about the great event. Cameras often lied as they focused exclusively on the weepers who cried on cue while mundane comments of the ordinary gawpers fell on the cutting-room floor. A myth was created that the whole country had gone mad.

Yet who didn't feel that gut-wrenching, visceral shock at the death of such a beauty mangled in a tunnel by an unsuitable lover's drunken driver? People needed someone other than Diana herself to blame, so Charles, his mother, and Diana's 'rottweiler', Camilla, were obliging scapegoats. For a time, the sheer power of the princess's radiant face was a daily rebuke to them, damaging them deeply.

If now, apart from the obsessive acolytes with altars bedecked with mugs, dolls and tea-towels, the Diana cult is at last over, what was her legacy? A slight unbending in royal etiquette has not left the Windsors looking less alien or stilted on display in peculiar hats yesterday in the Guards Chapel. A BBC poll found 56 per cent said they were 'out of touch'.

The whole Charles and Diana saga, with its excruciating Squidgy and Tampax tapes of their affairs, ripped a veil or two off royal mystique. When last asked, half the electorate thought the country would be better or no worse off without a monarchy, according to Ipsos Mori. Even if there is no groundswell to make the monarch Elizabeth the Last, this marks a weakening of old bonds.

But what of yesterday's Channel 4 poll, suggesting that a quarter of us still believe Diana was murdered? Sometimes when asked daft questions, it's fun to give daft answers. For how could Buckingham Palace have wanted a dead Diana, saint of celebrity, people's princess up in the firmament with Mother Teresa and Marilyn Monroe, a taunting icon far beyond their control?

Alive, where would she be now? How much more easily the monarchy could have handled her were she now a jaded New York Jackie O, fading slightly at the edges, losing her cachet with a string of ever less appropriate suitors, shopping and bitching in toe-curling interviews, forever betrayed by 'friends' and therapists. True or not, how easily Buckingham Palace could have made her seem that way, demolishing her with acid briefings, leaking her expense accounts with rumours of unruliness and belittling of the good she did. Peace would not have broken out in the war of the Windsors. One of her last acts was to visit the Duke and Duchess of Windsor's apartments in Paris, a warning if ever there was one.

But Diana in the sky with diamonds has been untouchable for this last decade. Yesterday they must have hoped it was the last time they will have to kneel before her memory. *Requiescat in pace*, they prayed, and they may well have hoped the everlasting light would shine upon her a little less brightly from now on.

SEPTEMBER 5 2007

# 205mph but still three minutes late

## PATRICK BARKHAM

The sun shone brightly, Eurostar 9021 flashed along by the Thames and, at last, we could blame the French. For 13 years, our neighbours have relaxed on 186mph trains on their side of the Channel tunnel and arched a Gallic eyebrow at the branch-line trundle through the green fields of Kent.

Yesterday, the first passenger train to take the new £5.8bn, 68-mile high-speed British track from the tunnel into the revamped St Pancras International was all set to smash the two-hour mark between Paris and London until track maintenance at Calais forced it to slow down.

Despite a hold-up that, for once, was France's fault, the train reached speeds of up to 205mph and set a record for the fastest rail journey between the capitals of two hours, three minutes and 39 seconds. Things going faster and getting better is a curiously old-fashioned idea, but this was a genuine taste of the near future: the magnificently restored St Pancras station opens for international passengers on November 14. Eurostar has promised scheduled journey times of two hours 15 minutes on the 306-mile route to Gare du Nord – 20 minutes quicker than the fastest services currently running from London Waterloo – with basic fares frozen at £59 return.

Four hundred railway buffs, tourism officials and journalists were greeted with champagne, croissants and ragtime jazz at the beginning of their journey.

An 18-carriage, two-engine train travelling at TGV speeds for the entirety of its trip? '*Bof!*' shrugged the French contingent, slugging back Nicolas Feuillatte champagne and sneering at '*le doggy bags*', picnic hampers with *saumon fumé* and *quiche aux petits légumes* laid on by Eurostar to reduce the weight of cooked meals for the record-breaking trip.

The British passengers, however, were far more enthusiastic. David Morgan, 65, a lawyer from Norfolk, sported a top hat and Victorian frock coat once worn by the station master at Sheringham, part of the Midland and Great Northern railway familiarly known as the 'Muddle and Go Nowhere'.

'My grandfather had a butler who took me on the footplate of an engine on my local branch line when I was 10. There's a certain romance to steam but this is the next best thing,' he said.

'It's the most exciting new stretch of track since Brunel,' exclaimed another passenger.

Small boys in short trousers may no longer wave from bridges at record-breaking trains but their grown-up selves had paid £500 each to railway charities to ride on Eurostar. Some started to wonder about the fate of their *blinis et citron* as the carriage swayed at 200mph. 'Why pay to go on the big dipper at the fun fair?' joked Mike Schumann from near Kings Lynn. An ashen-faced tabloid reporter disappeared to be sick, although the diagnosis may have had more to do with champagne than speed.

Halfway through the Channel tunnel, the French driver, Francis Queret, handed the controls to his British counterpart, Neil Meare, who took the train up to 200mph over the Medway viaduct, flashing through the new Ebbsfleet International station in Kent and under the Thames in a new tunnel. 'It's nice to drive fast but we've got speed limits just like you've got in a car,' said Meare.

Shortly after fleeting glimpses of the Dartford bridge and Rainham marshes, the train dived into the 12-mile London tunnel, passing through Stratford and under Hackney and emerging with views of the Gherkin through the sunshine and construction dust behind King's Cross.

To the strains of *The King's Hunting Jig* played by a brass band, the train came to rest under the light and airy arches of William Barlow's Victorian shed at St Pancras, the wrought iron repainted its original sky blue.

Eurostar's chief executive, Richard Brown, said the record marked Britain's 'entry into the European high-speed rail club'. Eurostar hopes its 2hr 15min London-Paris service will boost annual passenger numbers from 8 million to 10 million by 2010. When a Eurostar train clocked 208mph and broke the UK speed record in 2003, it triggered a 30 per cent surge in bookings.

Tourist bosses on the train were also enthusiastic. Neil Wootton, of the travel company Premium Tours, said the shorter Eurostar times would help its day trips to Paris. 'Part of the excitement for the American tourist market is about getting on Eurostar and being able to go under the sea. It's amazing how many Americans get on and expect to see fish and whales from the tunnel.'

It may be no less miraculous that Britain is now, finally, a small spur on the European high-speed rail network. But for those whisked from Paris to St Pancras yesterday, their journey was only just beginning: with strikes paralysing the underground and the city's streets gridlocked, it would take many another two hours to cross London, and even more to find the slow train home.

SEPTEMBER 10 2007

# Lauren still a class act, 40 years on

## JESS CARTNER-MORLEY

Ralph Lauren, who celebrated 40 years as a designer with a catwalk extravaganza in Central Park, New York, this weekend, once said: 'I don't design clothes, I design dreams.' As a business model, this might sound a little sketchy. But Lauren, who opened his first shop selling men's ties in 1967, now sits at the helm of a global business with $4.3bn (£2.1bn) of sales last year. It seems fair to say the man is on to something.

The dream Lauren sells is a quintessentially American one, in two senses. It is a fairytale vision of upper-class American style, evoking shingled beach houses and Ivy League college ties, lawn picnics with monogrammed linen, cricket whites and silver cocktail shakers. But it is also the American Dream itself. Lauren was born Ralph Lifschitz, the son of Jewish immigrants in the Bronx, and now divides his time between a vast Fifth Avenue apartment, a ranch in Colorado, and a villa in Jamaica.

Both elements of Lauren's vision of the American dream were reflected in the 500-strong guest list who gathered to toast him at the Conservatory Garden in Central Park.

Both of modern America's most powerful political dynasties were represented: the Kennedys by Bobby Jr, and the Bushes by Lauren, the current president's niece, who is dating Ralph Lauren's son David.

But also present was Martha Stewart, who, like Ralph Lauren, made her fortune by creating a fantasy wherein the perfect Egyptian cotton pillowcase, just like the perfect cashmere scarf, becomes hugely desirable as a symbol of an aspirational lifestyle. Martha Stewart was born Martha Kostyra, the second of six children in a Polish-American family in New Jersey; like Lauren, she is an outsider who sells a vision of upper-class elegance to other outsiders.

Last year Ralph Lauren, who at 67 is chairman and chief executive of Polo Ralph Lauren Corporation, awarded himself a salary package of $25.9m. The celebration indicated the deep pockets of the host: the 500 guests dined on champagne, caviar and rack of New Zealand lamb (accompanied by 'heirloom tomatoes') under a crescent-shaped arbour that had been bolstered with temporary steel reinforcements in order to hold the weight of dozens of huge chandeliers. This was the first time the city had granted permission for the Conservatory Garden to be used for a party; as a token of his thanks to the city's mayor, Michael Bloomberg, who was among the guests, Lauren has made a substantial donation to the park.

The long reach of the Ralph Lauren brand is best reflected in the polo shirt, with horse-and-rider logo, which has found its way into millions of wardrobes worldwide.

So it was fitting that Lauren should choose to theme the catwalk show that immediately preceded the gala dinner on a day at the polo. Fitted satin jackets in bright jockeys' colours were worn with gleaming white jodhpurs and accessorised with striped caps; a floor-length yellow gown was printed all over with an illustrated, full-colour version of the horse-and-rider logo. Lauren can be over-literal in his visions of upper-class dressing, but this had a wit and sass that brought to mind the younger, hipper aesthetic of designers such as Luella Bartley. Ever the businessman, Lauren also sent out a collection of flattering, pastel-toned gowns, in poppy-printed silk plisse or floral silk georgette, to please his more conservative customers.

As an illustration of Lauren's consummate accomplishment as an eveningwear designer, the collection included a trio of dresses representing three classic eveningwear styles. The first, in jonquil yellow, was a simple, strapless floorlength column, precisely cut to create the longest, leanest line possible. The second, in purple, was twisted and gathered across the body from the bust to the hip before flowing to the floor, a deft trick to emphasise the curve of the waist. The third, in emerald green, was a chic, classic cocktail style, hemmed at the knee. To the social set who packed the benches at this show, such styles are as much an essential part of a weekend wardrobe as the cotton polo shirt is to Lauren's less rarefied customers.

To the accompaniment of Frank Sinatra singing *The Best Is Yet to Come*, Lauren strolled along the catwalk air-kissing a front row that included the actors Dustin Hoffman, Robert de Niro and Sarah Jessica Parker, as well as his fellow American designers Donna Karan and Diane von Furstenberg.

Then, with a magician's flourish, the curtain behind the catwalk was whisked to one side to reveal the gardens – china and crystal sparkling in the light of a thousand candles, waiters bearing trays of canapès and cocktails – and Lauren led the way to dinner, beckoning his guests to follow him into his fairytale world.

SEPTEMBER 13 2007

# Le Saux's honesty can help bring pride to English game

## LAWRENCE DONEGAN

You never know, the trustees of the sports book of the year award may yet have something to say about the efforts of Graeme le Saux, but for the time being the safest bet is to keep breathing normally and simply congratulate the former England fullback for making a compelling case that the troubles facing football are not limited to dodgy decisions by referees and Russian billionaires muscling into boardrooms.

In his new autobiography, *Left Field*, Le Saux tells of how wearing Pringle socks and reading the *Guardian* led him to be branded a 'poof' by some contemporaries (he's not, incidentally), including two of the more dim-witted souls ever to bring shame on the noble name of Robbie. 'I got plenty of comments from other players about being a faggot or a queer. Robbie Savage seemed to get a particular thrill out of it,' he writes, before going on to describe an infamous match in which an overweight, underachieving Scouse property developer offered him out for a ... well, I'll let Graeme take up the story. 'I looked at Robbie [Fowler]. He started bending over and pointing his backside in my direction. He was smirking. "Come and give me one up the arse," he said, repeating it three or four times.'

By the soporific standards of the modern football autobiography, this is eye-popping because we are talking about well-known, current players who have been accused of indulging in unforgivable prejudice. (If you think that is overstating the case, try substituting 'queer' with one of the objectionable racial epithets you might hear should you be unlucky enough to stumble into a BNP branch meeting.)

Fowler and Savage are not the only ones named by Le Saux, nor are they the most famous. In the interview accompanying the book's serialisation, but not in the book itself, Le Saux described an incident during a match against Manchester United when David Beckham allegedly called him a 'poof'.

That would be David Beckham; gay icon, the man in touch with his feminine side who made it so right to be wearing a sarong. Please say it isn't so, David.

Beckham wasn't available for comment but a spokesman pointed out that the incident in question happened seven years ago and even though Le Saux has known Beckham for some time the former Chelsea man had never mentioned it in their conversations. 'While we appreciate Graeme has a book to sell, we refute these allegations completely,' the spokesman said.

There is great irony in having a spokesman for Beckham, for whom apparently everything, including his credibility as a footballer, has its price, sneering at a former colleague for giving an insightful interview to help sell his autobiography. But to make a joke about the messiah of football in America and his apparent lack of self-awareness would be to miss the point.

A footballer's sexuality is not public property but nor should it be something to be hidden away for fear of ridicule, or worse. Over the past 20 years, only one player in this country, the late Justin Fashanu, has publicly said he was gay and he was hounded until his suicide.

Meanwhile, here we are in September 2007 and not one player in the British game is 'out'. You can say this is a statistical improbability, an insult to our intelligence or an assault on the dignity of the gay community. What you can't say is that it is acceptable in a modern society, especially where many people take their cue from the national sport.

Le Saux has done his bit to address the problem of homophobia within the game and now it is everybody else's turn: the authorities, managers, referees and the players themselves. If Beckham believes he can make Americans love football, surely he can make British fans love a player who loves another man.

SEPTEMBER 14 2007

# Fuchsia is the colour, politics is the game

## MICHAEL WHITE

As Lady Thatcher faced that old familiar door, did she fantasise, even briefly, that the call to return to power had come at last? If she did, her host quickly disabused her of the notion by making sure she turned just long enough for the photographers to get their shot.

The lady was for turning! And Gordon Brown had turned her! The next challenge was to keep her entertained indoors for a full two hours. No perfunctory granny's visit this one, but a full-dress theatrical coup to impress Middle Britain. It is hard to be certain whether Labour or Tory purists will be more dismayed. But never let it be said that Margaret Thatcher, even at a frail 82, was anyone's political patsy. Yes, there was a lot of vanity stepping out of that blue BMW, a fraction early at 2.58pm, to be accorded a rare prime ministerial pavement greeting: two big political egos, each the size of the public debt.

But she was also playing hardball politics in her own way. The timing, perfect for spoiling David Cameron and Zac Goldsmith's green policy launch, was said to have been a coincidence. But Lady T had not consulted party HQ. She is known to feel hurt that her young successor feels the need to step out from under her long shadow and move on.

Was she teaching him not to 'trash' her legacy, as Malcolm Rifkind put it? Or to start wearing a tie to work? To speak less kindly of Polly Toynbee? Or was a lonely old lady just accepting a kind invitation to tea with small children?

A bit of the latter perhaps. Her grandchildren live in Texas and she brought presents, a remote control car for John – four next week – a cement mixer for little Fraser. But any doubt about at least part of the motive must have been squashed by that suit: hers, not his.

The photographers thought it was fuchsia, the police officer called it 'shocking pink'. Sky's Adam Boulton tried 'cerise'. Anyway, it certainly wasn't blue. In wearing it and sanctioning the presence of cameras (after initial hesitation) Lady Thatcher and Suit were fighting their way on to TV's evening bulletins and this morning's front pages. Not since Princess Di wore that little black number to upstage Prince Charles has a lady's chosen lethal weapon been her wardrobe.

Tony Blair had often praised Lady Thatcher and had her round to tea until they fell out over the detention of General Pinochet. But Brown was never like that, was he?

When you think what the earnest Scots socialist and the hand-bag-waving English monetarist must have said about each other in the nine years they shared in the Commons, yesterday was either a miracle – or just politics.

Yet it transpires that as a new MP, Brown was startled to receive a letter from the then-prime minister, expressing interest in an economic speech he had just made: they met and, top sources said yesterday, 'disagreed on nearly everything'.

When Blair left in June Lady T sent a routine 'good luck' note. The novelist Anthony Powell once said that people who write fiction have more in common with other people who write fiction than with anyone else: the same is true of the prime ministers' club.

So Gordon the strategist invited her in and last week pre-primed the occasion – 'one lump or six, Lady Thatcher?' – by praising her 'conviction politics'. One Thatcher intimate later said she was thrilled. 'We had to restrain her from writing a thank-you note.'

So yesterday no raised voices or broken tea cups could be heard from the street. There was a 50-minute private tête-à-tête, just Lady Thatcher and Mark Worthington, lobbyist turned loyal minder. Then came a tour of her old haunts to meet the staff, including a dozen friends from the old days; finally tea in the old flat above the shop with Sarah Brown, the kids and Alistair Darling's wife – another Maggie – who actually lives there now.

Waiting reporters were also fed titbits. 'I am reliably informed she met Sybil,' the new No 10 cat, said Top Source, who later revealed that Bill, one of the older uniformed custodians, had been invited up for tea. Bill was able to tell Mrs Brown: 'Lady Thatcher takes her tea black.' That colour may fit Cameron's mood this morning.

SEPTEMBER 19 2007

# In praise of the humble pork pie

## MICHAEL HANN

These are halcyon days for lovers of pork pies. Not salad days; we've no time for salad. We have been cheering on the Melton Mowbray Pork Pie Association in its battle with the foie-gras-and-carpaccio ponces of the European Union to secure for the Melton Mowbray pie (that's the one with uncured grey meat) 'protected geographical indication' – meaning only pies made by traditional methods in Melton Mowbray can claim the name, just as only sparkling wine from the Champagne region can be called champagne. And we thrilled to the news that, a fortnight or so ago, a pork pie from a Cannock butcher was chosen as the UK's tastiest food in the Great Taste awards.

Although Britain's snobbery about its own foods is slowly relaxing, pork-based snack products are still viewed by many as the lowest of the culinary low. We need to shout about the many ways we can make the most of a dead pig. Butchers and farmers' markets are selling fresh, delicious pies that banish the memory of the tasteless, soggy pies one buys (when desperate) from petrol station shops and second-tier supermarkets. At last, the meat of kings is getting the treatment it deserves: crumbly pastry that melts on the tongue; rich luscious jelly surrounding the meat; and firm flesh that tastes like pork, rather than the sawdust of the mass-produced variety.

I am a member of an informal luncheon society that meets irregularly to eat fine English pork products. In the light of recent improvements in pork pie standards we ask only one thing: that other pork-based snack foods are embraced and improved in the same way. We have noted, with approval, Waitrose's decision to sell free-range Scotch eggs made with Cumberland sausage meat as well as the growth of Scotch egg internet retailers.

We hope that the humble pork scratching – which has the potential to be the greatest pork-based snack food of all – becomes the obsession of some gifted young butcher. But until that day comes, as surely it will, we say only this: thank heaven for pork pies.

SEPTEMBER 27 2007

# Only Burma's neighbours can stop its dictators beating up the Buddha

## TIMOTHY GARTON ASH

*How long, O God, shall men be ridden down,*
*And trampled under by the last and least*
*Of men?*

The 19th-century poet Alfred Tennyson could not watch videoclips on YouTube of Poland's uprising being crushed, but his response perfectly captures the sense of impotent rage one feels as Burma's peacefully protesting monks and nuns are beaten up and tear-gassed by the country's security forces. It has been 19 years now since its first great movement for democracy in 1988, and 17 since Aung San Suu Kyi's National League for Democracy won a clear popular mandate in free elections. Yet under its Orwellian military regime, this beautiful land has sunk even further into poverty and oppression. How long, O God, how long?

As I write, shocking accounts of violence flash across my screen, including reports that several people have been killed. We do not know if the protests will persist, as some of the young monks promise, or be subdued. But two things are clear. Although the minister for religious affairs, General Myint Maung, rails against 'external and internal destructionists' and the sinister role of 'global powers who practise hegemonism', this was an entirely home-grown protest. Following sharp price rises in August, the cup of bitterness overflowed. No one in Washington, London or anywhere else outside Burma turned a tap. And this home-grown popular protest has – so far – been as peaceful as can be.

I have before me a joint statement from the All Burma Monks Alliance and the 88 Generation Students group which begins with a remarkable sentence: 'The entire people led by monks are staging a peaceful protest to be freed from the general crises of politics, economics and society by reciting the *Metta Sutra*.' The *Metta Sutra* reflects on the Buddhist virtue of *metta*, or unconditional love and kindness. (*'This is what should be done/By one who is skilled in goodness,/And who knows the paths of peace.'*) One demo banner read: 'Love and kindness must win over all'.

Who could not be moved by those videoclips, internet-streamed from digital cameras and mobile phones, showing the rhythmically striding monks and nuns, in their maroon, pale pink and saffron robes? And by that one grainy snapshot of Aung San Suu Kyi praying at her gate in the pouring rain as the monks strode past chanting: 'Long life and health to Aung San Suu Kyi, may she have freedom soon!' It is to this that the supposedly Buddhist generals, who often parade their piety in the Pravda-like pages of the *New Light of Myanmar*, are responding with gunfire, baton-blows and tear-gas. In effect, they are beating up the Buddha.

Tennysonian hand-wringing won't help the people of Burma. So what is to be done? For a start, as many of the world's leaders as possible should call for an immediate halt to violent repression. The UN general assembly is meeting in New York. It will probably not be possible to achieve a swift message of condemnation from the whole assembly. However, the UN security council was meeting to discuss the Burma situation yesterday evening – something China and Russia have previously resisted. Meanwhile, the UN secretary-general has asked for his special envoy to be allowed back into the country; at the very least, China must support that.

An old debate has flared up again about the relative merits of a tough policy of isolating the military regime with sanctions, as opposed to a policy of 'constructive engagement'. We probably could have done more in recent years to engage with civil society in Burma and to show the generals and colonels the advantages of coming out of isolation. In the longer term, they do need to understand that negotiating with Aung San Suu Kyi and other opposition leaders, and opening up to the outside world, would bring immense benefits to their country. They also need to know that it would not result in them ending up hanging from lampposts or sitting in prison. As Aung San Suu Kyi herself told me when we talked in Rangoon some years ago (when it was still possible to meet with her), they might even be reassured that they could keep at least some of what she nicely called their 'ill-gotten gains'. A change of junta supremo from the aged and obdurate general Than Shwe would be a good occasion for restarting that conversation. But such a policy of encouraging peaceful transition by constructive engagement is not something for today. For today, we need to stop them killing peaceful protesters.

George Bush has announced tighter sanctions to prevent the generals and their families travelling to or holding assets in the US – a sanction the EU has had in place for years. An experienced observer who knows the mentality of the Burmese military – call it superstitious or devout, according to taste – suggests that a far more effective sanction would be for someone to persuade them that beating up monks will result in very bad karma for themselves, their families, and their country. That is not, however, a message that one can imagine a western leader such as Gordon Brown conveying. It requires not a son of the manse but a priest of the pagoda.

Altogether, there is frustratingly little that western powers can achieve on their own. Symptomatically, Brown's first positive action has been to send a letter to the Portuguese presidency of the EU, urging the EU to take a strong stand. But even the EU and the US acting together in perfect harmony will make little difference unless Burma's Asian neighbours start speaking up. Everyone now looks to China, the biggest neighbour with the biggest involvement in Burma. China says it wants 'stability' in Burma. Certainly it does not want a bloodbath threatening its business interests there and spoiling the run-up to the Beijing Olympics. Of late, there have been small signs that China is concluding that stability in Burma requires change. But change kick-started by street protests is not the kind that ageing communist rulers are keen on.

Too little attention is being paid to Burma's other big Asian neighbour, India. Although it is the world's largest democracy, India has so far been quite pusillanimous in its relations with Burma's dictators. It seems more concerned about competing for influence (and energy contracts) with China than it is about the nature of the regime. As a result, Burma's rulers have been able to play India off against China, and vice versa. One thing the United States and the European Union could do is to suggest rather emphatically to our Indian friends that this is short-sighted. Ideally, India and China would also get together to see if they have common as well as competing interests in the unhappy land sandwiched between them. Two giants should not be played off so easily by a pygmy.

None of this seems likely to stop the generals from clamping down now. There is still a chance the repression won't succeed. History is always open. But even if this round of protests is suppressed, the world will have been dramatically and movingly alerted to Burma's plight; Burma's Asian neighbours will have been shaken out of their sluggish passivity; and we can hope that Burma's non-violent opposition will itself learn something from the experience, something for next time. If so, the monks will not have marched in vain.

OCTOBER 1 2007

# Review: *Carmen*

## ANDREW CLEMENTS

Having ended last season with a miscalculation of epic proportions in *Kismet*, the English National Opera begins the new term with an equally misconceived attempt on the dramatic life of one of the greatest staples of the repertory. Sally Potter's new production of *Carmen* will only reinforce the prejudices of those who don't like opera, or just regard it as pleasant music draped across an inconsequential plot. Her achievement is to turn one of the rawest, most intensely focused of dramas into a parade of half-baked, chic ideas totally lacking in dramatic logic and emotional power. Anyone who cares for Bizet's masterpiece should keep well away.

Potter and her designer, Es Devlin, transplant the scenario to the present day. We begin in London, with video footage shot around the Coliseum, but by the final act everyone has somehow reached Spain. José works for a private security company, while

Carmen seems to be a prostitute. All the dialogue has been jettisoned – why did the conductor, Edward Gardner, go along with such a decision? – and the action careers from one musical number to the next, without explanation or context. Christopher Cowell's translation plays fast and loose with the text, too; anyone who did not know the plot in advance would be hard-pressed to know what was going on.

What we get instead of dramatic logic is dancing – lots of it. Three choreographers are credited in the programme, but it's Pablo Veron's tango work that dominates, with some hip-hop thrown in. In the first couple of acts, Carmen can hardly open her mouth before a group of dancers materialises to gyrate around her, with the sequinned Veron himself very much to the fore. The routines seem to be a substitute for real stage direction. Though the singing of the four principals is the evening's only saving grace, none of them gets the chance to give their character any definition.

As Micaela, Katie van Kooten suffers most. Potter makes no attempt to integrate her into the drama, so she just walks on to the stage for her third-act aria, sings it beautifully and walks off again. David Kempster's Escamillo is reduced to cliched toreador swagger, while Julian Gavin works hard to make José flesh and blood. He nearly succeeds. But Alice Coote – who could be a fascinating, alluring Carmen, and sings her numbers ravishingly – is so constantly upstaged by the dancing and betrayed by the lack of direction that one of the most ambiguous heroines in operas is reduced to a mere cipher.

OCTOBER 4 2007

# An election? Bring it on now

## PATRICK WINTOUR

David Cameron yesterday called his party to arms in a virtuoso speech delivered without Autocue that goaded Gordon Brown to call an election and let the people pass judgment on 10 years of 'broken promises and old politics'.

At the climax of a closely argued and fluent address that marked no retreat from his modern Conservative agenda, Cameron demanded, to huge applause: 'So Mr Brown, what's it going to be? Why don't you go ahead and call that election. Let the people pass judgment on 10 years of broken promises. Let people decide who's really making the arguments about the future of our country, let people decide who can make the changes that we need in our country. Call that election. We will fight, Britain will win.'

In the hour-long speech, he repeatedly argued that change was required because Britain faced a new world in which the old centralised, cynical politics simply did not work. He promised to break down state monopolies in education, toughen the welfare regime, save district hospitals, end top-down reform in the public sector and recognise that the family is the best welfare system in the country.

In passages that drew some of the most enthusiastic applause, he also promised a cap on numbers of economic migrants, more powers for headteachers and to campaign for a no vote in any referendum on the EU constitution.

Afghanistan, Cameron said, would be his top foreign policy

priority. 'I think if we have learned anything over the past five years it's that you cannot drop a fully formed democracy out of an aeroplane at 40,000 feet.'

Brown, by his indifferent treatment of the armed forces, he said, had broken the military covenant.

In his strongest attack yet on the prime minister, he said Brown had a cynical plan 'to appeal to the 4 per cent in the marginal seats, with a dog whistle on immigration here and a word about crime here, wrap yourself in the flag and talk about Britishness enough and maybe you can convince people you are on their side. Well I say, God we have got to be better than that.'

There was no immediate sign that the speech had shaken the confidence of Brown's allies, who argued the speech lacked a unifying theme. But Labour will be watching the polls over the next three days before meeting again on Sunday to decide whether to press ahead with the planned November 1 poll.

The advertising agency Saatchi & Saatchi is producing a campaign for Labour's election team, and ministers are being asked to discuss their sections of the manifesto with Ed Miliband, the Labour election coordinator.

Shadow cabinet members, delighted at this week's show of unity, believe that if they can push the Labour lead down to three points, Brown will sense an election is too risky to call.

There is division within the cabinet and even some of Cameron's most senior aides remain convinced that Brown will pull back from an autumn election, recognising there is no demand for a poll. The Tory leader, however, still taunted Brown over the issue during his address.

He decided yesterday morning to use only a few notes when he was on his feet, reasoning it would help counter his perceived lack of authenticity. 'I haven't got a script. I have just got a few notes. It might be a bit messy, but it will be me,' he said.

He also addressed his other great negative – his privileged background – admitting he had no hard-luck story to tell as his father was a stockbroker and his mother a magistrate. He insisted he had the leadership and strength to become prime minister in a month's time at the age of 41, making him the youngest prime minister since William Pitt the younger. He alluded to this issue by saying: 'There's something else. It's about me. People want to know, are you really up for it, have you got what it takes, and I answer unreservedly, yes.'

Throughout his speech he contrasted the 'modern' Tories with Labour's 'cynical ... old politics', insisting Britain had to be roused from its sense of fatalism and pessimism.

'We can get a great NHS if we make doctors answerable to patients and not to politicians. We can get great schools if we break open the state monopoly, allow new schools in and insist on high standards.

'We can get safer streets if we strengthen our families and get the police onto our streets – if we really want it.'

He also refused to retreat on green politics. 'Some people say it is not popular to talk about green issues, I don't care. It is right and it falls to this generation to deal with this issue.'

OCTOBER 11 2007

# A triumph of wit, romance and neurosis

### ALEXIS PETRIDIS

Never has the seventh album of even such a feted band as Radiohead sparked as much coverage as *In Rainbows*. However, the debate has not been about its merits but its distribution method.

Out of contract with their label, they last week stunned the record industry by announcing they would release the album, four years in the making, as a download and ask fans to pay as much or as little as they liked.

With the band refusing to say how many people had downloaded the album, or how much they had agreed to pay, it was left to a survey by the record industry newsletter *Record of the Day* to put a price on Radiohead's art.

After polling almost 3,000 subscribers, it found the average purchase price for those downloading was £4. The most popular options were £5 or £10, although the average was dragged down by those paying only a nominal amount. Meanwhile, 12 per cent had opted for the obsessive's choice: a £40 deluxe box-set of the album containing CDs, vinyl, extra tracks and a hardback book. A similar exercise by nme.com put the average price at £7.

But for all the debate – and acres of free publicity – sparked by the novel distribution method, the only question that matters remains: is it any good?

Before it had even arrived in the world's inboxes, you would have been hard-pushed to call Radiohead's seventh album anything other than a triumph, at least of marketing.

The honesty box approach meant *In Rainbows* was discussed in areas not usually noted for their interest in leftfield gloom-rock. It turned up in a broadsheet's economics section, while one can only begin to imagine Thom Yorke's untrammelled joy at the piece by an advertising executive which claimed the singer's paralysed left eye was 'the perfect analogy' for the band's expertise in branding.

Elsewhere, the band's creative partner, the artist Stanley Donwood, rattled the collecting tin a bit, pointing out the album's lengthy, agonised gestation, which at one point entailed fraught discussions about splitting up.

This is hardly an extraordinary state of affairs – no Radiohead album feels complete without an agonised gestation – but, on listening to *In Rainbows*, it seems surprising. This does not sound like a band wondering what to do next. The lyrics may be as neurotic as ever – you're never far from the lights going out or being eaten by the worms – but as it flows seamlessly along it sounds supremely confident.

There's nothing tentative even about its more experimental moments, possibly because even its more experimental moments – *15 Step*'s clattering beats, the unsettling electronic pulse of *House of Cards* – are pressed into the service of fantastic melodies: the closing *Videotape* proceeds at the pace of a Soviet state funeral, but the tune is so glorious, it sounds graceful rather than lethargic, dreamy rather than dreary. Radiohead sound like they're enjoying themselves, not least on *Bodysnatchers*, which features a gleefully propulsive bass riff. In the parlance of the middle-American sports stadium crowds with whom Radiohead have such a troubled relationship, it rocks.

The most heartening thing about *In Rainbows*, besides the fact that it may represent the strongest collection of songs Radiohead have assembled for a decade, is that it ventures into new emotional territories: their last album, 2003's *Hail To The Thief*, had its moments, but it was scarred by the sense that the band's famed gloominess was starting to tip into self-parody and petulance.

Here, there's wit – at *15 Step*'s conclusion, Yorke's end-is-nigh keening is undercut by a children's chorus merrily crying 'hey!' – and warmth. With its strings and swooning guitars, *Nude* sounds lushly romantic. So does *All I Need*, which, moreover, ends in a fantastic, life-affirming crescendo.

Witty, romantic, life-affirming: these are not adjectives readily associated with Radiohead. In the years since *OK Computer* propelled them to superstardom, you could say the same about the phrase 'consistent album', yet that's precisely what *In Rainbows* seems to be. Whatever you paid, it's hard to imagine feeling short-changed.


OCTOBER 13 2007

# Al Gore wins Nobel peace prize. And this time, no one can take it away from him

## ED PILKINGTON

This is one prize the supreme court won't be able to take away from him. The five votes of a committee in Oslo yesterday awarded Al Gore the world's most exalted award, the Nobel peace prize, finally putting to rest the votes of the five judges who stripped him of Florida in 2000 and kept him from the White House.

It was the last laugh for a man who has, until recently, trod a lonely path to engage American opinion with the looming crisis of climate change and who was ridiculed by the beneficiary of that supreme court judgment in 2000, George Bush, as 'ozone man'. If seven years ago Gore suffered his *annus horribilis*, this year is undoubtedly his 'annus miraculous' – February: Oscar for his film *An Inconvenient Truth*; September: Emmy for his Current TV channel; October: Nobel peace prize.

The accolade was established in 1901 with the remit that it should reward the 'person who shall have done the most or the best work for fraternity between the nations, for the abolition or reduction of standing armies and for the holding and promotion of peace congresses'.

This year's choice risked controversy by widening the remit to include climate change, arguing that the crisis had the potential to increase the risk of violent conflicts and wars. The committee split the prize between Gore and the UN team of scientists, the Intergovernmental Panel on Climate Change. Of Gore, it said: 'He is probably the single individual who has done most to create greater worldwide understanding of the measures that need to be adopted.'

Bill Clinton's former vice-president said he was deeply honoured to receive the prize and seized the moment to renew his plea for the world's attention: 'The climate crisis is not a political issue – it is a moral and spiritual challenge to all of humanity.' The little dig at politics spoke volumes about Gore's long struggle to put the hurt of his failed presidential bid behind him. In recent months he has teased the American people, neither confirming nor stamping out rumours that he would stand for president once again.

Inevitably, the Nobel award has prompted a renewed flurry of that conjecture. Even before yesterday's announcement, the drum-beat had grown audibly louder: the nationwide coalition of his supporters, Draft Gore, this week took out a full-page advert in the *New York Times* that exhorted him to stand with the warning that if he did not 'rise to this challenge, you and millions of us will live forever wondering what might have been'.

Other influential figures added their voices to the chorus. Jimmy Carter, the former president and a fellow Nobel peace laureate (his 2002 award was famously cast as a 'kick in the legs' to Bush over the build-up to the invasion of Iraq), said in a TV interview that he hoped this might encourage Gore to 'consider another political event'. Carter added: 'I don't think anyone is better qualified to be president of the United States.'

Gore himself was studiously avoiding talk of a presidential bid. He maintained the ambivalent stance he has all year – neither in, nor out – in a way that has merely stoked the speculation and aroused further curiosity.

As a man with stakeholdings in both Google and Apple and a reputed $100m fortune, he could fairly easily raise the $100m needed to self-finance a primary race. But if he is to stand he has to move within the next couple of weeks to meet deadlines in several key states. And with Hillary Clinton, Barack Obama and John Edwards all proving serious contenders, observers of the 2008 race say there is no political oxygen left for Gore to breathe.

'The man's not running. Even if he won the Nobel prize for curing cancer, he still wouldn't run,' said Charlie Cook of the respected website the Cook Report. 'I don't know a single serious person in America who thinks he will stand.'

Even Gore's advisers were seeking to dampen down expectations of a dramatic announcement. 'He's spending all his time on the climate crisis. My sense is that this won't affect that calculation,' his adviser Michael Feldman said.

In the last analysis, the long and arduous journey he has travelled, not only to pull himself back up from the fall of 2000 but also to persuade the American people about the urgency of the climate crisis, has been reward enough even without gaining the keys to the White House.

Laurie David, who produced Gore's wildly successful film *An*

*Inconvenient Truth*, said the lesson of the Nobel was that he had found another way to make his mark. 'Al Gore has proven very eloquently that you don't have to be president to change the world.'

OCTOBER 16 2007

# End of the Ming dynasty

### SIMON HOGGART

At Mafia funerals it's always the *capo* who ordered the hit who makes the most fulsome speech over the coffin – about the departed's wonderful qualities, his integrity, his patriotism, his love of family.

So it was yesterday, when Simon Hughes and Vincent Cable emerged from Lib Dem headquarters to announce the resignation of Ming Campbell.

Earlier there was a mini media scrum outside the HQ. The news had broken too late for many to make the scene. The autumnal gloaming fell upon Westminster. Brisk young women marched out to tell us that there would be short statements from two of the conspirators (no, of course they didn't actually use those words) and there would be no questions.

Where was Ming? we inquired. 'He is not available,' the brisk young women said. 'But where is he?' we asked.

'He is not available,' they said, and for a politician, unavailable is as real a place as London, or Patagonia.

Norman Baker, the Lib Dem MP who believes Dr David Kelly was murdered, arrived to mutter imprecations. Ming should have been given more support, more time. Baker may believe that

Ming too was the victim of a massive conspiracy, and this time he might be right.

The two men emerged. They looked deeply solemn (though of course all Lib Dem leadership crises have a faintly ludicrous air – like watching monks trying to seize power in a Buddhist ashram).

What a paragon their late leader had been! The huge purpose and stability he had given to the Liberal Democrats. The 'successful preparations for the next general election' (how could they know already?) He had taken every decision in the interests of party and country! What a huge debt of gratitude we all owed him!

That was just Hughes, the party president. Cable, the deputy leader, came next. It was he who had announced yesterday that there was a 'debate' about Ming's future.

This is the political equivalent of the knife between the shoulder blades. Or even the machete into the skull. There must have been a bubble of rage in Sir Menzies's throat when he heard that. 'Et tu, Vince,' however, lacks a certain resonance.

Like the Walrus and the Carpenter as they surveyed the beach full of dead oysters, Mr Cable seemed to be close to tears. He spoke of the gratitude, respect and admiration felt by all the party for the lost leader. In his speech at the party conference (remember? It was less than four weeks ago) he had set out a superb vision of a 'fairer, greener, country'. Throughout, Cable's eyebrows were leaping up and down, as if he were trying to semaphore an entirely contrary message.

'Did you wield the dagger?' someone shouted. 'Where is he, what have you done with him?' yelled someone else. A voice demanded: 'Is he dead?' and I realised it was mine. As always at such times, you wonder, if the departed leader was such a cynosure, why did they want to get rid of him?

The door closed behind the two men, and the chill October wind blew in from the direction of the abbey.

OCTOBER 19 2007

# Before the tragedy, an emotional homecoming

## DECLAN WALSH

Benazir Bhutto had arrived full of hope. 'It's good to be home,' she said. 'A dream come true.' She hesitated on the top step, a flicker of nerves flashing across her face. Behind her was the plane from Dubai, the desert metropolis where she has spent much of the past eight years, battling to retain relevancy and waiting for this moment. Ahead was Pakistan, the fragile, nuclear-armed country she had once run, and hoped to do so again.

Call it a personality cult, feudal politics or genuine democracy, but overwhelming street power is the potent calling card of Bhutto's Pakistan People's party. It also proved to be a point of vulnerability. A sea of supporters washed up against the fortified bus carrying Bhutto as it crawled through Karachi.

Adolescents waved from tree branches; men danced, jigged and screamed, craning for a glimpse of their leader with the adulation of boy band fans; leather-faced 'aunties' – elderly female supporters – battled to hold on to the buses, which throbbed with disco music. 'Long live Bhutto!' they chanted, flinging petals into her path. 'Benazir for prime minister!'

Bhutto watched from the bus rooftop, jammed between party bigwigs in a green shalwar kameez. She smiled, waved and, in a nod to modern addictions, checked her email on her BlackBerry. 'It's really overwhelming,' Bhutto told the Guardian, looking over the sea of supporters. 'And we haven't even reached the main crowd yet.'

Acknowledging that it was 'not the same Pakistan' she had left, she said: 'The militants have risen in power. But I know who these people are, I know the forces behind them, and I have written to General Musharraf about this.'

The size of the crowd was impossible to gauge. News wires quoted a government official who said 150,000; Bhutto claimed 3 million. The clear truth, though, was that her party machine remains intact. 'Benazir's programme is for the poor. We are just waiting for jobs,' said Mansoor Ali Abro, an unemployed 24-year-old labourer who had driven 12 hours from a village in interior Sindh with 1,500 others. 'Criminal man is powerful. Poor man is on the ground,' said his neighbour, Mashuk Ali. 'I love Benazir.'

The journey started in Dubai, where Bhutto bid goodbye to her husband, Asif Zardari – who used to be known as Mr Ten Per Cent and has also faced corruption charges – and two daughters.

During her years of exile the local government was always keen not to publicise Bhutto's politics. Yesterday it was easy to imagine why. Bhutto supporters whooped and yahooed amid the airport's brand-name shops and plastic palm trees. On the flight, as a boisterous Bhutto rally erupted in economy class, flight attendants looked on helplessly.

Bhutto has excited such emotions and expectations before, only to allow them to evaporate in bitter disappointment. Crowds lined the streets in 1986 when she returned from exile in London. But when her second government foundered 10 years later amid scandal and corruption, few were weeping.

This time it will be different, she promised. 'I have gained a lot of experience. I'm older now, and wiser I hope.' Time will tell. For now her fate is tied with that of the president, Pervez Musharraf, who reportedly spent the morning at his army offices in Rawalpindi. Did she think he was watching on TV? 'You must ask him,' said Bhutto. 'But I am glad there's been no disruption of my welcome. This is a good sign of reconciliation.'

For critics, the 'reconciliation' is little more than a greasy political deal. Musharraf wants to keep power despite plunging ratings and Bhutto offers a solution. Many of those critics are within her ranks, and she will spend the coming weeks quietly convincing them.

Three hours after it had set out, her caravan had advanced one 10th of the 10-mile journey to the tomb of Pakistan's founder, Muhammad Ali Jinnah, where Bhutto had been due to give a speech.

OCTOBER 20 2007

# Riven by class and no social mobility – Britain in 2007

## JULIAN GLOVER

Ten years of Labour rule have failed to create a classless society, according to a *Guardian*/ICM poll published today. It shows that Britain remains a nation dominated by class division, with a huge majority certain that their social standing determines the way they are judged.

Of those questioned, 89 per cent said they think people are still judged by their class – with almost half saying that it still counts for 'a lot'. Only 8 per cent think that class does not matter at all in shaping the way people are seen.

The poorest people in society are most aware of its impact, with 55 per cent of them saying class, not ability, greatly affects the way they are seen.

Gordon Brown claimed at this year's Labour conference that 'a class-free society is not a slogan but in Britain can become a reality'. But even the supposedly meritocratic Thatcher generation of adults born in the 1980s appear to doubt that: 90 per cent of 18- to 24-year-olds say people are judged by their class.

The poll also shows that after 10 years of Labour government, social change in Britain is almost static. Despite the collapse of industrial employment, the working class is an unchanging majority. In 1998, when ICM last asked, 55 per cent of people considered themselves working class. Now the figure stands at 53 per cent. Of people born to working class parents, 77 per cent say they are working class too. Only one fifth say they have become middle class.

Despite huge economic change and the government's efforts to build what it calls an opportunity society, people who think of themselves as middle class are still in a minority. In 1998, 41 per cent of people thought of themselves as middle class, exactly the same proportion as today. The upper class is almost extinct, with only 2 per cent of those who answered claiming to be part of it.

The poll paints a picture of a nation divided by social attitudes and life-chances, with 47 per cent of those living in south-east England considering themselves middle class, against 39 per cent in the north and 35 per cent in Wales and the west.

Northern England remains a working-class heartland, with 57 per cent of people describing themselves as part of it.

Scots – 47 per cent of whom think they are middle class – are just as class-bound as English citizens. Almost half of Scots say that class plays an important part in the way people are judged by others.

Social change is taking place slowly. The middle class has grown: although 41 per cent of people think they are part of it, only 32 per cent say their parents were. In 1998, 69 per cent of people thought their parents were working class. Now only 63 per cent say so, and of those only 53 per cent say they are working class themselves. That shift mirrors the attitude of the ex-deputy prime minister John Prescott, who admitted 'I'm pretty middle class' despite working-class origins.

But many class attitudes have survived economic change. That suggests people are still judged by where they come from rather than how much they earn.

OCTOBER 25 2007

# Light on dogma, generous with laughs

## SIMON HOGGART

They laid Alan Coren to rest yesterday. Rest? Quite the wrong word; it would be hard to think of anyone less needing eternal rest. Right to the end he was joking, not just telling gags but revelling in the rich absurdity of all human life. Being dead means he is out of touch with his best source material. It must be appallingly frustrating.

He was buried in a beautiful plot on a slight slope, surrounded by trees, with a view over what may be the loveliest cemetery in London. It's in the heart of what he called Cricklewood, to the fury of local residents who insisted it was Hampstead, actually.

We were gathered round the grave for the service. Alan had been raised in orthodox Judaism, but he himself was – in Jonathan Miller's words – 'not really a Jew, just Jewish' and in any case, no orthodox rabbi would officiate in a municipal cemetery. So we had Rabbi David Goldberg, from a liberal synagogue, with a rich, rolling voice like an Anglican country parson.

It was quite a crowd. First the family, his widow, Anne, his companion for more than 40 years, and to whom he scurried home at the earliest possible moment rather than drink with colleagues. 'In that respect,' said Rabbi Goldberg, 'he was the Jonny Wilkinson of newspapers.' Their children, Giles and Victoria. There were showbusiness friends such as Maureen Lipman, Tom Conti and Esther Rantzen; folk from the radio, especially radio comedy, such as Andy Hamilton, Jeremy Hardy, Armando Iannucci, Mark Steel, Barry Cryer, Libby Purves and Sandi Toksvig, one of his closest friends, who may have taken his death harder than anyone outside the family.

And Mark Damazer, the head of Radio 4, newsreaders including Peter Donaldson, Brian Perkins and Corrie Corfield, friends from *Punch* days, such as Christopher Matthew, Michael Bywater, Valerie Grove and Dame Ann Leslie.

There was Jeremy Robson, who published an astonishing 35 books by Alan (and a memorial volume to come) and people who just liked being with him: Claire Rayner, and Michael Howard, for instance. The former Tory leader is cursed forever by Ann Widdecombe's 'something of the night' remark, which makes him such an appropriate guest at a funeral.

Round the grave we swapped stories. Christopher Matthew thought Alan's funniest line came after a news item about how the CIA was trying to extend its spies' careers: 'Bond tensed in the darkness, and reached for his teeth.' The service, being liberal, was largely in English.

At one point the rabbi said that in death our 'hope is for immortality'; so much more tentative than *The Book of Common Prayer*, which speaks of the 'sure and certain hope of resurrection'. But liberal Jews are famously light on dogma. At funerals there is usually one moment that makes your throat tighten and your eyes moisten.

For me it was when Anne Coren, on a stick because her hip has been broken, walked slowly to the grave to throw a handful of earth on to the coffin, and there was that terrible, yet horribly familiar sound, which implies eternity more than any words can.

OCTOBER 29 2007

# Country Diary: Lake District

## TONY GREENBANK

The top of Great Gable is a poignant place. In 1924 its bronze tablet war memorial was dedicated before a gathering of 500 by Geoffrey Winthrop Young to the members of the Fell and Rock Climbing Club who had fallen. On that same day his friend (for whom he was best man) George Mallory was last seen making his summit bid on Everest. In some way this scene of Mallory and his climbing partner Andrew Irvine disappearing into cloud was movingly relived recently as two *Guardian* books were launched on the summit of Great Gable in a biting wind and with tendrils of mists making figures on the skyline disappear and reappear as ghostly apparitions.

There were however 70 people making for the summit, not two, and such were the conditions the figures in various states of disarray among the vaporous mists boiling up around them resembled a Brueghel painting of hell. Martin Wainwright, editor of *Wartime Country Diaries*, gave a moving tribute to long-gone writers recording their observations in the 'damnable' conflict. One contributor wrote: 'I cannot help thinking that if only Hitler had been an ornithologist he would put off the war until after the autumn bird migration was over.' Richard Nelsson, the compiler of his kindred

*Guardian Book of Mountains*, also gave readings concerning conflict, though this was based upon the eternal struggle between mankind and hills. Rocks streaming with water added seriousness to the spoken words with droplets of blood red wine pooling in dimples among the rocks. Red too were remnants of aged poppies from last Remembrance Sunday left by walkers who attended the annual Gable-top service. In this respect the Fell and Rock Climbing Club has asked climbers this year not to bring poppies as they add to the litter. Their thoughts and sorrows will be every bit as sincere without these well-meaning tokens.

NOVEMBER 10 2007

# Not sensible, but, oh, the joy of it!

## STEPHEN FRY

And lo! The great day came.

I have been using an Apple iPhone now for more than four months. This is due to an unhealthy mixture of friendship with its designer, a slobbery and pathetic love of the new, the possession of an American billing address [necessary until today for the activation and use of the device] and a willingness to pay preposterous international roaming charges. It puts me in a good position, however, to tell you what you're in for if you decide to own one of these honeys.

I should first get out of the way all the matters that will please those of you wrinkling your noses in a contemptuous Ian Hisloppy sort of way at the sheer hype, pretension, nonsense and hoopla attendant on what is, after all, only a phone. There is much to support your case.

Proud techie owners of rival devices can say: 'What, only a 2-meg camera? What, no GPS? What, no 3G? What, no video? What, no third-party applications? What, no sim card swapping?' A whole heap of what no-ing can be done.

Proud non-techie people can say: 'I just want a phone that lets me make a call with the minimum of fuss. I don't want a "design classic" and I certainly don't want to be locked into an 18-month data plan, whatever that might be.'

Even those excited by the iPhone and likely to block their ears to the derisive hoots above, even they must allow themselves honestly to accept its drawbacks. Text entry is, despite the spine-tingling brilliance of a creepily accurate auto-correct facility, clumsy. There are perhaps a dozen niggles of that nature (though the camera isn't one: the iPhone's lowly 2-megapixel snapper easily outperforms higher-spec rivals). So what's to set against these drawbacks?

Beauty. Charm. Delight. Excitement. Ooh. Aah. Wow! Let me at it.

In the end the iPhone is like some glorious early-60s sports car. Not as practical, reliable, economical, sensible or roomy as a family saloon but oh, the joy. The *jouissance*, as Roland Barthes liked to say. What it does, it does supremely well, that what it does not do seems laughably irrelevant.

The iPhone is a digital experience in the literal sense of the word. The user's digits roam, stroke, tweak, tweeze, pinch, probe, slide, swipe and tap across the glass screen forging a relationship with the device that is like no other.

'But I don't want to "forge a relationship", I just want to get the job done,' you say? Well then, you know what? Don't buy one. And stop reading this. You're only doing so in the first place to lend fuel to your snorts and puffs of rage. Allow us our pleasures.

Whatever your view on Apple's new instant icon, you will not be able to deny that it has already changed forever what was already a colossal market.

There was pre-iPhone and there will be post-iPhone. All the competitors will have to come up with something better. I'm no red-in-tooth-and-claw capitalist, but actually, I can't think this example of mercantile evolution-through-competition is so very bad.

Conflict-traded rare earths and minerals, that's another matter. Someone wrote to tell me that the iPhone is full of Congolese metals. *Guardian* readers may want elucidation on this front. I'm not the man to give it, I fear.

The rest of the world can mock as much as it likes. If you're going to have a phone/video player/slideshow/music centre/web browser/camera in your pocket, is it so wrong to want one that makes you grin from ear to ear? Not with smugness (though heaven knows the enemies of the device will read that into the smiles) but with delight.

© *Stephen Fry 2007*

NOVEMBER 13 2007

# No need for cold feet over Leeds, Chelsy

### MARTIN WAINWRIGHT

Oh dear. It's a bit feeble if Prince Harry's girlfriend, Chelsy Davy, has really told friends she's abandoning Leeds because of the cold weather. We only had this autumn's first frost last night, and October was so mild that the leaves are still gloriously on the trees.

Woodhouse Moor, on Chelsy's doorstep in her terrace house,

looks just as vivid as the *msasas* in her native southern Africa, and the best is yet to come. Surely someone has told Chelsy that Leeds is drier than Barcelona. This makes winter lovely and bright, and the students become extra rosy-faced at the temporary ice rink outside the Civic Hall, plus visits to the Reliance bar. If you still have a cold corner after that, it isn't anything that won't be put right by a plate of toast and dripping from the Chemic, another pub just a handy walk from Chelsy's house.

She'll miss that, too. It may look a bit tatty in the *Sun*'s photograph, but Headingley's redbrick terraces are officially student heaven. I'm not of an age to say that definitively myself, but an academic study seven years ago described the Victorian suburb as 'a Shangri-la for young people'.

The excuse that a Zimbabwean like Chelsy suffers climate change more acutely doesn't really wash, either. You only have to take a detour through Leeds University campus to meet students from every part of the world. Goodness, we even had an African prince here once, Alamayou, the eldest son of King Theodore of Abyssinia. He lodged in Headingley too, in 1879. Actually, I've just discovered that 'he caught a severe cold and died within weeks.' But there are exceptions to every rule.

NOVEMBER 28 2007

# In praise of ... Gérard Errera

## LEADER

The Foreign Office lists 153 foreign ambassadors and high commissioners currently stationed in London, along with a further 22 acting heads of mission. In the nature of things, only a handful of this cosmopolitan herd of emissaries have either the national clout or the personality to make a wider impact in British life during their stay here. One of the few who has done so in recent years has been the French ambassador to Britain since 2002, His Excellency Gérard Errera, who will be packing his bags on Friday before returning to Paris to start work as head of the diplomatic service at the Quai d'Orsay on Monday. Mr Errera's predecessor left London early, after the *Daily Telegraph* outed him as the author of a nasty insult against Israel. But Mr Errera himself has not stayed long enough in a London that is nowadays home to more of his compatriots than many French cities. Through some turbulent times for the Franco-British relationship, especially on Iraq and the EU constitution, the ambassador has been an unfailingly approachable and informative advocate of his country's position, as well as a prominent figure in British social and cultural life. As much at ease on the lawns of Glyndebourne as in displaying his alarming familiarity with the works of Lonnie Donegan, Mr Errera has been one of the wittiest and wisest diplomats in modern times, a worthy follower in the footsteps of Talleyrand, living proof that French Anglophiles really do exist, and a true friend to this country as well as his own.

Orchids are moved into position for the RHS Chelsea
Flower Show, May 2008.

GRAEME ROBERTSON

Reggae Star Jimmy Cliff, June 2008.

SARAH LEE

Children play in the musical fountain outside
Beijing's Bird's Nest stadium, August 2008.

DAN CHUNG

Earthquake refugees in Mianyang, China, May 2008.

DAN CHUNG

American soldier holds the baby during a food handout, Baghdad, June 2008.

SEAN SMITH

# Winter

# Bankers party even as fears grow for City bonuses and jobs

## JILL TREANOR

The sub-prime debt crisis may have cost Barclays £1.3bn but it has not vanquished the Christmas spirit at its investment banking arm, Barclays Capital.

This week 3,000 or so bankers are expected to swap their glass-fronted offices in Canary Wharf for a marquee erected beside the Houses of Parliament.

Filling most of Victoria Tower Gardens on Millbank, the sound-proofed structure has a licence for two nights of entertainment. The party – rumoured to have cost £600,000 – is evidence that though the credit crunch has caused pain in the financial markets in the past four months, some bankers can still enjoy gains made in the first six months of the year.

The Centre for Economics and Business Research has forecast that bonus payments across the City will be down by 16 per cent on last year's record £8.8bn, but billions of pounds will still be poured into some bankers' pockets early next year.

The bonus round starts within days, when the likes of Goldman Sachs and Morgan Stanley reveal the extent of their payouts to employees. Goldman star players are tipped to do particularly well because it has weathered the sub-prime crisis better than its rivals. The bank's total compensation bill is expected to reach $18bn (£9bn), higher than last year's $16.5bn, and even though it wrote down $1.7bn of loans in the sub-prime crisis, its profits for the first nine months of the year are up on last year.

DECEMBER 15 2007

# Hotel checks out: Last day of cucumber sandwiches before Savoy closes its doors

## MAEV KENNEDY

Five winters ago Tony Cortegaca opened the doors of the Savoy as the hotel's last permanent resident left – on a stretcher.

As he was carried past the door to the Grill Room, the Irish actor Richard Harris managed to prop himself up on one elbow and shout to stunned guests, in that unmistakable voice blended from honey and sandpaper, 'It was the food ... the food!'

He died in hospital that night, and Cortegaca and the other staff who had known him and the rest of his gang of merry hell-raisers, including Richard Burton and Peter O'Toole, for decades, mourned him as a death in the family.

'A lovely, lovely man,' Cortegaca recalled – even though the hotel sometimes stuck him behind a screen in a corner of the grill room when he insisted on coming to eat in tracksuit and raincoat – 'one of the special ones'.

Today feels like another death in the family to 500 staff who between them have given thousands of years' work to the Savoy. Yesterday afternoon it was business as usual. Afternoon tea has been served every day since the hotel opened 118 years ago, and as the lights twinkled on the Christmas tree, and *Moon River* tinkled from the white grand piano, waitresses began to circulate the hundreds of rounds of cucumber sandwiches with the crusts cut off.

But today there is no honey still for tea, and after next week's auction there will be no honey spoons, sugar bowls, pink-rimmed tea cups, silver tea trays, cake stands or pink tablecloths either.

After breakfast Cortegaca will hail taxis and carry luggage as the last guests check out, and then he will lock the doors as the hotel closes for at least 16 months, for the most comprehensive refurbishment since it opened in 1889. Then, over three days next week, Bonham's will auction thousands of pieces of hotel history, including sofas, beds, mirrors, chandeliers, and the mahogany screen behind the reception desk commissioned at fabulous expense from Viscount Linley 15 years ago.

However, the novelist Fay Weldon, who in 2002 became the hotel's first writer in residence, occupying a riverside room where a mouse once ran over her foot, refuses to be sentimental.

'Things have to change. Hotels are not like homes. Carpets wear out, mattresses need replacing, windows need to be rust-free and to open and close, the current clientele are hardly literary or bohemian. Say Oscar Wilde to them and they look blank and think you're talking about Stephen Fry.'

The auction will include the contents of rooms once occupied by Wilde, by Humphrey Bogart and Katharine Hepburn, by Harris, and by the artists James Whistler and Claude Monet, although the decor and furnishings of their day have long gone.

'Those artists and writers who were up to much will be remembered by their work, not by the sofas they sat upon or the glasses they drank from,' Weldon said. 'So be it. Let the new world come and make ready for a new wave of mice, cockroaches and celebrity chefs. I only hope the lighting is good enough to read a book by.'

Almost all the staff have jobs to go to, but they have worked together for so long in the hotel once billed 'the palace by the river', that it feels like being orphaned. Cortegaca is losing his righthand man, Tony Harvey. The two Tonys have flanked the door on 12-hour shifts together in all weathers, sporting real white rose buttonholes supplied each morning and replaced in mid-afternoon with a fresher rose; coming to one another's aid with drunks; watching out for drivers who don't know that pub quiz staple: that the turn into the hotel is the only road in Britain where you drive on the right.

After Christmas they will both be back on the doorstep – but Tony Harvey will be at the Kensington Gardens hotel and Tony Cortegaca at the Lanesborough, one of five that vied to get him.

In its day, rival hoteliers came to stare at the Savoy in amazement. When Richard D'Oyly Carte decided to add some rooms on to the theatre he built to house Gilbert and Sullivan's Savoy Operas, he took careful note of the luxury hotels they had stayed in on tour in the States. His opened with lifts, hot water, central heating, showers and, most astonishing of all, electric lighting.

The latter proved a mixed blessing: like ageing actors terrified now of high-definition television, society beauties were horrified at the truths revealed by the bright artificial light. The hotel's famous pink tablecloths were introduced specifically to try and give a more flattering glow to the dining areas.

Two years ago the hotel was sold to the Fairmont group, which is now proposing to spend more than £100m on the refurbishment.

'I can't guarantee that the pink tablecloths will be back,' said Kieran MacDonald, the general manager. 'But I would be very surprised if there weren't some element of pinkness. Our intention is to restore what is best, what makes it the Savoy, not to destroy any of the atmosphere that makes this place so special to so many people.'

DECEMBER 19 2007

# Why I love supermarkets: (and why people who don't should get a life)

## JULIE BURCHILL

I read Jeanette Winterson's recent *Guardian* article about the joy of small shops and the evil of supermarkets with bemusement, amusement and amazement. Whose ego could possibly be so big and yet so fragile that whenever they nip out to the shops they demand 'passion, commitment – something more than the transaction', because, 'I'm not here to make a profit for somebody who couldn't care less about what they are selling, about how it is made, or about me'?

Maybe I'm lucky, but personally I find I get all the validation, passion and commitment I need from my family, friends, religion and voluntary work; that I might go looking for proof of my worth over the wet fish counter seems quite eye-wateringly daft. But then, as with so many of those who idealise small shops and demonise big shops, Winterson's arguments seem to be based around prejudice and superstition rather than fact.

Though they use the word 'pleasure' a lot, I can't help thinking that there is something rather sad about people who bang on about the joys of 'slow shopping', and its kissing cousin 'slow food'; this always seems to mark out a dull and dreary nostalgia-hound with too much time on their hands and a morbid fear of modernity. A Tesco-hater in my local paper recently fumed, for instance, that 'Tesco is rampaging through Hove like Attila the

Hun – it's also ruining things around the world. Onions have been flown in from other countries even when they are in season in England. Tesco is trying to make everything uniform; that makes for a uniform life.' Bloody foreign onions, coming over here, taking our shelves …

I love Tesco; here in Hove we have six of the beauties. Of course the less unhinged among us will always go for speed and convenience over drudgery and difficulty, and we can also grasp that the very same small shopkeepers who get into a sweat about Tesco didn't go into their racket to make the world a better place, despite their mealy-mouthed protestations that they are working for the benefit of the 'community'. They chose to go into their kind of business because they are capitalists who wanted to make a profit – as did the man who started Tesco.

In 1919, after serving with the RAF during the first world war, 21-year-old Jack Cohen invested his £30 demob money in surplus food stocks and a stall in the East End of London. On his first day he had a £4 turnover and made £1 profit; now £1 in every £8 spent by shoppers in this country is handed over in his shops. The idea that Tesco has always been a corner-shop-crushing colossus is a lie, one perpetuated by bitter, third-rate businessmen who would dearly love to have achieved a quarter of what Cohen did but lacked the ability and luck to pull it off, and who now seek to clothe their envy and hypocrisy in the rhetoric of care for the community. But with a bit less moaning and a bit more ingenuity, what's to stop them doing the same? Instead they would rather spend their time whining, in the manner of one Ken Stevens of the Federation of Small Businesses in East Sussex to the Brighton Argus newspaper, 'Where they start selling everything cheaper, that can be very damaging.'

Gosh, selling things cheap to people – burn them down, let's, and make the world safe for greedy, over-charging rotters! Don't get me wrong; small local shops are all very well, abroad, where it's sunny and one doesn't have to stagger through the streets in the pissing rain for six months of the year in search of the perfect pain au chocolat. But there can be few humdrum feelings more satisfying than knowing that one has bagged a week's worth of shopping in 45 minutes, and that one is now free to party the remaining days away and sleep in late every morning, safe from the fear that the cupboard is bare. If one can also find cheap books, CDs and pet insurance under the same roof, so much the better.

Far from making our lives limited, supermarkets open us up to taste thrills from all around the world at any time of the year – as opposed to laying down the law that we can only have strawberries in a month with 'J' in it, or whatever small-minded voodoo the foodies subscribe to. And let me please declare that I, for one, wasn't put on this earth to make life easy for British farmers, who are a reactionary and misanthropic lot as a rule – gaily destroying wildlife, backing blood sports, feeding animals the remains of their relatives and driving them mad. The EU has done enough to feather their nests; I don't need to add to their nest eggs when I go shopping. This sort of backward thinking, taken to its logical conclusion, would also see the return of morris dancing, inbreeding and operations without benefit of anaesthetic; no thanks, make mine modern!

I love the lights and rush and exhilaration of speeding round the supermarket; let those saddoes who want to dawdle their day away over errands, but some of us love the buzz of getting things done quickly so one can then move on and do something one loves, be it sex, conversation or lazing away the day on the sofa or the beach with a good book. People who are against Tesco are the sort of people who 50 years ago would have been against labour-saving devices on the grounds that they might conceivably give women time to put their feet up, have a cup of tea and watch daytime telly for half an hour.

Winterson dismisses supermarket employees, in all their diversity, as 'phoney', 'robotic' and full of 'fake helpfulness'. That's certainly not my experience of these good-humoured people, and speaks of a snobbish and unimaginative view of a whole swathe of humanity. She also attempts to convince us that small shops keep 'communities' – always a slightly shady word, as conservative as it is comfy – together. And she fetishises the family, as slow-shop lovers so often do, as in her comment that 'in every European city, family-run bars and shops have held their own against global-market madness', and her later reference to 'family-run concerns who spend much of their income where they live'. Whenever I hear the word 'family' used as a moral absolute, I immediately reach for my amyl nitrate and my whistle. Families are only as good or as bad as the individual family in question; seeing the word used as shorthand for all that is good and pure is ridiculous.

I am neither old nor poor, but I am able to put myself in the cheap chain-store shoes of people to whom supermarkets have proved nothing but a blessing. This is probably because I have no fear of the modern world, a fear that runs like mad mercury through those who celebrate small shops. But it is the modern world that has given so many of us the right to follow our hearts, live our dreams and hold fast to our freedom. The traditional world Winterson now worships, on the other hand, would have seen her living a lie and being forced by convention into a joyless marriage with a local lad, to eke out her days in the sort of rainy English provincial town she so despises.

One of the lowest blows used by the enemies of supermarkets is that old people, especially, feel frightened and alienated by them. This argument drives me mad: a) what an ignorant and condescending view of a generation who faced Hitler (a man who actually wanted to ban chain stores and give back the power to the small shopkeeper, fact fans!) and have more spirit in their little toes than we do in our entire scaredy-cat, food-intolerance-ridden bodies. And, b) they should get out a bit more, beyond the chi-chi 'family concerns' they breathe the rarified air of, and see the very different looks on the faces of the old people I see shopping in my local pedestrianised parade of small shops and in my local big, beautiful Tesco. It's so sad to see them stumble from shop to shop in the teeming rain, weighed down under their shopping bags; so lovely to see them strolling in the warm, dry brightness of the supermarket, leaning on their trollies like they were leaning on the backyard walls of their younger days, blocking the aisles without a care as they bump into their similarly strolling friends and set up a gossip-station right there. Then home – to await a big strong man lugging all that heavy shopping for them at their convenience. Perfect.

DECEMBER 22 2007

# Gout is no joke. This I know from painful experience

## MARTIN KETTLE

When I mention to someone that I suffer from gout – and I try hard not to bring it into the conversation too often – I can predict that they will respond in one of three ways. In response number one they say: 'I thought gout was an 18th-century thing; I didn't know people got it nowadays.' Response number two is to say: 'Been drinking too much port, have you, old chap?' The third response is to laugh.

To which my own reactions go like this. First, you can bet your life that people still suffer from gout today, and in growing numbers. Second, I think I last had a glass of port at Christmas 1995 or thereabouts, and drink normally has very little to do with it. Third, when someone laughs about gout, I have to try hard not to hit them.

Until I had my first attack 18 months ago, I was one of the ignorant majority too. When the word gout cropped up, I thought of Dr Johnson and Pitt the Elder, not Tony Soprano or Harry Kewell (all gout sufferers). But then the gout crept silently into my foot in the night – a common initial assault – and my world changed. Ever since, I have become aware that ignorance about gout is normal. Like many mainly guy things, gout is rarely discussed. But it is one of the most excruciatingly painful things that it can ever be your misfortune to encounter. I'm also told it makes you irritable. Damn right it does.

When I say 'one of' the most painful, this may be too modest. For the pain of gout may even be unmatched. It is no surprise to me that in a survey two-thirds of US gout sufferers ranked their attacks as 'the worst pain possible'. Some readers may bridle at this assertion. Right-thinking people have long accorded a unique status to childbirth as the most painful of all experiences. Yet, strapping on my tin-hat in anticipation of the response, it was a female GP of my acquaintance, who has had four children by natural delivery, who assured me that gout is indeed worse than childbirth. That is something I can never know, and I do not seek to make the worst the enemy of the bad but, please, reader, at least accept my assurance that gout is agonising.

Nevertheless, the idea that gout is a bit of a joke runs deep. Even the revered *Guardian* can treat it as a bit of a giggle. A month ago there was a revealing intro in this paper on a story about supposedly work-shy benefit claimants. 'Tiredness, gout and acne,' the story began, 'are some of the illnesses cited by incapacity bene-fit claimants, according to a Department for Work and Pensions document.' I don't think I am being paranoid in seeing the brack-eting of those three conditions as implying that none of them is a legitimate reason for not working.

All I can say to that is that, if I hadn't been a journalist with a good employer, able to work from home in bare feet or wearing soft slippers for large parts of the past 18 months, there's no way I could have held down a regular job. Your life changes when you can't get your shoes on because your feet are periodically swollen and full of pain. If your job depends on your feet, as it does for dancers, postal workers or footballers, then gout means it's curtains for work until you recover. No police officer could walk the beat with gout. No bus driver could safely get behind the wheel. Everything alters, even in your everyday life. You can't nip out to the shops the way you used to. Queueing is a misery. Sitting in a theatre seat is uncomfortable. Long plane journeys can be excruciating.

So, whatever else there is to say about incapacity benefit abuse, there is no excuse for the idea that claimants suffering from gout are somehow on the skive. I'm prepared to bet that every one of the 3,000 people who claim the benefit because gout prevents them from working is telling God's truth. If I were work and pensions secretary, I wouldn't be trying to shove gout sufferers off the benefit rolls, that's for certain.

Earlier this year, a rather grand figure of my acquaintance actu-ally congratulated me on getting gout. Such a distinguished disease, he assured me. Only the most interesting people get it. I retorted that you could say the same about syphilis. Anyway, the figures do not bear out this snobbery about gout being the patri-cian malady. Emperors and philosophers may indeed suffer from gout – as both Alexander the Great and Kant did. But so too do binmen and clerks. There was a piece in the paper the other day about a Heathrow security guard who started getting gout at 23. When he was diagnosed, he said exactly the same thing that we all say: 'How have I got gout? That's a disease rich old folk get.'

But it is not. Once you get gout, you soon realise that it is more common than you supposed. I know three *Guardian* colleagues with gout and I bet there are others. You soon see the world through fellow gout-sufferers' eyes too. Steve Bell pointed out to me an incisively brilliant 18th-century cartoon about gout by James Gillray – the devil is biting into the side of a man's toe joint. Only a sufferer could have done that drawing, just as only another sufferer, Ivan Turgenev, could have drawn for Pauline Viardot the witty little sketch of him climbing the stairs on his backside with his foot swathed in bandages stuck out in front of him. When I studied the 17th century, I never had any time for the Earl of Strafford, arguably the most dangerous over-mighty subject in English history. Yet I could feel even Strafford's pain when I read about his awful gout in John Adamson's recent book about the overthrow of Charles I.

The good news is that a combination of dietary watchfulness and modern medicine eventually equips you to overcome gout – or so I am told and hope. I can vouch for the fact that it isn't a quick process. Daily pills reduce the levels of uric acid that form the crystals which lodge in the joints to produce gout. Who knows, in 2008 I may even go on a walking holiday again. Provided I go easy on the port over Christmas, of course.

DECEMBER 27 2007

# Obituary: Oscar Peterson

## JOHN FORDHAM

After the phenomenal jazz-piano virtuoso Art Tatum died in 1956, the Canadian pianist Oscar Peterson, who had already been waiting in the wings for a decade, eased his formidable frame on to the throne. Like Tatum, Peterson had a Liszt-like technique (classical music's star pianists came to marvel at both of them), and could transform any melody into streams of spontaneous variations, sustain any tempo, use his left hand as freely as his right, and keep a faultless built-in rhythm section at work in his head. These skills made Peterson, who has died of kidney failure at the age of 82, one of the best-loved stars of the jazz mainstream.

Less charitable jazz purists might have held that he was the unfortunate victim of his spectacular technique. All his performances would feature the same mix of flooding arpeggios, cascading introductions and codas, ragtime and barrelhouse pastiches and solos at impossible tempos. Even after a stroke in 1993, he fought to rebuild much of his sweeping technical authority. The standard Peterson trio offering would be the uptempo tune (either a standard or an original that sounded like a standard), starting either solo or with minimal accompaniment. It would grow in volume from piano and drums in the second chorus, and by the third become an unbroken cascade of runs the length of the keyboard, resolving in thumping chords, thumbs-down-the-keys ripples and churning, repeated phrases.

With cavalier glee, Peterson would apply this treatment to tunes ideally suited to it as well as those that were not, with ballads relapsing bizarrely into caresses at the end. Yet there was a true artist in him too. Deliciously liquid arpeggios and arching, yearning phrases would sometimes emerge once he was sure he had given his audiences what they initially expected, and such contrastingly patient and spacious music might then allow the eloquence of his frequently superb accompanists to flower, notably the work of the double-bassist Ray Brown.

Peterson had received classical piano lessons from the age of six in his native Montreal. The impetus came from his father, a railway porter and self-taught pianist. At 14, Oscar won a local radio talent contest, worked in his late teens on a weekly Montreal radio show and was also a regular member of the Johnny Holmes Orchestra, playing in an elegant swing keyboard style drawn from Teddy Wilson, Tatum and Nat King Cole. Though he had studied trumpet too, childhood illness led him to abandon it for the piano, and he practised constantly, an irrepressible enthusiasm mingling with natural gifts to build a fully two-handed technique that rivalled that of classical recitalists (some 1940s jazz pianists made relatively perfunctory use of the left hand). Though Cole was perhaps the artist with whom Peterson felt most in sympathy stylistically, the speed, orchestral richness and lyrical sweep of his music made Tatum the only fitting comparison once the Canadian's mature style formed.

Peterson resisted offers to come to the US at first but made his American debut at Carnegie Hall, New York, with Norman Granz's Jazz at the Philharmonic in September 1949. Granz saw in Peterson just his kind of charismatic, communicative performer who reaches out from the subculture of jazz to a much wider audience, and he managed the pianist's career through the 1950s, recorded him and included him in regular tours with Jazz at the Philharmonic.

Initially, Peterson adopted the Cole trio's methods, frequently playing simply with guitar and double-bass and allowing his own, unerring rhythmic sense and driving swing to take the place of drums. Through the 1950s, his bassist was usually Brown, with Herb Ellis on guitar, but from 1958 Ellis was replaced by the subtle drummer Ed Thigpen, one of the few percussionists who could complement the storming Peterson without appearing to compete with him for the maximum number of sounds that could be squeezed into a bar. The group recorded extensively, and Peterson's reworkings of classic standards were so exuberant and upbeat that his recordings found their way into the collections of jazz fans and fascinated non-enthusiasts alike.

In 1960, Peterson founded the Advanced School of Contemporary Music in Toronto, assisted by Brown, Thigpen and the composer/ clarinettist Phil Nimmons, and he remained there for the next three years, devoting much of his time to running the institution. He continued to perform and record, and developed another string to his considerable bow by singing on a Cole dedication, *With Respect to Nat*, in 1965.

In the 1970s, though jazz was in retreat against the swelling popular and commercial pressure of rock'n'roll, Peterson continued to prove that his talents were robust enough to be less affected by the changing climate than most. He took to performing unaccompanied and delivered astonishingly self-sufficient performances in which he frequently seemed to resemble two or three pianists playing simultaneously. By this time one of the most secure of mainstream international jazz stars, he was invited to perform in all kinds of contexts, including work with symphony orchestras and guest appearances on many all-star jazz get-togethers with artists including Ella Fitzgerald, Stan Getz, the trumpeters Dizzy Gillespie and Clark Terry, and the guitarist Joe Pass.

In later years Peterson frequently worked in duet with Danish bassist Niels-Henning Orsted Pedersen, a remarkable virtuoso of complementary gifts to the pianist's. Pared-down accompaniment always suited Peterson best, as his devastating technique often meant that the more musicians there were in a Peterson group, the more they would all try to keep up, like a party full of non-stop talkers.

Peterson had a prolific output as a recording artist, in some years releasing as many as half a dozen albums. *Affinity* (1963) was one of his biggest sellers but his catalogue includes interpretations of the songbooks of Cole Porter and Duke Ellington, a highly successful single on Jimmy Forrest's compulsive *Night Train* (perfectly suited to Peterson's churningly machine-like style), and *Canadiana Suite* (1964), an extended original nominated as one of the best jazz compositions of 1965 by the National Academy of Recording Arts and Sciences.

He furnished the soundtrack to the movie *Play It Again Sam* (1972), hosted a TV chatshow, toured Russia in 1974 and influenced musicians as varied as Steve Winwood, Dudley Moore and Joe Zawinul. A dedicated spreader of the word, he also published educational works for student jazz pianists.

Though Peterson has sometimes been criticised as a musician in thrall to his own runaway technique, he remained an effective populariser of jazz among those who might otherwise not have encountered it. He was the kind of performer who invited a sometimes daunted general public in, and he always performed as if making music was the most fun a human being could possibly have. When he performed to a packed Royal Albert Hall two years ago, he delivered a startlingly ambitious programme for a man who looked as if the journey from the dressing room to the piano stool had been a considerable effort. That show could have been a wistful tribute to the past, but with musicality, courage, skill and energy, Peterson made it a performance that stood proud on its own two feet. It was the story of his life.

Also in 2005, he became the first living person other than a monarch to feature on a Canadian commemorative stamp, having already seen his name adopted for streets, concert halls and schools.

He is survived by his fourth wife, Kelly, their daughter Celine, two sons and three daughters from his first marriage and a son from his third marriage.

*Oscar Emmanuel Peterson, jazz pianist, born August 15 1925; died December 23 2007*

DECEMBER 28 2007

# Straight talking and war stories help make McCain the oldest Comeback Kid in town

### EWEN MACASKILL

John McCain wiped a tear from his eye. It had been a routine campaign meeting until that point, a stop at a staff canteen in Concord, New Hampshire. There had been the same lines and the same jokes as on earlier stops, until someone asked him about his heroes.

He mentioned Reagan, Teddy Roosevelt, Lincoln ... and Mike Christian. McCain, held for five-and-a-half years in a jail in North Vietnam, shared a cell with Christian. 'He exemplified everything that is best about America,' McCain said. He made a stars and stripes from assorted bits of cloth, sewed it inside his shirt and the prisoners had each day hung it on a wall as they took the pledge of allegiance. The North Vietnamese found it and

Christian, though severely beaten, immediately started work on making a new one.

He has told the story many, many times but it still has a resonance for Americans. The staff, who work for a big financial centre, stopped shuffling in their seats and listened to him in silence. There are no doubts about McCain's patriotism, given his military record, and his Republican rivals cannot match it, no matter how hard they try, whether it is Rudy Giuliani on his role in the aftermath of 9/11 or Mitt Romney recounting his presence at an airport in Boston as the body of a soldier killed in Iraq came off a baggage conveyor belt.

McCain, an Arizona senator, is having the best weeks of his campaign so far. He began the year in expectation of being the favourite but then spent the next 10 months behind Giuliani and Romney in the polls and, since November, Mike Huckabee. His campaign almost went bankrupt in the summer and he laid off staff.

He has since concentrated his time and limited resources on a win in New Hampshire, where the first primary is to be held on January 8. And the strategy appears to be working, producing a remarkable recovery that makes him this campaign's Comeback Kid. In a *Boston Globe* poll on Sunday, Romney's lead over McCain in New Hampshire was cut from 15 points last month to three.

In an email to supporters, McCain's campaign manager, Rick Davis, set out the strategy: 'a strong finish' in Iowa, where McCain was campaigning yesterday; a win in New Hampshire; a 'well-positioned' showing in Michigan; a win in South Carolina and a 'unique ability' to compete in Florida.

But McCain's war record, his years in the senate, and his experience in foreign affairs may not be enough. It could still turn out that his best chance was in 2000 when he stood against George Bush, winning New Hampshire but crucially losing the South

Carolina primary. If he was to win he would, at 72, be the oldest president to enter office.

Tim Fraser, 45, a salesman, said he had voted for McCain in 2000 but would not be doing so this time round. Fraser, a registered independent, said: 'I came along to have a look at him in case I was missing something.' He supported him in 2000 but McCain had since shifted to a more conservative position. He did not intend voting for any of the Republicans but would vote in the Democratic race.

McCain needs the backing of independents such as Fraser, who make up an estimated 44 per cent of the New Hampshire electorate and can choose to vote in either the Democratic or Republican nomination contest.

At a meeting in a public library in Concord McCain addressed a group of independents. Asked if he would stand as an independent if he failed to secure the Republican nomination, McCain joked he would rather stand as a 'vegetarian' candidate. On the face of it, that is not the way to go about winning over independents, but they laughed.

He has a habit of these quips; the media following him love it. At a meeting in an American Legion hall in Hillsborough he identified a questioner as the 'guy in the dorky hat'. The man was pleased rather than offended.

McCain revels in his reputation for saying what he thinks and hardly a speech goes by without him referring to 'straight talk'. He tours New Hampshire's town halls, homes, bars and anywhere else there are voters in his 'Straight Talk Express' bus.

One of the reasons he is not campaigning much in Iowa, whose caucus is on January 3, is that he has been honest enough to say, unlike all the other candidates, that he is opposed to federal subsidies for ethanol, the petrol-substitute from corn, one of the main staples of that state's farmers.

Nick Gervasio, 65, who was at the American Legion meeting and who described himself as a liberal Republican, said he appreciated that McCain gave an honest answer, though unwelcome, to a questioner demanding more social security. Gervasio said he would vote for him: 'He is not a typical politician. He tells the truth even if people do not want to hear it.'

Both McCain's father and grandfather were US navy admirals. His father commanded American forces in Vietnam while McCain was a prisoner of war. The North Vietnamese, on becoming aware of his father's position, offered to release him but McCain refused to be treated differently from his fellow PoWs.

He was tortured in Hanoi, one of the reasons he describes the CIA practice of 'waterboarding' as torture and is opposed. Although liberal on such issues, he has been a consistent conservative: pro-death penalty, opposed to abortion, hostile to European-style national health services and promising to be tough on federal spending.

He has struggled this year because of his support for the war in Iraq. Although he regularly cites reports that the Bush 'troop surge' is working, the war remains unpopular. He wears a black bracelet, given to him by a mother in memory of her son killed in Iraq.

He has also lost support because of a shift to the right, decrying Christian evangelicals in 2000 only to make an uneasy peace with them last year. And what has cost him Republican support more than anything was his championing this year, with the Democrat Ted Kennedy, of a bill that would have provided a route to citizenship for an estimated 12 million illegal immigrants.

In one of the wealthier suburbs of Concord, a family of McCain supporters threw open their huge home to neighbours to meet the senator. McCain, as usual, could not resist a joke, referring to the house as being in the 'projects' (social housing).

Crowded into the house was Mary French, 75, a real-estate broker and grandmother, who described herself as a pro-life conservative Republican. Before McCain spoke she said she was torn between him and Giuliani. Afterwards she said she would vote McCain. 'He has what a lot of them do not have: a moral compass. On his personal life he has a better track record.'

At the house party McCain recounted another story he regularly tells. He ran through the long list of candidates from Arizona, such as Barry Goldwater, who had sought the presidency and failed. In Arizona, McCain said, mothers, unlike in other states, 'do not bother to tell their children they might one day grow up to be the president'. McCain might yet find himself on that sorry list.

JANUARY 12 2008

# Obituary: Sir Edmund Hillary

## JIM PERRIN

I first met Edmund Hillary, who has died aged 88, in the Travellers club – a powerful figure in his mid-60s, broad of beam and shoulder, bear-like, inclined to paunchiness, the hair still dark, the energy superabundant. It was that competitiveness and drive that propelled him, as a 33-year-old New Zealander with a relatively limited mountaineering background – along with the Sherpa Tenzing Norgay – to be first to the summit of the world's highest peak.

Hillary was born of Yorkshire stock in Auckland. His martinet father had the pride, moral conservatism and fierce independence that typified the colonial pioneers. Educated at Tuakau district school, Auckland grammar and briefly at university in Auckland, two factors lent direction to Hillary's youth – his intoxicating encounter, initially through skiing, with mountains, and his father's move from journalism to beekeeping. Hillary also became an apiarist, and manhandling 90lb boxes of honeycomb built up the strength and endurance that was to serve him so well. His was an interesting family, practising Herbert Sutcliffe's theories of 'radiant living', exploring the ideas of Rudolph Steiner, pondering the teachings of Krishnamurti – all of which found expression in the practical and ideological romanticism of Hillary's later social policies in Nepal.

Hillary's mountaineering days began in New Zealand's Southern Alps in 1940. By 1944 he was a navigator on a Royal New Zealand Air Force Catalina flying boat. His squadron was stationed in Fiji – where he read Frank Smythe's books about 1930s Himalayan mountaineering – and in the Solomon Islands, where he was burned in an accident and invalided out of the service just after VJ Day. His recovery, however, was rapid.

A meeting with Harry Ayres, the outstanding immediate post-war New Zealand climber, led to an instructive tutelage. In 1948 the pair made the first ascent of the south ridge on Mount Cook, New Zealand's tallest peak at 3,754m (12,316ft). Later that year Hillary's role in a mountain rescue confirmed his 'growing belief that technical skill was not the only worthwhile characteristic of the first-class mountaineer'.

By 1950, he was ready for Europe, scaling many of the major Stubai Alps and the Bernese Oberland summits. As he wrote in his autobiography *Nothing Venture, Nothing Win* (1975): 'Our equipment was second-rate and our techniques no doubt mediocre. Nearly every party we saw was conducted by a guide and we struck a great reluctance to give any information or advice very different from the more informal and helpful atmosphere in our own sparsely populated mountains.'

On returning home, he accepted an invitation to join a 1951 New Zealand expedition to attempt Mukut Parbat, a difficult 7,242m (23,760ft) peak in the Garhwal Himalaya. En route, Hillary wrote to the British climber Eric Shipton asking if he might join the 1951 Everest reconnaissance expedition. Shipton responded with an invitation to Hillary and a companion to join his party. Hillary, as the fittest and best-acclimatised (though by his own admission not the most technically competent) set out immediately for Nepal. It was the start of a lifelong love affair. With Shipton, too, there was immediate rapport: 'I felt a sense of relief at his unshaven face and scruffy clothes.'

The two of them kept company for that first crucial view up into the Western Cwm, and after six months, Hillary's romance with Nepalese mountain travel was firmly established.

His performance in 1951 earned him a place on the 1952 British expedition to the unclimbed 8,201m (26,906ft) Cho Oyu – envisaged as training for an Everest expedition. Unfortunately, the peak lay directly on the Tibetan border, and the Chinese had just garrisoned the nearby town of Tingri, leading to the failure of the expedition.

The failure on Cho Oyu brought about the disgraceful and Machiavellian removal of Shipton from the leadership of the May 1953 expedition. Hillary stood by Shipton but was won over when John Hunt, Shipton's replacement, admitted that the change had been handled badly and called for his support.

It is significant that the three climbers who performed most strongly on Everest – Charles Evans, Hillary and Tenzing – were disaffected, either by the treatment of Shipton or by resentment on Tenzing's part at his own shabby treatment. Hillary had initially hoped to partner his fellow New Zealander George Lowe, but Hunt ruled this out. However, a growing warmth and respect had become apparent between Hillary and Tenzing.

As he was walking down to Kathmandu after the historic ascent, a letter arrived by runner, addressed to Sir Edmund Hillary KBE. Rather than feeling pleased, he was aghast. Nor was he any more delighted by the class of people with whom his new fame was to bring him into contact. 'I met the well-connected, the powerful and the rich; it was tremendously entertaining although I saw little to envy or, indeed, much to admire. We were being lionised by a class of society with which we had little in common.'

Another problem he faced was constant questioning over whether he or Tenzing had first taken the final step on to the summit. In fact, Hillary was always quite clear in his account of this, and a party line was agreed that they reached it simultaneously. This explanation did not appease popular feeling on the sub-continent that wanted Tenzing to have been the dominant partner in the final day's climb, and in some places, in both India and Nepal, Hillary was met with considerable animosity and coldness.

One benefit of his new fame was the confidence it gave him to stop off in Australia on his way home and propose to a musician, Louise Rose, whom he married weeks later and with whom he had three children. He wrote later in his autobiography that he could 'remember no occasion in the last 20 years that I could have wished for any other companion'.

In 1954 he went to the 8,462m (27,762ft) Makalu with Charles Evans, a trip that saw him suffer an attack of what appears to have been pulmonary oedema that was to herald the end of his career as a mountaineer at extreme altitude. Then, there was Antarctica, variously between 1955 and 1958 on Sir Vivian Fuchs 'Last Great Journey in the World' extravaganza, on which he proved that 'if you were enthusiastic enough and had good mechanics, you could get a farm tractor to the south pole'. When Hillary and his team on their Ferguson tractors reached the pole on January 4 1958, they were the first to have done so for 46 years.

Then it was back to the Himalayas with an American expedition in 1960 in search of the Yeti. In his book about the 1951 reconnaissance trip, Shipton – a notorious practical joker – had included a photograph of a Yeti footprint (Hillary stated to me that he believed it had been substantially 'improved' by Shipton). The expedition gathered local evidence and relics that were sent back for analysis, but the views of all the experts who examined them were unanimous that they were of more common Himalayan fauna.

Rather more valuable research was done on the same expedition – the first on which Hillary's wife accompanied him – into the long-term effects of altitude, and a further result was the building of an airstrip in the Solo Khumbu village of Mingbo, the first of Hillary's many community projects in the hill country of Nepal.

On his 1961 expedition to Makalu, he was forced down from 23,000ft with mild cerebral oedema. Although he undertook a few climbs at lower altitude in later years, this essentially marked the end of his serious mountaineering. However, the trip saw the completion of the first sherpa school at the village of Khumjung. 'It seemed an ideal way to repay the sherpas for the help they had given me,' Hillary said later.

Thereafter, his primary concern was the channelling of American corporate sponsorship into high-profile, low-technology and relatively low-cost community works in Nepal. He built schools at Thyangboche, Thami, Chaurikirka, Phortse, Pangboche and Junbesi; hospitals at Khumjung and Kunde; a water pipeline to Khumjung; a bridge over the Dudh Kosi to Namche Bazar; an airstrip at Lukla – the one now used by thousands of Everest trekkers each year.

His view of the effect of this work on the sherpa community was profoundly ambivalent: 'Those of us who loved the sherpas often felt they would live happier and more adequate lives if they were left untouched by contact with the outside world. But there was unfortunately no chance of this. Lukla ... hastened the onset of officialdom and tourism into the Everest area. Already the Khumbu has received many of the 'blessings' of civilisation – forests are being denuded, rubbish is piled high around the campsites and monasteries, and the children are learning to beg. The sherpas have a hospital and half-a-dozen schools, and more work is available – but is it sufficient recompense? At times I am racked by guilt.'

In most of these projects his wife was heavily involved. On March 31 1975, she and their youngest child, Belinda, were flying in to join him at the construction of a hospital at Paphlu when their plane crashed on take-off from Kathmandu. Both were killed. The blow was devastating. Rather than succumb, he redoubled his efforts on behalf of the Nepalese people.

In 1977, with his son, Peter (who developed into a formidable high-altitude mountaineer in his own right), he took part in 'From the Ocean to the Sky', a journey up the Ganges from its source to Badrinath, culminating in an attempt on the Garhwal peak of Nilkanta, close to where he had begun his Himalayan career. Four years later, even this doughty combatant had to acknowledge the effects of age during an American expedition to the east face of Everest. His glory days nearly three decades gone, he succumbed gracefully thereafter to the elder statesman role – a part he played well, and often with a sharp critical edge and robust tongue as the years and generations rolled by.

Hillary will be remembered as having been the right man in the right place at the right time. But the vigour and boldness with which he seized that opportunity, and the altruistic use to which he put his celebrity, are worthy of the highest respect. He could be brusque, tendentious and dismissive, but he was also kindly, direct, decent and incorruptible to a degree seldom found among those of great fame.

His books are all good, plain writing, the style graphic, the romanticism of outlook palpable, the philosophy surprisingly radical and tolerant. His 1953 account, *High Adventure*, in particular, is a much more engaged and vigorous piece of writing than the official expedition volume, and a classic of its genre. Ultimately, no doubt, his fame must rest on that single ascent and the thrusting, bold way in which it was accomplished. But as one of the first two men to step on to the highest point on Earth, thereby becoming mountaineering's first and perpetual ambassador, his position is unassailable.

*Sir Edmund Percival Hillary, mountaineer, born July 20 1919; died January 10 2008*

JANUARY 18 2008

# Review: *No Country for Old Men*

## PETER BRADSHAW

The bleak and unforgiving borderlands of Texas by the Rio Grande are the setting for this triumphant new movie by Joel and Ethan Coen, based on the western thriller by Cormac McCarthy. It's their best since *The Man Who Wasn't There* in 2001 – and it's the best of their career so far. The Coens are back with a vengeance, showing their various imitators and detractors what great American film-making looks like, and they have supplied a corrective adjustment to the excesses of goofy-quirky comedy that damaged their recent work. The result is a dark, violent and deeply disquieting drama, leavened with brilliant noirish wisecracks, and boasting three leading male performances with all the spectacular virility of Texan steers. And all of it hard and sharp as a diamond.

The setting is 1980, though the period is not signalled with any of the traditional giveaways. Tommy Lee Jones plays Sheriff Ed Tom Bell, an intelligent and sympathetic lawman, from a proud family of lawmen, who is, however, preparing to quit, having become disenchanted by society's inability to contain the criminals' evolutionary leap to a new level of ruthlessness. The twang and roll of Jones's voice is controlled with a musician's flair and the craggy folds of his hangdog face are a Texan landscape in themselves. He has a goosebump-inducing opening voiceover about sending unrepentant young killers to the gas chamber, superimposed on prospects of the western terrain photographed by Roger Deakins; it recalls the famous aria at the top of the Coens' first film, *Blood Simple*, in 1984.

Sheriff Ed Tom is nonetheless a welcome voice of sanity and humour in a world of evil. When he stumbles across a ring of decaying corpses and shot-up trucks and SUVs in the remote desert – the grisly remains of a drug deal gone sour – his callow young deputy remarks, plaintively: 'It's a mess, ain't it, Sheriff?' And Ed Tom replies, tersely: 'If it ain't, it'll do until the mess gets here.'

The second player is the psychopathic hitman Anton Chigurh, played by Javier Bardem, who has been hired by shadowy interests to recover a satchel of $2m in cash that has gone missing after this failed drug deal. Chigurh has an appalling hairstyle, and a habit of killing people with the air-pressure boltgun generally used on livestock, but there is nothing funny or ironic about him; he has a fanaticism that goes beyond the icy commitment of an assassin for hire. He is in effect a serial killer, an existential devotee of murder, a connoisseur of fear and victimhood, and finally appears to forget about the money in his pursuit of slaughter. The scene in which he bullies and threatens the gentle old proprietor of a local gas station is scalp-pricklingly disturbing. (Has the Coens' pre-eminence at the Cannes film festival caused them to imbibe the style of fellow auteur Michael Haneke?)

The third player is the Coens' great find: they have made a star of him. Josh Brolin is absolutely superb in the plum role of Llewelyn Moss, the taciturn Vietnam veteran who has innocently stumbled across this drug money while out hunting and headed off over the Mexican border with it, followed by the sinister Chigurh and the long-suffering Ed Tom, who knows that Moss is just a good ol' boy who needs protection and whose decent wife, Carla Jean, (Kelly Macdonald) is worried sick about him. Brolin gets some of the best lines in the film. 'If I don't come back, tell my momma I love her,' says Llewellyn. 'But your momma's dead,' replies Carla Jean. 'Well, then I'll tell her myself,' says Llewellyn, after a thoughtful pause.

The tone of the film, like that of McCarthy's original novel, is apocalyptic: it gestures ahead, darkly, to an utter annihilation of norms and restraints. The Coens' adaptation in fact omits the details of Ed Tom's experiences in the second world war and with it some of the Sheriff's internal life and his need for redemption, but this omission has the effect of intensifying the motiveless, ahistorical quality of the action, the sense that the contest between the good guys and the bad guys under the Texan sun has become even more eternally brutal. The Coens are true to the pessimistic severity of the book's ending – darker, arguably, than the ending of McCarthy's great novel *The Road*, to whose horror this story can, in retrospect, be seen to be heading.

The savoury, serio-comic tang of the Coens' film-making style is recognisably present, as is their predilection for the weirdness of hotels and motels. But in McCarthy's novel they have found something that has heightened and deepened their identity as film-makers: a real sense of seriousness, a sense that their offbeat Americana and gruesome and surreal comic contortions can really be more than the sum of their parts.

Tommy Lee Jones and the actor Barry Corbin have a wonderfully modulated scene, in which Ed Tom calls on his old Uncle Ellis, another retired police officer, who has seen enough of the unequal struggle against evil to have even fewer illusions than his nephew. But he tells him that America has always been like this, that it is a tough country, cruel and harsh, eating its sons like Saturn. Watching this film has something of the elemental thrill of watching a cloud-shadow spread with miraculous speed over a vast, empty landscape: it has a chilly, portentous intuition of what America is.

JANUARY 22 2008

# The city is mine

KATE PULLINGER

I've always loved the city at night, even before I knew what it was like. I come from a rural suburb of a small town on the west coast of Canada and I spent my adolescence dreaming of cities in the dark. To go anywhere when I was a kid you had to drive; there was no public transport. And when you got there, wherever There was, there wasn't anything to do, except drink. I knew that when I finally made it to the city the night would sparkle and shine and pulse and that when I walked down the street, night music – Roxy Music, the Velvet Underground, Curtis Mayfield, Ultravox even – would accompany me.

My first ever city was Montreal, where I spent a dissolute 18 months struggling with the concept of university. Montreal at night was always romantic but bipolar: a continuous street party during the summer – hot sweaty nights in cafes and bars that spilled on to the streets; phenomenally cold, encased in ice, in the winter. I would bundle up in multiple layers before heading out. In January and February I would wear both my coats. Montreal at night involved a lot of trudging, carrying your party shoes in a bag, stamping the snow off your boots. Falling snow at night in the city is irresistible; it squeaks and crunches beneath your boots on the pavement and comes to rest on your eyelashes and cheeks like glitter, only even more precious, more fleeting.

Walking by myself through Montreal at night was to feel a kind of freedom that was completely new to me – the people are sleeping, the city is mine, all mine. Through the frozen air I could hear and see myself breathing – walking at night always makes me feel more aware of my own physicality somehow, it's the unexpected silence, the unsolicited peace – and my joy at escaping the suburbs was complete: I'm alive, I'm my own person, and I'm at home in the city.

After Montreal I came to London, where a lot of women are afraid to walk alone at night. When Jacqui Smith, the home secretary, said at the weekend that she wouldn't walk at night in Hackney, or Kensington and Chelsea, she was just being honest, despite her aides' subsequent attempts at spin. In a world where we are afraid to let our children cross the street by themselves, this is hardly surprising. Our levels of fear bear little relation to the statistics – Smith was right that crime rates have fallen, too – but we are told to be afraid, so many of us are, both despite of and because of our experience. But not me.

For me, growing up was all about becoming free, becoming who I wanted to be, not who other people expected me to be, and

London was a part of that. It was the 1980s and London had an urgency to it, made all the more vivid by the fight to the death between that era's David and Goliath – Ken Livingstone and Margaret Thatcher. I was young and broke and needed to save my money for pints, books and movies: walking was the cheapest way to get around and most nights out ended with a long walk home. The city was huge, and foreign to me, and I needed to map it out in my mind by stalking the twisty streets with their ever changing names: Eversholt Street becomes Upper Woburn Place becomes Tavistock Square becomes Woburn Place becomes Southampton Row becomes Kingsway all inside 15 minutes. It was only through walking that this would ever make sense, and it was only when walking at night that I witnessed the secret lonely heart of the city; for a time it seemed as though every other doorway in the centre of town was temporary shelter to at least two homeless people. Alone at night I could repeat the street names and practise the English-as-in-England words that were new to me: 'wanker', 'loo', 'pants', 'tuppence', 'sacked', 'fanciable', 'shag'.

I had a bicycle some of the time and there is nothing to match riding a bike by yourself through the streets of London late on a summer's night when the air is so soft it feels like velvet and your wheels spin and your hair gets messed up under your helmet but you don't care and you have to peel off the layers to stop yourself sweating. I was living in Vauxhall and working in Covent Garden at a catering job that required an early start before the tube was running, and crossing Lambeth Bridge on foot at 5am provoked in me a kind of epiphany, an ecstatic communion with the city and its only-just-buried layers of history. At night it's as though the city's history comes alive, bubbling up from where it lies dormant beneath the tarmac: when the crowds are gone, modernity slips away, and the city feels ancient and unruly. How could anyone not love London late at night, or early in the morning? How could the wide black Thames with the city reflected upon it not remind you of everything that is most desirable and glamorous in life?

But sinister, too, of course, and this is part of what makes the city at night such a grown-up, adult, provocative space. There are parts of town that always have been, and always will be, creepy. In London: the backend of Whitechapel. Stockwell on a rainy night. Acton when you're a bit lost. And Hampstead, because everyone there seems to go to bed very early.

In attempting to recant her comment about not walking alone at night in Hackney, Smith named the parts of the city where she does feel comfortable (for her, Peckham), and this is something that most women would recognise: we make our routes, we do what we feel comfortable doing, and it's not possible to ask anything else of us, home secretaries included.

I've lived in Shepherd's Bush, west London, for 11 years now and I always feel safe on the Uxbridge Road. It's one of those wide, long streets that is full of life, full of commerce and connection, full of people I sometimes know and often recognise. The walk home from the tube feels safer than the shorter walk home from White City, with its looming football ground and empty pavements, cars zipping past too quickly. Just before Christmas I walked home by myself from a party; several people asked if I would be OK before I left. When I got outside the night was foggy and the street lamps glowed through the freezing mist; a black taxi passed with its yellow light blazing, the low purring sound of its diesel engine reassuring. I wandered along, a bit drunk, bundled up, and the residential streets were completely empty. When I got into bed I put my cold hands on my husband's warm back and woke him up, happy.

I wear sensible flats and carry my party shoes in a bag still, not because of the snow, obviously, and not because I want to be able to run away if I can, but because I like to do my walking in comfort. I don't walk at night as much as I used to, but that's because of children and work and the fact that the days and nights aren't as long as they used to be. It is true that I would not take out my mobile phone on a dark street for fear that someone might think it worth snatching. It's also true that I do not listen to music through headphones when I walk by myself, but that's because I've never liked listening to music through headphones: it has always made me worry that someone is about to sneak up behind me, even when – or especially when – I'm lying on the couch in an empty house.

Plenty of people don't love London, I realise that, and plenty of people probably love it even less at night; I'm well aware that it might take only one incident for me to change my mind about walking alone at night. I have been mugged in London, but that was in broad daylight in Finsbury Park on the way to the tube station; I lost volume one of a two-volume *Complete Plays By Shakespeare* that my mother had given me. The young man who pushed me against a brick wall to wrestle my bag away from my shoulder had a look of desperate determination; the police later found the bag and the wallet, but not the Shakespeare.

I've walked these streets for 25 years now. I'm not a young woman any more – aren't the young more likely to be victimised? – and I'm fairly tall – aren't little women more preyed upon? – and on dark winter nights I walk quickly with a hat jammed down over my head. But when I look up from the pavement and see the sparkling lights, I hear the night music; could it be that I am who I always wanted to be, and the city at night belongs to me?

FEBRUARY 2 2008

# Munich 58: presses stopped in Manchester as *Guardian* man confirmed dead

## RICHARD WILLIAMS

They stopped the presses for 10 minutes when the confirmation of Donny Davies's death reached the offices of the *Manchester Guardian* on the evening of February 6 1958. The city was full of funerals in the days that followed and crowds of bystanders joined the entire staff of the newspaper as they lined the street to salute the cortege of a man whose Monday-morning football essays, appearing under the byline 'Old International', had entertained and instructed his readers for a quarter of a century.

Davies, who perished in the Munich air crash, was a small, smiling, cloth-capped man of Victorian virtues, a broad range of accomplishments and such literary talent that his colleague Neville Cardus called him 'the first writer on soccer to rise above the immediate and quickly perishable levels of his theme and give us something to preserve. Old International was not only the best of soccer reporters; he was also something of a poet.'

According to the Dean of Manchester, addressing a memorial service for the eight journalists killed in the disaster, Davies had done for football what Cardus did for cricket. Another sporting clergyman, a Methodist minister in Cumberland, expressed his admiration in a letter to the *Guardian*'s editor. 'His reports were stylish essays – cultured, humorous, a sheer delight,' the Rev W Winchurch wrote. 'One found in them classical allusions, quotations from Shakespeare, anecdotes, humorous examples of Lancashire dialect, as well as a perfect picture of the match and the players.' Among the dozens of correspondents who offered their condolences to the paper Joseph Fox of Edgbaston asked: 'Who else would have thought of an exhausted and defeated cluster of goalmouth defenders on a muddy day as "like a stricken gun crew at Sebastopol – glorious in death"?'

Such letters came in from all over the country, mourning the loss of a man whose audience had been broadened by his weekly radio appearances on the BBC's *Sports Report*. 'Being a woman, football does not hold a great interest for me,' Mrs Dorothy Bennett wrote from Faversham, Kent, 'but I always listened to Mr Davies's commentaries each week. His clever and original similes always fascinated me and I thought he must know his Bible well.'

Harry Donald Davies knew many things well. He was born in Pendleton, Lancashire, in 1892, the son of an orphanage boy who, at the age of 17, had walked from Kidderminster to Manchester with nothing but sixpence in his pocket, in search of the employment that eventually took him to the position of mill manager in Bolton, where his eldest son was born. Don grew up accompanying his father to cricket and football at Burnden Park and Old Trafford, and showed his own early promise in both sports.

After leaving Bolton school he played on the right wing for Northern Nomads, the equivalent of the south's Corinthian Casuals, and won the first of his amateur international caps in 1914, when he toured Austria, Hungary and Romania with England. He had agreed to join Stoke City, who promised to cover the cost of his history degree course at Manchester University, when war broke out. Instead he signed up with the Officer Training Corps and served as an infantry lieutenant before transferring to the Royal Flying Corps.

A fortnight after receiving his wings, and after only a day in action on the Western Front, he was shot down over Douai and captured before being sent to a series of prison camps. At the last of them, Holzminden in northern Germany, he captained the camp football team, studied German and French, read Gibbon's *Decline and Fall of the Roman Empire*, helped with the construction of escape tunnels and suffered so badly from a three-month gap between food parcels that on his return to England, weighing less than 6st, he was given six months to live.

'I must get a job' was his response and in 1919, while beginning to study for his university degree in the evenings, he took a teaching post at the apprentices' school run by Mather and Platt, a Manchester engineering firm. He remained there until his retirement in 1957, eventually as headmaster and finally as education officer, jobs that formed the core of his working life but also left weekends and long holidays free for sport and other diversions.

A prolific batsman and a gifted cover fieldsman, he captained Bradshaw CC in the Bolton League. After graduation he had the time to play as an amateur for Lancashire, whom he represented for several seasons. In the winters he continued to play football, and came up against George Abbott. 'I first met him in 1920,' Abbott wrote to the *Guardian* the day after the crash, 'when, as a Manchester YMCA full-back, I tried, without much success, to cope with a sprightly and elusive outside-right playing for Old Boltonians in the Lancashire Amateur League.

'It was some consolation to learn after the game that this was Don Davies, who had been capped for England. We played together for three seasons, 1925-28, for Northern Nomads, during which a friendship formed between us severed only by his untimely death yesterday. He was a grand companion and a great sportsman in the very best sense of the term. May the soil rest lightly on him ... '

Davies married Gertrude Quinn, also a teacher, in 1921; they had two daughters. He loved music, dance, poetry and art – he played the piano, attended Barbirolli's Sunday concerts at Belle Vue, saw Nijinsky and Pavlova, loved Shakespeare and Dickens, read Goethe and Schiller in the original, and brought prints by Albrecht Dürer back from football tours of Germany. He also stood up against oppression and is said to have been the first donor to Manchester's collection for the victims of the Fascist bombing of Guernica. For more than 30 years, too, he was active in the scouting movement. 'He pushed you into things you never dreamed you could do,' one of his former Rover Scouts wrote after his death, 'and, thereafter, he stood on the touchline of your life shouting encouragement.'

All these interests informed his writings on football, beginning in 1932 with his first piece for the *Guardian*, whose sports editor devised his nom de plume, and ending with his final report on Manchester United's 3-3 draw in Belgrade, in which he singled out the first of the two goals scored by the 20-year-old Bobby Charlton. 'Dispossessing Costic about 40 yards from goal,' he wrote, 'this gifted boy leaned beautifully into his stride, made ground rapidly for about 10 yards and then beat the finest goalkeeper on the Continent with a shot of tremendous power and superb placing. There, one thought, surely goes England's Bloomer of the future.'

He had almost not made the Belgrade trip. John Arlott had asked for a greater variety of assignments and was delighted when the sports editor invited him to travel with United to the second leg of their tie with Red Star in place of Davies, who had another engagement. On the Saturday before departure Arlott covered United's visit to Highbury but on the Sunday, when he telephoned the office to check his copy, he was told Old International had expressed a wish to accompany United after all. The following Thursday a disconsolate Arlott was mooching around a London bookshop when the office tracked him down, gave him the news and asked him to write Davies's obituary.

Arlott produced an appropriate piece but neither he nor the

great Cardus could improve on the tribute contained in a letter to the paper's editor from a reader in Norbury, south London. 'One of the most tragic deaths in yesterday's air crash was that of Old International,' J M Boakes wrote. 'Many people, including myself, although never having seen the Manchester United team, felt that we knew the individual types of play of these great footballers because of his outstanding descriptive writing. Byrne, Colman, Taylor, Whelan and the others are not just names to us; we can see them coming away with the ball, sweeping it through to the player gliding into open space, firing in the unstoppable shot. They will always be alive in our imaginations because he painted their movements so vividly.'

FEBRUARY 5 2008

# Super Tuesday: there's been no contest like it. Not since never

### MICHAEL TOMASKY

Ever since those days and weeks in late 2006 when this longest of presidential campaigns began to assume form, commentators have been reaching back into history to find the most apt and dramatic comparison to insert into that evergreen sentence of American punditry, the one that begins 'Not since ... '

Some landed on 1976, when contested nomination battles in both parties lasted well into the spring and summer. Some went back to 1952, which is the last time both parties' nominations were truly 'open' – no incumbent president seeking re-election, and no vice-presidential heir apparent on either side.

Some, anticipating the possibility that the nomination of one party or the other might not be settled by the time of the party's summer conventions, invoked 1924, that tuneless cacophony of a year when the Democrats weren't able to unite around a candidate until the 101st ballot at their convention.

And finally, the more erudite among them showed off by mentioning, say, 1876 or 1828 (never mind, you don't need to know they were messy).

Now, with the race in full swing, we can say that all of those analogies are wrong. My 'not since' sentence consists of three words:

Not since never.

I'm not usually given to hyperbole or (I hope) to purple prose, but I believe this to be absolutely true: there has never been a presidential race quite like this in the history of the United States.

It has genuinely impressive candidates. It has a grand theme. It's really, meaningfully about something. It may result in a woman or, perhaps more incredibly still, a black person being the president of the United States. Or, if not one of them – this is footnote-ish by contrast, but still quite interesting – maybe then the oldest person ever elected president, a man who would, if he served two full terms, have 80 candles to blow out on his last White House birthday cake.

And not least, as spectator sport, it has been joyously, raucously unpredictable. Hillary Clinton's eleventh-hour comeback win over Barack Obama in New Hampshire is the single most stunning election result I've seen in 20 years of doing this stuff. And there have been numerous other surprising, even stupefying, plot twists besides.

But let's talk big picture.

The grand theme of this contest, to hear the candidates tell it, is 'change'. That's a shallow buzzword that doesn't say much, and to listen to the candidates strain to persuade the public that 'I represent change too!' (Obama was first) is to be reminded of schoolchildren in pursuit of gold stars from teacher.

But amazingly enough, it's not entirely inapt. This election is fundamentally about whether a majority of Americans are prepared to give liberalism another chance. The story goes like this.

The modern conservative movement in America was founded in the mid-1950s. We had conservatives before then, Lord knows. But this was something new. This was conservatism as a dedicated project.

Clarence 'Pat' Manion, a dean at the University of Notre Dame and a founder of the movement, convened groups of conservatives to get together and start infiltrating (legally and above board – by winning elections) their local Republican parties. Rich conservatives in various walks of life started putting massive amounts of money into conservative-movement politics – financing candidates, starting ideological magazines, publishing rightwing books. If you drink Coors beer or have ever visited the California theme park called Knott's Berry Farm, you've pitched in yourself.

The Republican party of the day, I should note, was a mostly moderate amalgam. Dwight Eisenhower as president embraced the New Deal. There is a quote of Ike's, famous now in the era of George Bush and Dick Cheney, and piquant enough in light of current circumstances to warrant reproducing here in full:

'Should any political party attempt to abolish social security, unemployment insurance, and eliminate labour laws and farm programs, you would not hear of that party again in our political history. There is a tiny splinter group, of course, that believes that you can do these things. Among them are a few Texas oil millionaires, and an occasional politician or businessman from other areas. Their number is negligible, and they are stupid.'

Ah well. By 1964, this faction had taken over the Republican party. It nominated Barry Goldwater. But he was massacred that

November by Lyndon Johnson, and the wise observers of the day declared this strange conservative thing, this malformed aberration, mercifully deceased.

But it turned out that that was liberalism's high-water mark. The changes, political and cultural, set in train that year – the House of Representatives passed the historic civil rights bill the very day after we Americans first saw the Beatles, on Ed Sullivan's TV show – had, within four or five years' time, unleashed uncontrollable forces.

By that time, the American left – broadly construed to include everyone from Hubert Humphrey to Noam Chomsky – was at war with itself. I expect you know the litany: on race, women's rights, the war in Vietnam, the generation gap, Israel, the developing world and more, liberals were at loggerheads. In the 1970s, things got worse – crime, energy crises, a hostage crisis, malaise and turpitude. Meanwhile, conservatives – who believed some of their negative press in 1964 and retreated for a time – decided enough was enough and rededicated themselves to pouring still more millions of dollars into building an infrastructure of interest groups and media outlets to promote conservative ideas and denigrate liberal ones. They met with a willing public.

Then came Ronald Reagan – history's first 'movement conservative' president. Obama was right, in his now-famous remark of three weeks ago, the one the Clinton campaign ran with (and distorted, eventually to its detriment in South Carolina), that Reagan changed the country in profound ways. It's true that a sizeable minority did not care for the man or his politics. But for most Americans, the Reagan years showed that conservatism worked and had answers.

For 25 long years, it remained so. It remained so even during the term of Bill Clinton, who felt he had no choice but to govern as a moderate progressive in a fundamentally conservative era. It remained so after September 11.

But many Americans' faith in conservatism was injured on the streets of Baghdad and finally died in the flood-soaked streets of New Orleans.

Furthermore – Americans look around themselves and see a middle class that is prosperous but deeply anxious; a healthcare system that works reasonably well, except when you really need it; a world that hasn't reacted very positively to our attempts at bullying it; a planet that might indeed be suffering for our, pardon the pun, sins of emission.

Americans have given up on George Bush. That much we know. What we don't know is whether they've given up on his ideology. It may be that they look at Bush's failures and see an ideological failure, a failure of conservatism. But it may also be that they see only an execution failure, a failure of competence.

So these are the questions – and they're very important and profound questions – this election will answer: will American voters say that they want a 'change,' to go back to the key word, only from incompetence to competence, keeping basic conservatism intact (John McCain, arguably)? Will they say they want a shift away from conservatism, but the cautious and incremental shift that Clinton represents? Or will they want the broader change that Obama signifies – a change not dramatically to the left of Clinton in ideological terms, because he is not, but potentially a vast change in the political culture, toward something that does not accept our red v blue divide and culture wars as a given and would redeem America's most solemn original sin of racism?

Liberals around Washington, indeed around the country, are upbeat because it feels like it might be one of those moments. It feels like enough Americans are tired of conservatism, not just of incompetence. It feels like enough of them see that conservatism doesn't have good solutions to some of the new problems America confronts. Not that many Americans, still, are willing to call themselves liberal; just about one adult in five. And no one is hankering for a return to the 1970s or seized with a burning desire to pay higher taxes. But the current mood in the country seems to indicate that Americans are willing to give liberalism that second chance.

And if liberalism gets that chance and succeeds, the modern conservative movement will enter into a period of introspection and recrimination unlike any it's ever experienced. What in this context does 'succeed' mean? As little as two things. If a Democratic president and Congress – and everyone expects that Congress will stay in Democratic control – can 1) pass healthcare and 2) articulate and implement a strategic foreign policy vision that defends America and charts a new course in the world, then Americans will embrace this new liberalism. Movement conservatism will be forced to transform itself so utterly as to be unrecognisable as its erstwhile self which is another way of saying that, short of its 60th birthday, it will in essence perish.

That's all that's at stake.

But of course most voters don't think about these big ideas. Elections are always about a thousand things, little things, some silly things, some not-so-silly things, emotional things. Ah, emotion; now that's a very political word.

In the past year or so, there has arisen a certain vogue in brain research and political behaviour. Why, of all things, brain research? Because some scientists have been studying how citizens arrive at political decisions. They have concluded that voters use emotion far more than reason.

We should always remind ourselves that this election will be about these things, too. It already has been. Clinton did not reason her way to victory in New Hampshire – voters felt sorry for her after she showed a human response to attacks many saw as unchivalrous. Most people couldn't tell you three specific policies Obama advocates, but they sure can tell you how he makes them feel.

Those researchers have also found that among the various emotions, the negative ones – anger and especially fear – are usually better motivators. They have even found quite specifically that scenes or thoughts of death make most people adopt more conservative political views (see *The Political Brain* by Drew Westen, from which this paper ran extracts in August last year).

Republicans know this, and they understand what they're doing when they allege that Democrats won't protect the country from more terrorist attacks. Democrats, except for Bill Clinton, haven't understood the role of emotion very well. Al Gore and John Kerry seemed to think voters did things like read the details of healthcare plans. And they responded very weakly to attacks, allowing conservatives to define them in many voters' eyes (remember how the swift boat veterans tarnished Kerry).

So another interesting question: will the Democrats finally understand that a campaign isn't a college debate but is an obstacle course that must be negotiated with a velvet glove on one hand and a switchblade in the other?

We head now to super-duper Tuesday. We will probably have a candidate on the Republican side, McCain. On the Democratic side, if Clinton wins all the large states, especially California, she will probably be able, to use a metaphor from American football, to run out the clock on Obama, eventually winning – one officially 'wins' by amassing 2,025 delegates, which one does by winning state primaries and caucuses – in March or April.

But if Obama does well tonight, and especially if he wins California, look out. The inevitable candidate, Clinton, will start looking awfully ... uninevitable. It would be fitting to the extent that that's the kind of election it's been. Remember Rudy Giuliani? He led his Republican opponents almost the entirety of 2007 –

only to experience in 2008 one of the most astounding flameouts in presidential history. Giuliani was on top back when McCain was finished, dead, kaput.

If you've been watching, you know what I mean. And if you haven't – well, start tuning in. This will be one to tell the grandkids about.

FEBRUARY 14 2008

# Review: Pina Bausch – Tanztheater Wuppertal

## JUDITH MACKRELL

London has an intense relationship with Pina Bausch; her season at the Wells sold out weeks ago. Yet it is only now the city is seeing the two early productions that mapped out her choreographic terrain: *The Rite of Spring*, created in 1975, and *Müller* in 1978.

They are an astonishing pairing – one hot, dark and terrifying; the other pale and elusive. Both show how Bausch, even at the beginning of her career, was able to combine movement of shocking visceral intensity with stage visions of often hallucinogenic strangeness.

In her setting of *Rite* she returns Stravinsky's music to its most primitive logic by covering the stage in thick dark earth and by choreographing on a huge scale. Some 32 dancers confront each other in thudding convulsive groups, ranked across a sexual divide. As they unite in great wheeling circles then scatter into a collective frenzy of coupling, Bausch makes it appear as though they are galvanised by some savage, biological imperative. As they run and fall, dirt smears their sweaty bodies. By the time the chosen maiden (Ruth Amarante) is led towards her sacrificial solo she seems to be only thing standing against her tribe and their absolute terror of extinction. Her dread and her ecstasy leave us shaking.

*Müller* is a far more intimate work – based on Bausch's childhood memories of her parents' establishment. Her grown-up self (danced by Helena Pikon) re-enters the cafe as a sleepwalker, eyes shut tight, arms outstretched as if remembering the scene by touch.

Five other people are present – but their behaviour appears both pointless and obsessional. The action is seen as by a naive child, but also as by an adult who understands the tragedies and disappointments the cafe once harboured. There is the woman (Aida Vainieri) who keeps leaping ardently into the arms of her lover who in turn weakly, sorrowfully keeps dropping her. There is the man anxious and bespectacled (Jean-Laurent Sasportes) who races through the cafe knocking away chairs and tables in case someone might get hurt or the second woman (Nazareth Pandero) in a red wig who ineffectually gestures kindly intentions but is unable to attract any notice.

At first sight this piece looks bleak, a forensically pared-down study of lost souls. Yet the way the action is layered around the wispy presence of Bausch's dream figure gives it a magical quality of remembering.

FEBRUARY 19 2008

# They're all guilty? 'Definitely'

## STEPHEN BATES

It was some time during the afternoon that counsel for the Metropolitan police outlined the extent of the international conspiracy to kill Diana, Princess of Wales, and her companion Dodi Fayed, as outlined by Dodi's father, Mohamed Al Fayed, in court 73 of the high court in London yesterday.

Shortly after Tony Blair and Robin Cook had been added to Fayed's list of conspirators, Richard Horwell QC, a note of incredulity rising in his voice, said: 'So that's MI5, MI6, the CIA, the DGSE – the French intelligence service – Judge Stephan ... the French ambulance service ... Lord Condon, Lord Stevens ... Mr Burgess, the Surrey coroner and Lady Sarah McCorquodale?' He could have added several more: two bodyguards; the French pathologists; a photographer called James Andanson, who was allegedly driving the white Fiat Uno that brushed against the Mercedes shortly before it crashed in the Alma tunnel in Paris on August 31 1997; Henri Paul, the chauffeur; a reception clerk at the Ritz hotel; Sir Michael Jay, the then British ambassador; Sir Robert Fellowes, the Queen's private secretary, who was Diana's brother-in-law; Lord Mishcon, her solicitor and – of course – Prince Philip and Prince Charles. Time and again, Fayed answered: 'Definitely.'

'You don't care what you say about anyone, do you, Mr Al Fayed?' said Horwell. 'You truly do not care about the interests of other people, do you, Mr Al Fayed? You don't care about the evidence, do you?'

Day 71 of the inquest and – after more than 170 expert and other witnesses – it was finally Fayed's day in court, which was only right and proper, given the number of barristers he is employing to represent him and the Ritz, Paris, which he owns. It proved to be six hours on Planet Fayed as the Harrods owner repeatedly outlined his allegations against virtually anyone, it appears, who has ever crossed him.

His counsel have repeatedly refrained during the inquest from raising some of the more extraordinary claims, possibly for lack of evidence – as Fayed's former director of security admitted in court last week. But that did not abash him in the least.

There was the Duke of Edinburgh, masterminding the murder of his former daughter-in-law from Balmoral: 'It is well known he is Nazi, a racist. Fine. It's time to send him back to Germany from where he comes. You want to know his original name? It ends in Frankenstein.'

And the Prince of Wales: 'He participated [in] it. Definitely and I am sure he knows what is going to happen because he would like to get on and marry his Camilla. And this is what happened. They cleared the decks. They finished her. They murdered her. And now he is happy.' And Lord Condon and Lord Stevens, the two former Met commissioners, for concealing the note they were given by Mishcon three weeks after the crash in which Diana had disclosed two years earlier that she feared she was going to be killed. And Mishcon himself, for asking them to keep it confidential. Stevens had produced 'a completely false report' when, after a three-year investigation, he decided the crash was an accident – and he finished off all the Harrods champagne, Fayed added for good measure.

The French ambulance service was implicated too, for driving Diana to hospital so slowly, in order to make sure she died. And the French intelligence service and the French magistrate investigating the crash, who determined it was an accident: they also conspired. 'The French are not renowned for doing the bidding of the British, Mr Al Fayed, are they?' said Horwell drily.

As for Andanson's car, Horwell asked: 'Why, with the might and power of the royal family, the British government, would MI6 choose a Fiat Uno, one of the world's lightest and least powerful cars?' Lord Scott Baker, the coroner, chipped in: 'A clapped-out Fiat Uno', mindful that others claim the car could no longer be driven and was only used to store rubbish. Horwell added: 'Can you tell us why James Andanson took his dog on this criminal enterprise?'

Fayed replied: 'Well, it's his own car and he chose to use his own car.' As for the motive, the British establishment did not want Diana to marry a Muslim and had discovered she was pregnant. The fact that she had just ended a two-year relationship with the Pakistani surgeon Hasnat Khan and had emerged unscathed: 'All this baloney. It was just a casual relation with this guy, a friend but nothing serious. You cannot say marry someone like that, lives in a council flat and has no money. How do you think a guy like that can support her?' Horwell: 'She could not possibly marry a man on the income of a surgeon?' Fayed: 'Why you ask such silly questions? What you are saying is just bullshit.'

The conspiracy was all the more remarkable, counsel suggested, because the news that Diana and Dodi were going to get engaged and that she was pregnant was only disclosed in a single brief telephone call to Fayed an hour before the crash.

Horwell: 'Do you ever pay any attention to the evidence? The answer to my question is no. All you are interested in is your assumptions. This inquest is being held in part for your benefit.'

Fayed: 'What you want to prove? You are talking absolute rubbish.'

Horwell: 'This elaborate conspiracy has minutes to be formed and put into operation.'

Fayed: 'No. They knew what they had been discussing.'

He seemed incredulous that anyone should question his word. He said: 'It's proved, there are dark forces. My version is the right version because [I] don't take any garbage from anybody who can pretend they are important ... It's just a great tragedy that they don't let her to be happy and enjoy her life.'

Horwell did extract one admission: Fayed said he would accept the jury's verdict, expected in April.

The coroner said: 'Do you think there is any possibility, however remote, that your beliefs about conspiracies may be wrong and that the deaths of Dodi and Diana were in truth no more than a tragic accident?'

Fayed: 'No way. I am 100 per cent certain.'

FEBRUARY 19 2008

# Review: Daniel Barenboim

ALAN RUSBRIDGER

And so, after eight concerts, 32 sonatas and 101 movements, we came to the conclusion of this extraordinary cycle, with 3,000 people on their feet cheering the begetter of it all. At the end, Daniel Barenboim impishly pushed the piano stool under the keyboard, closed the lid and gestured that he had no more to say.

This intense series of concerts has been so festooned in critics' stars, so garlanded in superlatives, that late joiners may have been beguiled into expecting pianistic perfection. In fact, Barenboim, at 65, is by no means a perfect piano player. It may sound trite to say he is greater than perfect, but that is how it seemed. The interesting question is in whether his greatness lies in his imperfections.

We know what 'perfect' sounds like. But how many pianists alive are so willing to risk so much, to think aloud, to feel their way so openly and generously – even at the cost of wrong turnings? Barenboim can rush passages, fumble notes, blur intricacies and even, on occasion, depart from the score – though he can also draw gasps at the fastest, lightest pianissimo fugal dexterity you could hope to hear. But so what? He moved the audience onto another plane where they stopped thinking about technique, or mere pianism, and came face to face with the music, with Beethoven himself.

After 50 years or more of playing these pieces, there is no doubting Barenboim's intellectual grasp or the confident sense of narrative – all conveyed through an endlessly fascinating physicality. He signals a sound he is about to create; he looks up in wonder at a sound he has just created. His left foot skips and kicks with excitement; the left hand drops three feet on to a fugal entry in *Opus 110*. In the first movement of *Opus 7*, he practically stands to attention.

Not in *Opus 111*, with which he ended. Having created this bond with the audience and taken them on an epic journey, he turned in on himself. The last movement forced a degree of awed concentration out of the listeners, finding release only with the final chord.

Two-thirds of the way through the movement, there is the heart-stopping moment where two notes, separated by the length of the piano, hang suspended. Barenboim seemed to hold them for an eternity as if emphasising this metaphor of apartness in life, the apparent impossibility of resolution. When it finally came, the relief was overwhelming. There was a kind of euphoria in the hall, something beyond perfection.

FEBRUARY 20 2008

# The future's orange

## TIM HAYWARD

The ante has been upped in the food world recently. It used to be enough to arrive at a dinner party with some staggeringly good wine or an obscure cheese, but now, with the return to traditional foods and a bubbling subculture of fashionable self-sufficiency, it's de rigueur to bring something you have made yourself: a jar of chutney, a pot of recherché preserve or, to really get the other guests hissing with thwarted envy, a jar of home-made marmalade. So this year I resolved to knock up a few jars.

The Seville orange season is short – from December to late February – so it is now or never for 2008. The thick-skinned fruit are unbelievably fragrant, but inedibly bitter. They have no real use in the UK except for making marmalade – so greengrocers don't often stock them and, when they do, they disappear quickly as word spreads through the marmalade underground. I get a tip-off that Waitrose has some, but the three branches I visit are out of stock by the time I arrive.

I finally unearth a wholesale fruiterer in south London who promises to keep some for me – as long as I buy a 12kg (26lb) case.

Twelve kilos doesn't sound too much. A dozen jars maybe. It all seems manageable – until I load the damn things on to the kitchen table. I phone Fi Kirkpatrick, author of *Debrett's New Guide to Easy Entertaining*, who is to marmalade, what Howard Marks is to marijuana. 'I'll be right over,' she says.

Kirkpatrick explains that the sugar balances the bitterness, so quantities are adjusted for either proper, punishing, lip-shrivelling posh marmalade or a softer, less challenging breakfast spread for the weak-minded. Little room is allowed for debate. With her innate preserving skill, Kirkpatrick surveys my fruit and calculates that we will need 9kg of sugar.

She has brought along the family preserving pan, 'the Behemoth', which we half-fill with whole oranges and top up with enough water to cover them. The oranges are poached for half an hour then allowed to stand until cool enough to handle.

The idea is to separate the thinnest outer layer of the skin from the pith, pulp, pips and juice. Boiling the oranges makes them wonderfully soft, so you can chop them in half and scoop out the entire contents in one sweep of a melon-baller – at least Kirkpatrick can. The guts of the oranges, pips, pith and pulp go back into the reserved poaching water for another hour's simmering. These gungy bits are important because they contain the pectin that eventually sets the marmalade.

While the pulp is simmering, we cut up the skins, a moronic yet convivial process that gives Kirkpatrick time to explain the important quality signifiers in marmalade production. Thin shreds of peel are indicative of machine preparation or unseemly 'faffiness', so only hefty artisanal chunks are allowed. An over-sweet marmalade will mark you as a ghastly parvenu and, though competition marmaladers go for a clear, light jelly, true connoisseurs know that long cooking creates a darker preserve with a richer, more complex flavour.

I glibly suggest the addition of whisky or ginger to the mixture but Kirkpatrick extinguishes my attempt at innovation with a look of wounded disappointment.

With the skins chopped to Kirkpatrick's satisfaction, we ladle the pulp into a jelly bag – a muslin sack the size of a small pillow-case, which is rigged between two chair backs. The liquid elements of the fruit pulp drain slowly through, back into the Behemoth, which is balanced on four volumes of Delia Smith and the bathroom scales. Wringing out the hot jelly bag feels like trying to juice a piglet, but finally the last dribbles are collected and weighed. We dissolve a socially impeccable three-quarters of the weight of sugar into the juice.

This syrup, brought to a rolling boil, must be watched, stirred and nurtured constantly. Depending on the size of your pot, this can take 20 minutes or several hours but under no circumstances can you walk away. If it boils over, at worst you will be badly burned, or at best you will still be scraping orange toffee off your kitchen floor at Christmas.

Proper cooks who worry about this sort of thing recommend a 'cold-plate test' to check how the marmalade is gelling. You're supposed to keep a stack of saucers in the fridge on to which the hot jelly is dropped: when a decent layer sticks rather than runs, then it is ready.

Kirkpatrick scorns this as yet another instance of faffiness and, sure enough, after about 45 minutes, there is a subtle but noticeable change in the bubbling surface of the marmalade. The plopping sound becomes more of an angry hissing. We quickly stir in the chopped skins and Kirkpatrick, sounding like an 18th-century ironmaster, announces that we're 'ready to pour'.

In 10 minutes the jars are closed, cooling and beginning to set. After a couple of gins we crank up the toaster to produce test slices of wholemeal toast. The set is perfect – big soft chunks of peel in a rich mahogany gel – and its deep flavour will mature beautifully over the coming year. The whole process was achieved in a little more than five hours.

Kirkpatrick congratulates me. Her work here is done and she is required on the other side of town where someone is having trouble folding napkins. Picking up her two-jar fee, she heads to her car. I turn back to the oddly undiminished crate of Sevilles and start on the next batch.

... It's now 2am and I've just got the lids on to the fourth batch and scraped the last marmalade off the kitchen surfaces. My body feels as if I've been stirring molten pig iron, my eyes are red with citrus steam and there's orange peel in my ear. My larder shelves are straining under the 48 jars I have produced. No one will escape the gift of marmalade this year. I shall be dishing it out instead of business cards, handing jars to buskers and leaving it as tips in restaurants. One thing I won't be doing, however, is eating it for a while. I swear, if I see another bloody orange I will scream.

FEBRUARY 23 2008

# Shaun Hill, the thinking diner's favourite cook

MATTHEW FORT

He looks an unlikely saviour. With his chef's jacket, unruly locks and specs on the end of his nose, Shaun Hill has the manner and appearance of a mad chemist. However, he's the man bringing new life to the Walnut Tree near Abergavenny, the dynamo in the kitchen and the smiling face in the dining room. Though I find it hard to see Hill as a dynamo – he always seems much too laid-back for that.

For those who are too young to remember, the Walnut Tree is a restaurant that was raised to iconic status by Franco and Ann Taruschio during their quarter-century at the helm. It was loved by locals and critics alike, but after they sold the place, it went through an unhappy spell from which it's now being rescued. As I sat with Shaun in the dining room, a couple stopped to say how lovely it was to see the place 'getting back to normal again'. They had been regulars since the 80s. 'It was pushing at an open door,' Shaun told me after they'd gone. 'A load of people want it to be right again.'

It wasn't quite what Shaun had planned. When he sold his much-lauded Merchant House three years ago, he'd planned a life of playing with his grandchildren and restaurant consulting. But he soon realised he wasn't cut out for the consulting side of that master plan: 'It's hard to have a whole conversation with people who don't agree with you without losing your temper.' More, he missed the adrenaline rush of service and of 'doing what I prefer doing and, in truth, what I'm better at.'

Look at a Hill menu and you see the results of more than 40 years of doing what he's better at, immaculate taste and the confidence of a man who knows what he likes to cook: smoked haddock boudin with shrimps and dill; calf's sweetbreads with wine-braised sauerkraut; lemon sole with salsify and watercress beurre blanc; poached veal knuckle in its cooking liquor, salsa verde and gherkins. Shaun describes his cooking as 'the nice side of coarse. I like the spirit of generosity in the grub.' This isn't a restaurant review (Matthew Norman will be doing that in a week or so), so I won't go into detail beyond saying there are few, if any, chefs on this planet whose food, or company for that matter, I look forward to more.

The thing is, Shaun Hill is a chef of rare parts. He has cooked high-end food and lower-end food. He's cooked for other people. He's cooked for himself. He's won Michelin stars for both. He's written books that have won awards, and books that explained the mysteries of Roman cooking. With a few others, he helped make Ludlow the gastronomic capital of Britain. And now he may be helping to do the same thing for Abergavenny. 'Around here there's the Foxhunter Inn at Nantyderry, the Hardwick on the Old Raglan Road and the Swan at Whitebrook. They're all run by seriously talented chefs. It's good for all of us.'

He may be one of the grand old men of Britain's restaurant business, and his food and his approach to kitchen craft are as far removed from the new generation of molecular gastronomes as it is possible to be, but he is cheerfully open-minded about the new wave of British chefs. 'The man's a star,' he says of Heston Blumenthal. 'I just worry about the imposters without the talent who try to imitate him. Anyway, listen,' he adds, 'I was Heston's predecessor at one of the molecular gastronomy conferences at Erice. I gave a speech on The Meaning of Fresh As a Culinary Term. I only did it because I failed all my science O-levels – and I was speaking ahead of the Nobel prizewinner for physics that year. There's nothing like sticking your tongue out at the past.'

And Shaun Hill is still sticking his tongue out. He was planning the music for his funeral the other day, he said, when he came across a prewar German close harmony group singing *Happy Days Are Here Again*. 'That'll do for me,' he said.

FEBRUARY 25 2008

# The kindness of strangers

PETER PRESTON

It is, they promise, totally random. Call up the electoral register, press a computer button and you get the 450,000 jurors a year the system needs. The waiting area at Blackfriars crown court is much like the departure lounge at Luton airport in a February fog. But, against expectation, it is also the most heartening, cheery, life-affirming part of two weeks in a different world.

Gloom comes easily in the columnar business. The newly anointed columnist of the year, returning to Britain after a winter break, based a 950-word diagnosis of national decline on one dirty toilet at Gatwick airport. The revered columnist who lives next door to me wrote incandescently the other day about mad, rich motorists trying to run her down on a Chelsea zebra crossing. And another makes us shed a tear for her 12-year-old daughter, 'hardened by 18 months of secondary school travel' so that 'being pushed, sworn at and squeezed on the overcrowded trains and buses is already routine'.

Even without a whisper about Jacqui Smith walking the fear-soaked streets of nocturnal Hackney, all of this leads to the grisly conclusion that we live in dangerous, vicious, booze-crazed times. But there's nothing remotely uncivilised here while you wait for hours for a case. Against almost all columnar wisdom, this is a gentle, patient place.

You're not supposed to write about the trials you've heard or the jury's discussions so I won't. And I won't bang on about the uplifting role of juries in national life, because there's a piece from the *Guardian* 2006 stuck on the waiting-room noticeboard saying precisely that. But, meanwhile, we chosen many are just getting by, sitting and chatting over 85p machine coffee, tapping at computers, revising for exams in electrical engineering, reading gloomy articles in gloomy papers.

I'm the oldest repository of possible justice in sight. The rest are varied: young men in T-shirts and sneakers, young women reading *Grazia*, housewives, mobile phone junkies, Nigerians, Arabs, West Indians, South Americans, cockneys, members of every religion and none. They've got the vote, so they're not a total cross-section of polyglot London. But they are as random a group of ordinary strangers as you'll ever meet, and they are still utterly nice in that old, familiar, English way. I'm crippled by arms that won't stretch over my head. Somebody hangs my coat up, then puts it on me again at the end of the day and straightens my collar. Somebody gives me a hand out of the jury box. Somebody calls a lift. The court's ushers and jury managers apologise for delays as though they mean it and know us all by our first names within a week.

It may be pathetic – even bathetic – to write about simple concerns and friendliness thus. But none of us know each other. The computer has brought us together, so we're making the best of it, reminding ourselves (I think) that co-existence is the natural order of things.

And because this crown court is a bus ride away from home, I'm taking the bus across south London every day. Nobody's pushing, swearing or squeezing here and, going into town, a black youth in his late teens hops up to offer me a seat; going back, a little lad who can't be more than eight makes the same unprompted offer. That's the way it is time and again. The old and the sick and mums struggling with prams have almost unfailing priority. On buses, as in jury rooms, we're in it together.

'What happened to you in court today?' they ask when you get home. Nothing happened, you say. No muggings or home secretary quaverings no *Daily Mail* horrors or shivers of terror; no fear in an alien land, where ways of life are under threat. Totally by chance, and yet again, you encountered a few hundred people who turned out to care about living together. No news in that, and a very atypical column.

FEBRUARY 28 2008

# In praise of ... Lincolnshire

## LEADER

Shaken but not stirred, the people of Lincolnshire went about their business almost as usual yesterday, despite the fact that in the wee small hours they had endured Britain's biggest earthquake in a quarter of a century. At the epicentre, in Market Rasen, masonry fell off the church, but the Rev Michael Cartwright told the local paper he was grateful that nothing had actually fallen through the roof. Stoicism is in keeping with the character of a county which, despite being England's second-biggest, does not like to make a fuss. In the 1970s its great size was diminished by Whitehall bureaucrats, who lumped its northern districts – along with Yorkshire's East Riding – into the cooked-up county of Humberside. Glanford and Grimsby endured their fate with less grumbling than was heard from Yorkshiremen on the other side of the Humber. Nonetheless, Lincolnshire yearned for unity once again – something it finally achieved in 1996. The flattish landscape and rich soil mean it is better known for arable farming than panoramic views. Even so, it can offer the visitor as many draws as many more boastful shires. That great Victorian John Ruskin dubbed Lincoln cathedral 'the most precious piece of architecture in the British Isles', and it remains breathtaking today. Pretty market towns abound, the loveliest of all being Louth. Then there are those Skegness sands, famous for being 'so bracing'. It would take much more than yesterday's tremors to shake the spirit of Lincolnshire from its rock-solid foundations.

# Spring

# The thrill of the chase

## STEPHEN MOSS

'Why do you want to write about the Cheltenham festival?' my wife asks me menacingly. 'Racing is corrupt and it's cruel.' I sense that convincing her, and possibly you, that the festival – which starts today – is an event of grandeur and poetry is not going to be easy.

It's a matrimonial battle we have most weekends. I am very keen on jump racing, and especially steeplechasing, where horses have to clear large fences rather than the smaller (and, paradoxically, more dangerous) hurdles. She dislikes it intensely, seeing only injured horses and impoverished punters. The conflict usually comes to a head on Grand National day in April.

I may be genetically programmed to like racing. My chief recollection of my grandfather is visiting him in his little two-up, two-down, where he would invariably be in his armchair with the racing on. The *Express* was always open nearby, with Peter O'Sullevan's daily treble ringed. The generations change and now, each Saturday morning, my father and I swap tips, deciding where to put our 50ps. I think he does it only so he can eliminate my generally misguided selection from the race to improve his chances of finding the winner. Sometimes I study the form assiduously; other days I just stick in a pin or choose a name I like. The pin-sticking generally works better than the close analysis.

As an anally retentive child, I used to keep a book in which I would make selections in every race. Once, when I was about 11, I 'went through the card' – chose the winner of every race – at Nottingham, not something I've managed since. For a while, in adulthood, I thought I could make money out of backing horses – by putting largish amounts on short-priced favourites, 'buying money' in the punting lingo. But one day I came spectacularly unstuck at a wretched little course called Southwell (which, as if as a warning, also stages a meeting today), and thereafter packed in the serious stuff.

Backing horses, really going for broke on them, is exhausting and painful. I've known one or two professional punters, and their lifestyles are draining: every day is financial life or death. I also knew a keen amateur punter, and he told me he had to feign illnesses in meetings so he could get out to watch a race. Or maybe he wasn't feigning illness: the gambling was the illness.

Now, apart from the odd small wager and my filial 50ps, I've given up betting. Yet my love of racing, reborn as aesthetic appreciation rather than financial calibration, has deepened. Or, rather, my love of a branch of it. Flat racing, with its sheikhs and high-rollers and Ascot fashions, I no longer much care for. It hasn't been the same since Lester Piggott and Willie Carson retired. But National Hunt racing – the winter game, peopled by trilbied toffs and anoraked toughs who brave the lashing rain at Uttoxeter or Market Rasen – I have come to adore. This, for me, is the heart of racing, and when at 2pm this afternoon a throaty, Guinness-fuelled roar greets the start of the first race at this year's Cheltenham festival, it will be beating fast.

'Festival' is the vital word. This is a gathering of the racing clans, a meeting of friends, with thousands making their annual pilgrimage from Ireland. Watch the jockeys after that first race, the way the first and second embrace after they have passed the finishing post. They have just slogged their way round this most demanding of tracks, deadly rivals for two or three miles, and now, with the race over, they salute each other.

The great sport writer Hugh McIlvanney, a Cheltenham addict

for half a century, has written lyrically of the 'festival spirit': 'No event in sport has a more seductive capacity to accentuate the positive, whatever the doom-laden reality suggested by the results. Even if the financial ship is going down, *Abide With Me* won't be on the songsheet, because few at the festival accept that the eventide need ever fall. The occasion has so much life force it could kill the unwary.'

The Irish influx, the punting priests and beer-soaked sinners, gives Cheltenham its character. Horses are not a leisure activity in Ireland they are part of the country's soul. 'Every man and his cat has a horse in Ireland,' an Irish stable hand now based in England told me. 'Even people with just a couple of acres have a mare and they breed from it.' They save all year for Cheltenham week, and bet fearlessly. There is a famous story of a Dublin man who made enough on the first day to pay off his mortgage, then lost so much on the second that he had to sell his house.

Every race at Cheltenham – 25 spread over four days – is ultra-competitive, every prize huge. To get a winner at the festival marks out trainer, jockey and horse as special (punters, too, so hard is it to identify the likely winner in most races). That's why the 'racing is corrupt' charge, here at least, can be forgotten. Corruption – horses being made to lose or not to run to their true ability – occurs in low-grade races. At Cheltenham, the potential honour and the size of the pot mean everyone is trying like hell.

The cruelty charge is harder to dismiss. Two years ago at Cheltenham nine horses died during races, and two others died later of injuries they had sustained there. The eventide did fall for some wonderfully brave animals. Horses are killed most years, but the loss of life in 2006 was unprecedented and led the pressure group Animal Aid to dub Cheltenham the 'festival of death'.

Last Friday, to limber up for Cheltenham, I went to Sandown for the slightly batty 'military meeting', where half the crowd seems to be made up of retired brigadiers, and many of the jockeys – taking part in special races for amateurs – are serving soldiers. It was an enjoyable day and I even made a few quid, but I was reminded that serious injury is never far away.

In the last race, I backed a horse called Blackthorn Boy. It led for most for the way, jumped brilliantly – big, bold leaps that led the track commentator to say, in a well-worn racing phrase, that it was 'jumping for fun' – and was still in contention as it came to the final hurdle. That, though, is where racehorses are at their most vulnerable: they're going flat out but are also tiring, limbs and brains no longer perfectly coordinated. Blackthorn Boy took a crashing fall.

The signs for Blackthorn Boy looked grim: he lay on the floor twitching the jockey removed the saddle and began a long, lonely walk back to the Sandown stables; screens of funereal black were erected. When a horse is killed at the track by the on-course vet, it is horrible; when a horse you have backed dies, you feel somehow implicated, an accessory to the slaughter.

A crowd gathered at the trackside, close to the final fence. I took this as a sign of concern. In fact, they were just waiting for the screens to be moved, so they could cross the track and get to the car park. Mundane life goes on. And, miraculously, life also went on for Blackthorn Boy. A horse ambulance drew up, he staggered to his feet, and shakily climbed aboard. Blackthorn Boy survived. But he had broken a bone in his knee and it's 50/50 whether he will race again. The early spring day had ended in an evening chill.

I don't know if, as the horse fraternity say, racehorses live (and sometimes die) to jump, or whether they are being pushed beyond their limit. But I do know that trainers and their staff adore their charges. The totemic tearjerker in racing is the stable hand who, after a horse has been put down at the course, has to go back home in the empty van. She will have loved the horse, lived with it, doted on it; now she has lost it. No lover could be mourned more.

I wanted to hear from the horse's mouth what the festival means, and how this spectre of death is kept at bay. So, on Saturday morning, I drove to the village of Naunton in the Cotswolds, where the trainer Nigel Twiston-Davies has his yard. He has 20 horses entered at the festival, including Knowhere in Friday's Gold Cup.

Twiston-Davies, a former amateur jockey, has been a trainer for 20 years, and has twice trained the winner of the Grand National. He's a boyish, curly-haired 50-year-old, a survivor and a success in an arduous, round-the-clock occupation. The morning I visit, he is up on his windswept gallops watching the horses work, before returning to his cluttered office to file final entries for Cheltenham, take frequent calls from owners, and prepare the departure of horses for that day's meetings. He has to be trainer, businessman, accountant, diplomat and master strategist – plotting which races to aim at and how to win them. 'Everybody heads for Cheltenham and that's where you really want to have a winner,' he says, between fielding calls and checking weather forecasts – he thinks this week's rain will aid Knowhere's cause. 'The Grand National is the FA Cup, but Cheltenham is the Premier League. The National's the biggest thrill in the world, but if you win the Gold Cup then you're meant to have the best horse.'

Like many of those in jump racing, he is taciturn and down to earth – there are too many vicissitudes in training to make bold claims or predictions. But when I raise the issue of danger and death, he is almost lyrical. 'They're bred for the job,' he says, 'and what are they going to do otherwise – stand around in a field rotting? This death thing is blown out of all proportion. We put too much human emotion into it. Say I dropped dead now or tomorrow, I'm happy as a lark. If I died now, I wouldn't have a shabby old age with teeth falling out to look forward to. It's those you leave behind who suffer. If you die doing something you're good at and you enjoy, you die happy.'

I ask Knowhere's stable hand, Eva Kicmerova, how she copes with the threat of the empty horse box. 'You worry about them, of course,' she says. 'It's the races, so you know those things do happen. But if it's a horse you look after and ride as well, it hurts. We hope Knowhere can win on Friday, or get a place, but the main thing is that he goes around and comes home all in one piece.'

On Friday Knowhere will line up against two horses who some believe are the best chasers for a generation – Kauto Star and Denman. Their first ever encounter is being written up as if it was Ali v Frazier, and at Sandown last Friday a pre-Gold Cup lunch was held at which their respective owners, the cerebral millionaire golf-course developer Clive Smith and the larger-than-life professional gambler Harry Findlay, squared up to each other in true pre-title fight style.

It was designed to hype up a clash that the racing industry, always looking for the next star, hopes will bring the country to a near-standstill at 3.15pm on Friday. But Findlay said one striking thing: 'When you own a horse like Denman, it's as if it's not really yours any more. It's become public property.' Nor was he complaining: he and Smith accept they now share ownership of their horses with the punters and fans.

It is chasers such as these to which, above all, the public responds. Think of Arkle, Red Rum, Desert Orchid. Kauto Star and Denman have yet to join that pantheon, but it is early in their careers and all things are possible. We identify with chasers because they are big, brave, beautiful and, unless injury intervenes, can race for year after year. A jumper will usually retire at around 12; flat horses, because of their value at stud, will rarely go on beyond four or five; many top performers leave the stage at three, to protect their glittering reputations – they have become commodities. We can get to know jumpers in a way we never can with flat horses, follow their literal ups and downs. 'Narrative' is a word much heard in sport, and the narrative of a great chaser is an edge-of-the-seat one.

At Sandown last week, I was reminded of what I love about jump racing. Its racketiness: this union of high-bred ladies (Princess Anne was handing out the prizes) and low-born hustlers joining forces in an anti-puritanical alliance against the middle class, who reckon you should work on a Friday afternoon. Its absurdity: that army officers who fight wars should, in their leisure time, choose to negotiate obstacles likely to cause them serious injury. Another of my selections was brought down in an earlier race, and I heard the announcer say later that its rider, a Captain Wallace, was too badly hurt to be able to attend the stewards' inquiry. War zones may well be safer.

Animal Aid, along with my wife, would no doubt like racing banned (though it shies away from proclaiming this as its aim). 'Beneath its glamorous facade,' it insists, 'commercial horse-racing is a ruthless industry motivated by financial gain and prestige. Cruelty? You can bet on it!' On the issue of whips, I (and the TV pundit John McCririck) agree with them: excessive use of the whip is bad jockeyship and should be outlawed. With them, I would mourn every horse's death. And yet I go on admiring the beauty of chasing, and marvelling at the courage and skill of horse and rider. Which ultimately counts for more: the heroic life or the tragic deaths?

On my early-morning visit to Twiston-Davies's yard, I was introduced to Bindaree, winner of the 2002 Grand National, now 14 and enjoying retirement. 'He has a home for life here, and more or less owns the place,' said the trainer. I stroked the horse's neck, and it felt as if I'd shaken Pele's hand. 'Almanacked, their names live,' wrote Larkin in his lovely poem *At Grass*. He was hymning flat horses, but jumpers are even more more securely locked in our collective memories. They give their all, and sometimes give too much. Let this afternoon's roar be one of pure admiration as well as punting excitement.

MARCH 4 2008

# Mountain roads are a greater risk than the police

## JONATHAN WATTS

For foreign correspondents in China, the past week's unrest in Tibet and neighbouring provinces is arguably the biggest story for almost 20 years. It is definitely proving the toughest to cover.

The pitfalls are enormous. Political sensitivities over Tibet can hardly be greater than in Olympics year. The two sides – the Chinese leadership in Beijing and the Dalai Lama's government-in-exile in Dharamsala, India – are projecting vastly different interpretations of what is happening. Casualty figures, arrests, riot-damage and paramilitary violence are all disputed. The only way to be sure of anything is to see it with your own eyes. But even that has been impossible for most journalists most of the time.

Trouble has been breaking out hundreds of miles apart in an area roughly the size of western Europe. Chasing the incidents is like racing from London to Zurich to Lisbon, while trying to dodge the police and avoid putting sources in danger at the same time.

Rugged mountain scenery provides the spectacular backdrop for the story, but creates a logistical nightmare. The roads are a greater risk than the riots and police. We have driven through a snowstorm, across an icy stream and through an area prone to rockfalls.

In the past seven days, we have taken seven flights, been driven for 30 hours and covered a distance roughly equivalent to 10 times the length of Britain. Even so, most of the time, I have felt as if I should be somewhere else.

Security restrictions have not helped. I have twice woken up before dawn to avoid checkpoints on six- to eight-hour journeys that ultimately ended in failure, when the police stopped me, found I was a journalist and sent me back.

According to the Foreign Correspondents Club of China (FCCC), there have been at least 30 cases of reporting interference by the authorities in the past week. Most times, it simply means being stopped at a checkpoint and sent back by police. But there have also been cases of journalists being detained for two hours (Canadian TV), having the hard drives of their computers searched (Newsweek) and being aggressively treated by paramilitaries with guns (Telegraph and Associated Press). In one instance, a wire reporter was forbidden to board a flight he had a ticket for.

Very little independently verified news has emerged from the controlled zones. There are a few notable exceptions, such as the text and video report that my colleagues Dan Chung and Tania Branigan were able to file of a demonstration in Xiahe last week. That area is now locked down.

The best-placed insider was James Miles of the *Economist*, who happened to be visiting Lhasa when the protests erupted. As far as the English-language world is concerned, he will play a significant part in writing the history of what happened. But perhaps the biggest scoop so far was the footage taken by two Canadian TV reporters – Steve Chao and Sean Chang – of a clash between Chinese police and Tibetan horsemen, monks and bikers in Hezuo, Gansu province.

To avoid unwanted attention by the authorities, reporters in China take many precautions. Because all passports are stamped with 'journalist' visas and all hotels must inform the local public security bureau when a correspondent is in town, it is better to check in very late and leave very early. Because calls on regular phones are monitored (or so most of us believe), reporters buy prepaid sim cards if they want to talk to a source about a confidential issue. And because mobile phones can be used as bugging and tracking devices, many journalists remove the batteries when they want to be sure no one is listening.

There is no doubt the government has blocked many websites to prevent people in China from seeing a critical view of its actions. But for me, the main technological problems have not been caused by cunning authorities, but by dismal communications facilities in remote areas. Many hotels in such areas lack reliable internet connections. I have filed two stories from internet cafes, but even that is not always an option. In Linxia, there is a midnight curfew on internet cafes. The rule can of course be broken, but only if you agree to be locked in until morning.

Having worked in China for more than four years, I should be used to the inconveniences. They are usually a small price to pay for the privilege of covering one of the most compelling stories in the world. But what is galling is that this year was supposed to be different. Ahead of the Olympics, the government promised that reporters would have full freedom to report on all aspects of China. There had been positive signs of change. Correspondents have been allowed to choose where they live (they used to be restricted to diplomatic compounds) and who they hire (they used to be obliged to recruit from the government's diplomatic service bureau).

The FCCC, which has never been granted legal status, has pushed for a relaxation of travel movements. Encouragingly, the authorities were willing to talk, and from the start of last year, they introduced special Olympics regulations that eased travel controls. The obstructions of journalists in the past week, however, has shown China only applies the new rules when it is convenient.

MARCH 19 2008

# In pursuit of the 'God shot'

## TIM HAYWARD

I bought my first espresso machine in the 1990s. It was a La Pavoni Europiccola, a small, retro-looking chrome job with a big lever you yanked down to express the coffee. It looked great on the counter but made vile coffee, was a bugger to clean and constantly threatened to explode in a shower of steam and shrapnel. When, one glorious day, it blew a gasket, I seized the opportunity to upgrade, but I needed advice.

A reasonable person might assume that coffee obsessives would gather in coffee shops, but these days they lurk in the labyrinthine OCD souks of internet chatrooms. In pursuit of the perfect home espresso – what they call 'the God shot' – I gleefully joined their ranks, kicking off the most expensive and pointless addiction of my life.

The ideal espresso (according to the Instituto Nazionale Espresso Italiano) is a 25ml beverage extracted from around 7g of finely ground coffee, using water at a temperature of 88C, passing through the grains at a pressure of 9 bar. See, dead easy. It should be thick-textured, having emulsified many of the oils, retain most of the volatile aromas and flavours of the bean and be capped with a thick colloidal foam layer – 'crema' – reddish, creamy and flecked. Each one of those factors is minutely variable, potentially causing thinness, bitterness, under- or overextraction or – the ultimate humiliation – a thin or patchy crema.

My first mistake, according to my online coffee-nerd chums, had been to buy a manual machine – they are spectacularly inconsistent. So I invested in the legendary Rancilio Miss Silvia (£310), the cheapest acceptable electrical-pump machine and, for a few blissful weeks, I chucked in a couple of scoops of ground Illy every morning and got out a nice little espresso. Then, one day, the crema failed to appear.

I returned despairingly to the chatrooms, where it was suggested that my problem was with the grind of my beans. Who knew? After much debate and guidance, I purchased a Rancilio Rocky (£180), one of the cheapest grinders operating with 'burrs' rather than blades, which give a consistent grind without compromising the volatile oils. It was still expensive and took up as much counter space as a small shed. The fresh-ground beans definitely improved the flavour, but now the texture of my 'shot' was inconsistent.

Millions of people probably get great coffee every morning with a standard home machine and ground coffee from a supermarket. I was starting to worry that, with a process that has as many variables as pulling an espresso, once you're daft enough to go off piste, things get monumentally messy in a way only explicable with chaos theory. Emails flew, recommendations were exchanged and argued. I could, they suggested, work on my 'tamp pressure' – that bit where the barista scrunches down the grounds into the 'basket' on the machine is crucial to the brew. I was, they said, going to need a tamper, custom-made for my machine and tamping hand by Reg Barber in Vancouver. After shelling out £75, and hours of practice with my new tamper on the bathroom scales, I got the hang of applying consistent pressure when packing the grounds, but still the perfect crema eluded me.

'Temperature,', suggested the Nerds. 'The mechanical thermostats on the boiler of your machine can be inaccurate to at least 10 degrees either side – you need to PID your machine,' wrote one.

A PID is a small computer used in labs and industrial-process control to manage temperature. To fit it, you need to find secret instructions written by obsessed academics, hidden deep in websites. You need to ignore all the disclaimers about blowing up yourself and your coffee machine, you need to persuade obscure component suppliers that you are not a bomb-maker, and then you have to take your machine apart and rewire it, thus invalidating any manufacturer's warranty. 'It's like a Jedi building his own light sabre,' the Nerds said. Which, in truth, is how it felt, until I switched the damn thing on and watched the entire PID unit quietly melt. Obviously Darth Vader never confused the blue and the brown wires.

Another hundred quid and a fortnight later, my machine was PIDded, accurate to within a hundredth of a degree and still turning out crap coffee, which was when they recommended I take an angle grinder to it. This is a fashionable new modification where you chop off the bottom of the portafilter (the bit you put the coffee in that attaches to the machine) so there is nothing between the bottom of the basket and the top of the cup. This allows you to examine obsessively the flow for the characteristic 'tiger stripes' of the perfect shot, but shoots half the coffee up the front of your shirt when you hit the 'brew' button. Things were getting out of hand. In the following months, though I tried 18 different types of coffee, rebuilt the brew head and fitted an electronic timer to allow the machine to get up to temperature before I woke up, the God shot eluded me.

Today, my kitchen bench looks like a Bond villain's lair. I have invested hundreds of pounds and countless hours only to produce average coffee inconsistently. And what do the Nerds have to say?

Apparently, the real pros are drifting away from espressos to experiment with syphon pots, those things resembling two spherical glass vases stuck together that put so many 1950s hostesses into the burns unit.

I've learned a painful lesson. When Giovanni Gaggia filed a patent for an espresso machine in Milan in 1947, it was designed to make coffee in industrial quantities at serious speed. Professional baristas get results because they use huge machines that deliver a thousand shots a day. The hand processes like tamping become consistent after the first hundred. To become barely competent could take me years. The boys in the chatrooms will denounce me as a heretic, but I now know that, for me, the best espresso will always come from an Italian standing coolly behind a big machine, not an obsessive Englishman throwing money at a small one.

MARCH 19 2008

# A sore that still festers

GARY YOUNGE

Some will wonder in years to come how, with markets wavering, the Fed ready to pronounce and the American economy flirting with stagflation – or, worse still, recession – the top political story in the US became a story about race, even for a few hours. Not even a story. A speech. A good speech – a speech that could have been delivered any time over the past 30 years, but also, somehow, had to be delivered now.

Essentially, Senator Barack Obama's speech in Philadelphia yesterday said nothing new, even if it contradicted what he has said before. Back when he was addressing the Democratic convention in 2004, he claimed: 'There's not a black America and white America and Latino America and Asian America; there's the United States of America.' Such realities are not created by fiat, and the past few weeks have proved how audacious such hopeful statements were.

The 'racial stalemate' that he referred to acknowledges that race is a festering sore in America – not because some people are sensitive and others are mean, but because for as long as there has been an America, black and white people have had completely different experiences of what being an American means. It is difficult to believe that Obama had only just written yesterday's speech. If it had not been his former pastor, Jeremiah Wright, someone or something else would have opened that wound on which Obama has so eloquently been applying balm these past few months. To most African Americans, the Rev Wright's fiery critiques of the US were as banal as Bill Cosby's screeds against bad parenting as common a thing to find around a black dinner table as hot pepper sauce.

But he had to say it now because he is not standing to be head of a black supper club, but president of a country where most white people have probably never had dinner with a black family, let alone gone to their church. He said it for those who seriously believed that everyone had bought into and benefited from the American dream. To those who did not hear, could not understand or would not listen, it was news that some were disaffected not just with what America has become but what it long has been. With Wright's sermons zipping around YouTube, Obama had to speak both to those who found his statements banal and to those who believed them to be ballistic. He had to intervene before Wright became Willie Horton with a dog collar.

To that extent, the speech probably worked. He acknowledged

white disadvantage and black alienation. He refused to disown Wright for the same reason he refused to disown his own white grandmother – because good people in bad societies will sometimes say and do bad things. He acknowledged there were problems and then said 'Kumbaya'. He hoped for better times and said everyone had to do their bit. That may be enough for now.

It may even, for the time being, put to rest the notion, peddled by the former vice-presidential candidate Geraldine Ferraro, that he would not have got as far as he has were he not African American. We know nothing about the pastors of Hillary Clinton and John McCain – or how offensive their views might be to African Americans. I think we can safely say that had Obama been white he would not have had to make this speech.

We can, with equal certainty, say that it won't be the last time that race comes up, particularly if he becomes the nominee. Last month *US News & World Report* put Obama on the cover with the question: 'Does Race Still Matter?' Those who believed his candidacy was evidence of a post-racial America now have their answer.

MARCH 27 2008

# 'Look at me! I'm at the castle!'

### ANGELIQUE CHRISAFIS

To a royal salute, the *Marseillaise* and the crunch of white horses trotting over gravel, Nicolas Sarkozy pulled up at Windsor Castle yesterday, barely containing his excitement at sharing the Queen's carriage.

Despite the new sombre, presidential manner that had been

promised on terra firma, in the carriage he was chatting eagerly to the Queen, hands gesticulating, fingers pointing and tanned face smiling and nodding. Never mind the promise to look more like a straight-faced Francois Mitterrand or Charles de Gaulle, this was vintage Sarko. He had not lost the quirk that he likes playing on with protocol: the boyish glee of his 'son-of immigrant made good' persona, a smile that seemed to be saying: 'Look at me! I'm at the castle!'

From greeting Prince Charles and Camilla at Heathrow to the carriage procession through the streets of Windsor, he also set out to address his harshest critics' complaints.

He pulled down the sleeves of his sombre navy coat to avoid any glint of a flash watch, he sighed serious sighs, furrowed his brow. As he crossed the quadrangle with Prince Philip to inspect the guard of honour he looked so serious he even stooped. And if there was one issue he wanted to address it was the merciless ribbing he has taken for his notoriously non-existent English.

Despite the Queen's fluent French, it was clear that as he prepared to go into lunch he was trying out a few short phrases in the monarch's ear, to which she could be seen saying 'yes'.

Crucially, he wanted to be speaking the language of Shakespeare when in earshot of a small crowd of Her Majesty's press assembled by the entrance to the Queen's apartments. Seizing on a small metal irregularity on the quadrangle's gravel pathway, he projected a theatrical: 'Careful!' in a heavy accent at the Queen. She politely kept looking straight ahead and went in.

In the five-carriage state procession through Windsor, Sarkozy showed off his rainbow cabinet. First, himself with the Queen, followed in another carriage by his new, ex-model, Italian wife dutifully sitting on the edge of her seat and chatting to Prince Philip. Then in open-topped carriage number three came Prince Charles and Camilla with awe-struck humanitarian champion

Bernard Kouchner, who Sarkozy so proudly poached from the left. Finally, open-topped carriage four was the president's pride and joy: Rachida Dati, the glamorous justice minister and daughter of illiterate North African immigrants, nicknamed 'Dior Dati' for her style, who has charmed world leaders such as George Bush, who held a special meeting with her, impressed by this ambitious 'Muslim minister'. With her was Rama Yade, the Senegal-born junior minister for human rights and a Sarkozy protege.

In 1996, when Chirac was in the Queen's carriage, he made two gaffes – blowing a kiss to the crowd and touching the monarch. Sarkozy, whose protocol adviser was on hand to whisper guidance, was keen not to put a foot wrong, focusing his small talk on the army displays and the royals' love of animals.

After lunch the Queen indulged Sarkozy's hobby of stamp-collecting, presenting a gift of framed blocks of stamps issued in 2004 to celebrate the centenary of the Entente Cordial. He also received an honorary title, while Carla Bruni-Sarkozy was presented with a carriage clock. Sarkozy gave the Queen the book *Perfect Knowledge of Horses*, published in French in 1743, by Jean de Saunier, Louis XV's general inspector of horses, and two Lalique crystal equine sculptures. The duke was presented with a bronze statuette of a hunting dog.

Bruni-Sarkozy was once described by a woman she wronged as looking as if she was made out of wax. It was a fitting analogy yesterday as she stood demurely, presenting a perfect, almost mechanical smile. Her arrival outfit of a blue-grey suit and hat – despite a slight resemblance to a 1950s air hostess – carried a clear message from Sarkozy.

This was Jackie Kennedy: the belted retro coat, the little hand-bag, the hat. It was the president's way of reasserting his obsession with the Kennedys and his sense of a national family purpose, a glamorous and intriguing new dynasty. He once said of his ex-wife,

Cecilia: 'If you liked Jackie Kennedy, you'll love Cecilia.' He and his ex-wife tried to model their photoshoots on them. Yesterday Bruni-Sarkozy introduced herself as Jackie Kennedy mark three.

Sarkozy, despite a standing ovation for his Westminster speech, appeared in more modest form yesterday than when he declared after a campaign visit to London: 'They haven't seen the like of this since the Beatles.'

Back at Windsor Castle in the evening, he gave a speech at a state dinner in St George's Hall, restored after the Windsor Castle fire that was one of the catastrophes of the Queen's *annus horribilis* of 1992. As an opinion poll yesterday showed Sarkozy's approval ratings were falling yet further, he hoped to use the visit to stave off what could be an *annus horribilis* of his own.

MARCH 31 2008

# Bliss of the bus-crawl

### DAVID McKIE

To the catalogue of mostly desirable things one is not permitted to do until one is old enough, such as drinking, driving or getting married, there is now to be added another. Tomorrow sees the launch of the English National Concessionary Travel Scheme (ENCTS), under which the right of people over 60 to travel free outside morning peak hours in the areas where they live will be extended right across England. Thus elderly persons in Cumbria – along with some disabled passengers – will be able to roam free of charge through Cornwall, while the over-60s of Lancashire may explore at no cost the delights of Leicestershire (and there are delights in Leicestershire: let nobody tell you otherwise). This applies, be warned, to the humble service bus, not to the high-speed coach or to the train.

The joys of the pass are not confined to the picturesque. They are useful for routine journeys, to the workplace if you've still got one, or the shops or to visit the family. But perhaps this new countrywide freedom will be used most of all to explore. Not long ago, while compiling a book, I spent months travelling round the country by service bus, discovering as they deviated down byways on their way to their advertised destinations many delightful small towns and villages I had never previously heard of. Pub-crawling and church-crawling are well-documented pastimes, but bus-crawling (and my goodness, some of them really do crawl) is worth indulging in too. And for those who have yet to pass 60, there are many bus companies all round the country that will treat you to a full day's travel at quite merciful rates.

What you need to plan these outings is a decent map and a set of timetables. But always read the small print. In that strange confected mini-new town South Woodham Ferrers, Essex, I stood for a good half-hour awaiting a bus to Bradwell-on-Sea. Eventually I rang the operator. 'The bus isn't running today,' a doleful voice informed me. 'But it says in the timetable: Thursdays only,' I whined, 'and this is a Thursday.' 'Ah,' said the doleful voice, 'but it doesn't say every Thursday, does it.' And later in very small print I saw the warning I'd missed: 'Runs alternate Thursdays.' You are required to phone to ask which are the ones when the bus is in action.

Then there's the rural bus etiquette, which calls for vigorous waving. In Saturday's *Guardian*, Simon Hoggart mocked a service in North Yorkshire that warns its would-be passengers to give clear signals to the driver as the bus is approaching. I'm afraid such warnings are truly necessary. Outside the big cities, buses may not respond until they are waved at. On a 556 from Newquay to Padstow (a glorious ride: do get off and acquaint yourself with St Mawgan) I heard head office rebuking the driver for allegedly flashing past a stop without picking up passengers. He remembered the incident: he'd approached the stop quite slowly and seen there were people waiting but they hadn't given a signal and hadn't even stirred from where they were standing. 'Signal and stir' should be the traveller's watchword out in the sticks.

Hoggart also noted another peculiar usage: the practice of one country bus becoming another. Some of these buses are so deeply into metamorphosis you suspect they've been reading Ovid. Coming from Happisburgh on the Norfolk coast to North Walsham, I leapt from my Sanders Coaches 34 route in the fear that the 736 towards Potter Heigham might have already left. Just in time I noticed that the 34 from which I'd dismounted had now been transformed by a flick of the driver's wrist into the 736 and was just about to depart.

I have to say that apart from the odd curmudgeon, I have found the drivers of rural buses, including the one who had caused such offence between Newquay and Padstow, a friendly and helpful breed. The best companies too (which are often the small ones) will happily recommend their most enjoyable journeys (this is how I discovered the Western Greyhound 556 and now know that the 501 Newquay to St Ives, summer only, is worth trying too). In places such as Cornwall, the time to make these journeys is now, before its roads are clotted with cars, and buses run late, and connections are missed and the joys of the liberation that is ENCTS from tomorrow may not be quite so unqualified.

# Clarkson for prime minister?

JACKIE ASHLEY

Can we please have fewer women in politics? Let's be honest. After the feminist experiment, it has become clear that women are, frankly, not very good at big issues. It would be better all round if most of us retreated to the kitchen and the ironing board and left serious matters to the lads. I'm not saying that there is no place at all for women in public life. But they should be pretty, young, say nothing and stand a demure few inches to one side of their husbands.

Isn't it irritating when they open their mouths and start to yak away? Isn't it horrible when you get some older, and dumpier women appearing on telly as ministers, or opposition spokes-women? It's a man's world. So can we just rewind that whole suffragette thing and go back to politics by the boys, of the boys and for the boys?

OK, I haven't been at the cooking sherry and, obviously, I don't think any of the above. It's just that the past few days have been so horrible for women in public life that sarcasm, while cheap, has come to seem the only response. Harriet Harman is already getting pre-emptive sprays of male condescension because she is being 'allowed' to do prime minister's questions, clearly a big treat for the fluffy-headed thing. The fact that she was elected deputy leader of the Labour party and has an absolute right to stand in for Gordon Brown is apparently neither here nor there.

Ah, you don't like Harman? Fair enough, plenty don't. So how about Wendy Alexander, the Scottish Labour leader, whose clothes sense, style and competence have been so savagely ripped apart in the media? She seems perfectly normal to me. Or Jacqui Smith? I may not like her attitude to civil liberties, but she's at least as good a performer as any of her recent male predecessors at the Home Office. Glance over the water where Hillary Clinton is now being ordered to give up her presidential ambitions by a male group of Democratic fixers. Like or loathe her, she's shown extraordinary guts and staying power, yet she seems to get not an ounce of credit for being a better fighter than any man. There is a quiet but strong misogynist current flowing just now.

There has, however, been one female political heroine of the past few days. I refer, of course, to Carla Bruni, now Mrs Sarkozy, who has had the British media lying on their backs drooling, gurgling with delight and with a certain suspicious bulge in their collective trousers. Yup, agreed, she's quite a girl. Anyone who can see off Jerry Hall and slide so effortlessly from nude modelling to solemnly representing the people of France (though she's Italian herself) at Windsor Castle, is to be reckoned with. She has it all: the smile that manages to be both demure and debauched, the perfectly judged Parisian dress sense, the Audrey Hepburn-esque tilt of the head. No Hollywood blockbuster could cast such a perfect adult-fairytale princess as Carla.

My grouch isn't with her. I do think that Nicolas Sarkozy looks just a trifle silly trotting alongside her with the dazed-codfish expression of a man who's just swallowed a suitcase of happy pills; but Carla is only exercising a power that has been familiar since the dawn of time. No, it's that the adulation was so unrestrained, and contrasted so starkly with how normal women are treated in public life.

Brown has a reasonable number of intelligent women in his cabinet, most of them ridiculed each day with a harsh edge few men feel. But isn't our public life more male than it has been at any period since the 1970s? The Tories put themselves across as an almost men-only opposition. The most prominent Conservative woman is Samantha Cameron, with a touch of the Carla about her, and certainly lacking the political profile of Labour spouses. The Lib Dems are dominated by Nick, Chris and Vince. Then there's the London mayoral elections, where alpha-male Boris is romping ahead, and where the only female candidate is the almost unmentioned Green. Is this where we have come after decades of feminism, and all those hopes for a new and more balanced kind of politics? Yes, there are more women MPs and ministers. It's just that they are clustered forever in the wings, at the edge of the picture.

The question, then, is why? Except for those who truly believe women are not fitted for multitasking, information-absorbing life in the fast lane, isn't the most obvious culprit the media climate? Again, I am speaking impressionistically, not scientifically: but has not the rise of the internet coincided with a rise of the men's magazine culture? Blogworld is the future, and it will not be resisted; but at this stage in its development, it seems dominated by rightwing male individualists and libertarians.

A jeering tone has migrated from websites into the mainstream media, because journalists are the most suggestible species there is. The bullying swagger of American radio's male shock-jocks was until recently something we talked about with mild bewilderment. Now it's echoed from early morning to late night across Britain. All those raucous certainties, those casual dismissals. Men-only bars have long been illegal; we seem to have bar-room radio instead.

Maybe the mood is best caught by the online petition on the No 10 website to make Jeremy Clarkson prime minister, because 'Jezza is a legend and deserves a chance to run the country'. *Top Gear* is a fantastically successful programme, and Clarkson is a very shrewd man who controls his image cleverly. Like Carla, it isn't his fault he is a symbol of a culture poised between swagger and leer.

Thinking back to the 1970s, what was most potent about the feminist movement was a self-confident, even aggressive, cultural mood – not just the Greers and the Callils, but the millions of women who enjoyed a little swagger of their own. There were the magazines, the feisty broadcasters, the breakthrough authors, the argument-pickers; and collectively they were what mattered.

Since then we have gone soft, become a touch apologetic. Maybe we took victory for granted 30 years too early and drifted back to other things – maybe we are paying the price for that now. Women with any interest in politics are going to have to reclaim the new media and the airwaves. However, the first thing is to notice the need and to speak about it. We're going to have to fight a little harder for our place in the sun – to be a bit stroppier and tougher. Either that, or we're going to have to start taking demure-smiling and silence classes.

APRIL 2 2008

# Review: *Peter Pan el Musical*

## LYN GARDNER

An awfully big misadventure, this Spanish mauling of JM Barrie's masterpiece flies into the Garrick and crash-lands belly up. There are no survivors. Such is the mind-boggling awfulness of this family show, performed in Spanish with inept English surtitles, that you wish the Lost Boys had not shot at Wendy but taken aim at this great white elephant and finished it off instead. My youngest daughter – a stoic survivor of such theatrical catastrophes as *Fireman Sam Live on Stage* and *The Man in the Iron Mask* – refused point-blank to return with me after the interval.

*Peter Pan* is the most thrilling and heartbreaking of stories, but this travesty turns it into an all-singing, all-dancing laser show that makes the average English pantomime version look classy. Cristina Fargas's adaptation guts the narrative and robs the story of its emotional nuance. Every single song would fail to win the Eurovision Song Contest and the choreography hails from the dark ages. The Lost Boys are so irritating it is clear that they did not fall out of their prams but were pushed by parents desperate to be rid of them.

Substituting hyperactivity and cheerfulness for charm, this show gets almost everything wrong – from the Darlings' London home, which appears to be modelled out of Plasticine, to Nana the dog, who the family have mysteriously failed to notice is a terrifying shaggy mutant the size of a small rhino.

The show's publicity proudly announces that one million Spaniards have seen this show, which just goes to prove that there is no accounting for statistics.

APRIL 11 2008

# Here's to the mob, for its humiliation of dictators and hypocrites alike

## SIMON JENKINS

Come on, confess it, you have not enjoyed a story so much in years. A round-the-world marathon with all-in wrestling, kick boxing, rugby tackling and sanctimonious steeplechasing, staged free of charge in the streets of London, Paris and San Francisco by the International Olympics Committee – and before the Beijing games have even started. To add to the joy, nobody gets hurt except politicians.

On one side are Gordon Brown, the Chinese politburo, Tessa Jowell, Ken Livingstone, the IOC fat cats and 1,000 jogging police-men, all playing 'protect the holy flame' as if in a scene from Harry Potter. On the other side is an old-fashioned mob. The mob wins and the nation splits its sides with glee. The old left dares not walk the streets of London these days, but must tremble behind £1m worth of police protection. Sweet is the sight of the boot on the other foot.

I have decided that the mob is a much underrated political phenomenon. In London last weekend it reduced the Olympic torch parade to a Keystone Cops farrago. Then in Paris it extinguished the flame altogether, and in San Francisco it forced the proceedings to vanish into an early grave. Some pundits consider such demonstra-tions undignified and ineffective in an era of television studios, e-politics and blogs. But they said that of rock concerts.

The mob helped kill the poll tax, felled the Berlin Wall and brought Yeltsin to power in Russia. It toppled dictators in Serbia and Ukraine, and may yet do so in Kenya and Zimbabwe. A crowd running amok in the streets of a capital somehow outguns opinion polls and election victories in the minds of rulers. When those in palaces of power peer round their curtains and see the howling throng, their knees go weak and some primitive instinct communicates defeat.

This week's mob in London, Paris and San Francisco was tiny and unrepresentative of mostly non-violent Tibetan opinion. But by attaching itself to a publicity stunt, the mob delivered a humiliating blow to the mightiest dictatorship on earth, China. It also exposed the hypocrisy of the IOC's Jacques Rogge, now trying to pretend that, 'with hindsight', awarding the games to Beijing was not a great idea as they might be exploited politically. He should have listened.

The torch tour, shorn of the mental candyfloss about world peace and harmony, was political. It was conducted by Chinese heavies and patronised by has-been celebrities and publicity-hungry lobbyists. As for the IOC, it failed to withdraw its approval even when told the tour would climax in the former Tibetan capital of Lhasa. Rogge and his crew have spent so long immersed in five-star hotels that they cannot tell a Gandhi from a Genghis Khan. The Chinese have taken them for the mother of all rides. Never were so many conned so rotten by so few.

The mistake of this tour was its hubris. Had the Chinese and the IOC been shrewd, they would have avoided democracies altogether, or at least they would have run the torch inside stadiums, where they could ensure photo-opportunities with politicians smiling as they received free tickets for Beijing. Instead they craved geographical authenticity. They thought with Kipling that they could 'talk with crowds and keep your virtue'. They accepted the advice of the IOC, that playing to the mob would serve the glory of them both. They both got a raspberry.

That said, every catastrophe has a silver lining. The Olympics can now go in one of two directions. The costly-is-beautiful polit-buro-cum-New-Labour Olympics are irrevocably tainted and seem incapable of purging themselves. As the cameras roll, the anthems play and the flags fly in the forthcoming orgy of chauvinism, every contestant in Beijing must be pondering what political statement to make on the rostrum, whether about Tibet or George Bush or Tower Hamlets borough council. Hecklers will shout, banners will wave and thugs will beat up bystanders. Track and field will be way down the news list.

If London sticks to this agenda in 2012 – and Brown's £9bn pledge suggests it will – then it should make the best of it and plan a parallel Olympiad of protest. By then the event will be regarded globally as a festival of political activism, like G8 summits and United Nations assemblies. With so much publicity and so much hype, it will be the occasion for mass campaigning about anything and everything. The theatre of the street will out-dazzle the theatre of sport.

Unlike G8 summits, the games offer real leverage to a mob. Nobody but caterers cares if a G8 summit is disrupted or abandoned. But $20bn to $30bn is invested in an Olympics these days, with just two weeks to make a return. That time sensitivity offers street activists extraordinary power, power that may even induce the Chinese to lighten their repression at least until August.

London would be a splendid venue for a political Olympiad. It has long been a place of refuge and asylum. For the period of the games its doors should welcome any cause, however worthy or crackpot. Halls should be open for rallies and churches for protest. Let Trafalgar Square be standing room only for the duration. While the IOC tucks into the taxpayer's champagne at Fortress

Stratford, back in central London anarchism can rule and Jowell's torch of harmony become the torch of glorious discord. Much nonsense is uttered about the Olympics not being political. Anything rooted in blatant nationalism is political. Anything so expensive as to impose a multibillion-pound opportunity cost on the host nation is political. Anything 'awarded' as a prize to authoritarian states such as the Soviet Union or China is political. The Olympics were political to the Greeks, and included diplomatic parleys among the poetry competitions and beauty parades. Nor were the actual games gentlemanly and decorous. Robin Lane Fox, in The Classical World, describes 'smashed teeth, limbs, ears and bones, occasionally to the point of death'.

The revival of the games by Pierre de Coubertin in the 19th century was also political, albeit the facile politics of world peace and platitudes about the global fraternity of youth. There is no fraternity in international sport, which as Coubertin recognised is war by other means. Sportsmen are trained to beat hell out of each other to the greater glory of their country. All else is naivety.

To those who might find a political Olympiad distasteful, there is a clear and simple alternative. They can treat the Olympics as only about sport, and not about world harmony and the enrichment of the construction industry. Athletes can attend the games as individuals. The tarnished Olympic image can be cleansed by suppressing national anthems, flags and all visits and speeches by politicians. The games would become solely about running, throwing, jumping, swimming, riding – active verbs, not abstract nouns.

If that happened there would be no need of idle threats against China. There need be none of the political clutter that Rogge and others have brought to the Olympics, any more than there has been at this month's world cycling and swimming championships in Manchester. They passed off without anyone mentioning Tibet. But they did not have to justify $30bn.

Marmoset monkey, animal testing centre, May 2008.

GRAEME ROBERTSON

Cigar smoker, Monaco, March 2008.

GRAEME ROBERTSON

Pilgrims at Saut D'eau, Haiti, July 2008.

DAVID LEVENE

Mary Alingu breaks rocks near Katine, Uganda, December 2007.

DAN CHUNG

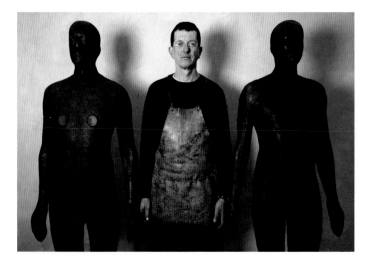

Sculptor Antony Gormley in his studio, January 2008.

GRAEME ROBERTSON

APRIL 16 2008

# Fields of gold

## ADITYA CHAKRABORTTY

Call it the revenge of Marie Antoinette. The French queen, who on being told that her subjects had no bread suggested they eat cake instead, has gone down in history as callous, unworldly and fully deserving of the guillotine. Last year, however, farmers in Pennsylvania began following her advice. As standard animal feed had become too dear, they started giving their pigs and cows chocolate – and banana chips and cashews and yoghurt-covered raisins, any of which were cheaper than run-of the-mill corn and beans. One farmer even supplied his cattle a special 'party mix' of popcorn, pretzels, cheese curls and crisps. This, he told reporters, saved 10 per cent on feed costs.

From hogs in the US to shoppers in the UK, we are all being hit by higher food costs. Bread, milk and other foodstuffs consumers think of as basic are nothing of the sort; instead, they are subject to a complex range of pressures stretching from London to China, from America to Australia. The price of that daily loaf is fluctuating according to what happens on the Minneapolis Grain Exchange, or the outlook for the Indian economy.

What all that means is that if you think bread is already pricey, think again: it will almost certainly go higher. A loaf of Hovis Classic White, that staple of school lunchboxes, now goes for around £1, already far above what it fetched a year ago. But the company behind Hovis, Premier Foods, warned last month that it would have to raise prices again. Premier also admitted that its profits from bread sales had nearly halved, thanks to what it termed 'an exceptional level of cost inflation'.

To get some sense of what Premier and other food sellers are battling with you must journey through a thicket of weird and wonderful names. Where shoppers see a loaf of sliced bread, experts think of US hard red winter wheat. But the basic picture is stark. Wheat prices, which were already creeping up, have doubled in the past year. And some types of the crop have risen more than that: spring wheat (a protein-rich variant that apparently goes into the better class of sandwich) has shot up from $220 (£110) a tonne last April to $578 now.

The most immediate reason for the spike is a traditional one: poor harvests. There was barely any rain in Australia last year and the year before that, so stockpiles of wheat have hit a 30-year low. This year's harvest, however, is set to be a lot better, and that in itself would not account for such a dramatic surge in prices.

Another factor is more recent: biofuels. As of yesterday, 2.5 per cent of all petrol and diesel sold in the UK must be made from plants. And that will rise by 2010 to 5.75 per cent. This is part of the government's push to combat climate change. In comparison with fossil fuels, energy derived from plants is touted as cleaner and greener. The problem is that they take up land and crops that might otherwise feed people. It's not just the UK that has got on the biofuel bandwagon. America is easily the biggest country on board, as it looks to reduce demand for petrol. The result has been that 20 per cent of the American maize crop has gone not into feeding people, but fuelling machines.

The precise effect of the biofuel craze on food prices is controversial; some experts claim it has had minimal impact. They get short shrift from people such as Amy Reynolds, senior economist at the International Grains Council. She says: 'At the start of the decade, a small amount of grain – 18m tonnes – was used for industrial purposes. This year 100m tonnes will go towards biofu-els and other industrial purposes. Can anyone really tell me that that hasn't had an impact on what we pay for food?'

So if you want to bring down food prices, one obvious thing to do is to call a halt to biofuels. But that would probably not reverse the trend. The long-term reason why prices are going up is simply that more people are eating more – especially in the increasingly prosperous developing countries such as China and India. In 1985, for instance, the average Chinese person ate 20kg of meat a year; now she eats more than 50kg a year. When you consider that it takes 10kg of feed to make 1kg of beef, the effects of these billions of new consumers is dramatic.

There are two responses to this. One is to quote Thomas Malthus and to argue that a rising population always means scarcity of precious resources. But that is probably melodramatic. The truth is that for a long time, the west has had access to cheap resources. Once you strip out inflation, what we paid for wheat dropped by more than 80 per cent between 1973 and 2000. Even now, after the record rises for wheat prices, what we pay is still below the levels of the 70s.

In an ideal world, we would simply adjust for the new wealth of the east by adjusting our spending: eat slightly less meat, or not throw away our leftovers. But this transition is unlikely to be so smooth. For one, while British shoppers have to pay more at the till, poor countries such as Bangladesh are struggling to feed themselves. And the consequences could be brutal.

This past weekend, Dominique Strauss-Kahn, managing direc-tor of the International Monetary Fund, said the food crisis posed questions about whether governments in some countries would survive. 'As we know, sometimes those questions lead to war,' he said. 'We now need to devote 100 per cent of our time to these questions.'

In the UK, too, as we face a slowing economy, higher food prices are just what we don't need. Over the past few months, Mervyn King, head of the Bank of England, has been sounding increasingly worried about the rising cost of living. 'The higher level of energy and food prices is a genuine reduction in our standard of living relative to where it would otherwise have been,' King said a few weeks ago. 'This is because of the higher prices that all of us are having to pay.'

Just ask Joseph Gazzano. He owns an Italian delicatessen in London serving a loyal bunch of customers, but lately he's been getting flak from what he calls his old ladies.

'The pensioners who come here look at the prices shooting up and think I'm the one to blame,' he says. His continental bread has gone up by 30p in six months, and biscuits have risen 20p-£1. What's happened to the pasta? 'Don't mention the pasta,' he says. 'All that lot' – he points to the shelves of conchiglie, orecchiette and tufoli – 'all that lot has shot up.'

And he's not responsible. 'One of my suppliers has been in the business 50 years and he says he's never seen an inflationary period like this. All the stuff I buy has gone sky-high. I can absorb some of the price rises, but not all. And it worries me: it doesn't matter if the price of petrol goes up – you can bike it. But food going up matters because you have to eat'.

# Country Diary: Yorkshire Dales

## PHIL GATES

Heavy rain threatened to wash out our walking holiday so, hoping to turn adversity into an asset, we headed for Yorkshire's limestone country to visit waterfalls. Torrential downpours quickly turn tame picture-postcard cascades into raging torrents, and the ever-popular falls at Ingleton didn't disappoint. Along the wooded ravine, the sound of rushing water grew steadily louder until we reached Pecca falls, where the exhilarating, concussive force of the raging white water of the river Twiss, tumbling over ledges and squeezing between rock walls, was enough to dispel any gloom that the weather could deliver.

In an atmosphere kept perpetually moist by clouds of spray, conditions were perfect for feathery mosses and scaly liverworts that smothered steep banks where the first spring flowers – golden saxifrage and barren strawberry – were beginning to open. Upstream, the river delivered its tour de force – Thornton Force – a 14-metre-high curtain of water at the head of the valley. And then we reached the open treeless landscape of broken limestone scars and dry-stone walls, filled with the bubbling calls of curlews, leaving the sound and fury of falling water behind. We crossed the river above the Force and followed the footpath that skirts Twistleton Scar End, with the great bulk of Ingleborough looming in the haze away to the south-east. Suddenly we found ourselves surrounded by 'chak, chak' alarm calls that seemed to come from every direction. We had arrived on this bleak, stony hillside at the same moment as a fall of wheatears, newly arrived at the end of their long migration. Immaculately plumaged in slate-grey backs, black eye stripes and pale orange bibs, they perched on barbed wire, foraged on the grassy slopes and flitted along the wall tops just a few yards ahead of us. The limestone hills of Yorkshire on a wet and windy April morning were a stark contrast to their tropical African wintering grounds, but their arrival was a welcome affirmation that spring had arrived.

APRIL 26 2008

# If Boris Johnson wins next week ... it might be time to leave England and move north

IAN JACK

Just before George W Bush was re-elected you would hear a certain kind of American say, 'I can't stand the thought. If he wins I'm going to live in Canada.' Like Scotland in English conversations, Canada is not a place much mentioned by Americans. What is it, after all, but some duller version of the United States situated somewhere to the north – fierce winters, lots of land and not many people, and the Queen's head on the money?

But with the Bush crisis and the feeling of liberal alienation some of its virtues were remembered. Canada didn't go about the world telling it how to behave or invading those parts of it that were behaving inconveniently, which the US was morally and economically less and less equipped to do. Canada had quieter manners, was more civic-minded, enjoyed enviable standards of healthcare and education. Shootings and muggings were far fewer.

In these new circumstances the hush of the arrivals hall at Toronto airport seemed less a gateway to a society of almost intolerable politeness and order and more like a welcome to an idealised version of the country the traveller had just left – that is, the US minus Bush, racial difficulty, manic Wall Street and the occasional high-school massacre. 'Provincial' had its up sides.

So it is now with Scotland. To my mind, Scotland is the new Canada. Some clarification is needed here, because in the 19th century the opposite was true. With Lowlanders financing the transcontinental railway and Highlanders clearing the timber, Canada was the new Scotland – Nova Scotia, founded as long ago as 1621. What I mean is that Scotland is becoming to England what Canada has long been to the US, at the very least since the Vietnam draft-dodgers crossed the border.

The two northerly countries share several similarities: frequent bleak weather, low population densities (the Highlands have eight people a square kilometre to Canada's three), but it is Scotland's emerging character and relationship with its bigger southern neighbour that make the case more powerfully.

Britain is now heading into its own Bush crisis. Next week 7 million Londoners may wake to discover Boris Johnson is their mayor. Some time before the summer of 2010, 60 million UK citizens may discover that David Cameron is their prime minister. If you live in London, as I do, that means living under a double yoke of old Etonians.

What do I have against old Etonians? Nothing much, some of my best friends, and so forth. But Johnson and Cameron share more than a public school. Like the shadow chancellor, George Osborne (an old St Paulian), they belonged as students at Oxford to the Bullingdon, described as a 'dining club'.

The group portraits of the Bullingdon Club showing Johnson, Cameron and Osborne are now an embarrassment to the politicians in them. There they stand in their made-to-measure blue tailcoats (£1,200 each), ready to take on the world by frightening a few waitresses and wrecking a restaurant.

You might argue that their haughty pose represents nothing more than youthful excess and a wish to be in touch with the world of Evelyn Waugh, but you must also wonder why the leadership of the likely next British government has been drawn from such a narrow and privileged seam of English society.

The front bench and Cameron's private office are stacked with old Eton boys. Journalists write about it continually, but with remarkably little sense of shock, as though the grammar school years of Heath, Thatcher and Major had never existed and the old routes to power (a school, a club, a good marriage, a trust fund) were just the inescapable, unalterable facts in the web of English life.

The question then arises: if this is what England is, if this is what England wants, do I belong in it?

I've never asked this of myself before. Like Gordon Brown, I subscribe to the idea of a British identity as well as, in both our cases, to a Scottish one. Unlike Gordon Brown, I've never tried to parse this identity in the abstractions of 'values' – show me a modern European state that doesn't claim liberty somewhere on its letter-head – but rather in the specifics of the things I grew up with: the BBC, the Royal Navy, the *Beano*, and a thousand other British bits and pieces that came out of centuries of shared history and aren't exclusively English, Welsh or Scottish.

Increasingly, we Britons are a lonely little crew and skipper Brown has too heavy a hand on the tiller. In Scotland, only a minority choose to call themselves British. In England, the thought has eventually dawned that 'British' and 'English' have

different meanings, and so this week on St George's Day pubs flut-
tered with red and white flags and writers such as Billy Bragg
laboured to evoke 'progressive nationalism', meaning Wat Tyler
rather than the Duke of Wellington.

To anyone who grew up in Scotland, this English angst brought
deja vu. In our history class 50 years ago, the same kind of argument was gone through very often. Were the Jacobite rebellions an
expression of Scottish nationalism or just a stupid wheeze cooked
up in France? Were bagpipes singularly Scottish? Did Logie Baird
really invent television?

I had a friend, Norval MacPhail, the only boy in the school to
wear a kilt apart from a few English children who sometimes
appeared in Hunting Stewart, presumably because their parents
believed, quite mistakenly, that it would help them 'fit in'. Norval
was also the school's only Scot Nat. We had playground discussions about the viability of an independent state.

'So what about the navy, what about the railways?'

'We're going to electrify the railways, like Switzerland.'

'How?'

'Scotland has lots of hydro-electric power. You'll see.'

What a prescient little boy Norval was back in 1959. Unlike
England, where the Department for Transport has spurned electri-
fication, Scotland intends to electrify some of its lines. Also, unlike
England outside London, it is building new ones: Alloa to Stirling,
Airdrie to Bathgate, a branch to Glasgow airport, 60 kilometres of
track that will reconnect Edinburgh to the Borders.

By the standards of mainland Europe these are quite modest
additions, but there is nothing like them in non-metropolitan
England. By 2011, travellers between Glasgow and Edinburgh will
have a choice of four routes 20 years ago they had two. Of course,
my boyhood friend's nationalism didn't spring from visions of
integrated public transport. Like most nationalisms, it came out

of romance, myth and history. But now the Celtic mists are beginning to clear. The benefits of Scottish devolution – to Scotland – can be seen concretely.

Listening on the radio this week to an English Labour MP criticising Gordon Brown for his want of radical social reform, it was impossible to resist the thought: 'But all these things have already happened in Scotland. You're living in the wrong country. Perhaps I am too.'

What has the Scottish government done differently from England under its old Labour-Lib Dem and new SNP administrations? The list is worth remembering: free personal care for the elderly and infirm; university tuition fees abolished (unless you're a student from England) and prescription charges reduced by £1.85 when south of the border they went up 25p, with a pledge that within the lifetime of the present Scottish parliament they will be abandoned altogether.

The SNP government has declared itself against nuclear power and a new generation of Trident submarines. It has restarted the building of council houses and by 2015 aims to be building 35,000 a year. This week it announced that the biggest and most expensive hospital in the United Kingdom would be built in Glasgow at a cost of £842m met entirely from public funds, rebuffing New Labour's belief in private finance initiatives.

The SNP is not a particularly ideological party and by no stretch socialist as one of its members told me last week: 'We're pragmatic and opportunistic, like the big Irish parties.' It will also be pointed out that this long free lunch is being subsidised by English taxpayers via subventions from Whitehall (to which the SNP would reply that an independent state would make up the difference with its share of revenue from North Sea oil). But this is clever politics. If the money well runs dry, Scotland's first minister, Alex Salmond, can blame Westminster perfidy.

No wonder, therefore, that Scotland has suddenly become attractive to many people just south of its border. Opinion polls in Berwick-on-Tweed show that a majority would like the town to become part of a country that it left in 1482. Anecdotal evidence suggests that the Tweed valley and Dumfries and Galloway are witnessing a growing flow of incomers from Newcastle, Yorkshire and Cumbria. Scotland could become not just a separate state but even a mildly expansionist one.

There is always the weather and geography to consider, but in the long term both might prove a blessing. Scotland has around 30 per cent of Britain's land mass but, with 5.117 million people, only 8.4 per cent of the UK population; a national average of 65 people to the square kilometre compared with 380 in England.

By 2031 the population of England is expected to grow by 20 per cent, in Scotland only by 5 per cent, after which it should begin to decline. 'Sustainability' might be more easily achieved than in England. As well as wind farms and hydro-electric dams, power could be harnessed from the constant Atlantic swell beating against the Hebrides and the currents of the Pentland Firth, schemes that are now attracting money and science.

Global warming is expected to expand Scotland's arable land westwards up the glens from the traditional farmlands of the north-east. Sea-level rise threatens Scottish fields much less than the fertile plains of East Anglia. Above all, there is rain, which in the words of Bill Slee, a researcher into land use at Aberdeen's Macaulay Institute, makes Scotland 'distinctly advantaged'. Unlike countries further south – around the Mediterranean and even parts of England – Scotland is unlikely to suffer water stress. If crops become scarcer and more expensive on the global market, Scotland could be well placed to take advantage. And, taking bleak futurism one step further down the road of James Lovelock and

Cormac McCarthy, Scotland's bloody tradition of militarism might help make it more defendable.

None of this can certainly be known and I won't be here to see it. The greater certainty, or so it seems this week, is that Johnson will win London and Cameron the country. Will I go and live in Scotland then, writing 'Damn you, England' as John Osborne wrote in his famous letter to *Tribune* in 1961, from his holiday villa in the south of France? 'There is murder in my brain and I carry a knife in my heart for every one of you. Macmillan, and you, Gaitskell, you particularly.' (An Etonian and a Wykehamist, as it happens.)

I don't think so. There are limits to self-importance, and in any case life is often too complicated to be reduced to choices of home. But I think that if Cameron wins he will be the last prime minister of Great Britain. If he goes two terms, he will become the first prime minister of England. Our united semi-states will be no more. Then there really will be a new Canada in the north.

APRIL 28 2008

# We should stop fooling ourselves. Our armed forces are no longer world class

MAX HASTINGS

The Ministry of Defence is plunged into a grim process described as a 'mini defence review'. Teams of service officers and civil servants are exploring every aspect of spending and procurement plans in a desperate effort to save money. Current year sums have been made to add up only by creative accountancy, pushing back some big bills to 2010. Whoever becomes defence secretary after an election that year will face a pile of yellowing, unpaid invoices.

Everybody knows that a major defence programme must be cancelled. The navy's cherished aircraft carriers? These would be the first choices of most soldiers, but because the ships mean jobs in Labour constituencies, they are almost certainly safe. Some frigates and destroyers? At least two planned escorts are likely to be axed. The army is fearful about its next-generation armoured vehicle. Several headquarters will have to go. General Sir Richard Dannatt, chief of the general staff, has failed in his attempt to persuade ministers to increase the army's numbers.

Dannatt's case is founded on the fact that his soldiers are attempting to fight one major war, in Afghanistan, with inadequate resources, while 4,000 troops are in another theatre, Iraq, to appease American sensitivities. The army also maintains a significant peacekeeping presence in the Balkans. It was announced last week that another infantry battalion is to be sent to Kosovo.

Yet the deep instinct of the government, and even more so of the parliamentary Labour party, is that Tony Blair's wars have brought Britain only embarrassment and grief. The last thing they want is to throw good money after bad by recruiting more soldiers, never mind deploying them in combat.

The scepticism is understandable, but the conclusion is mistaken. Many people, myself included, are dismayed by the huge mistakes made in Iraq and Afghanistan. Yet it remains essential for Britain to possess a credible army. A strength of 100,000 is insufficient. Whether we like it or not, the 21st century will produce new conflicts in which we are obliged to participate or at least provide peacekeepers.

Britain cannot alone fill the yawning gap in Afghanistan left by other Nato countries that refuse to do their share of fighting and supporting humanitarian reconstruction. But we can never hope to win this conflict, or any other, without more boots on the ground. Mass matters. It is not enough for western powers to announce in a given crisis: 'We are committing troops,' then to dispatch three men and a dog. No strategic purpose is attainable unless soldiers are deployed in sufficient strength, with convincing humanitarian backup.

I argued on these pages two years ago that the force that Blair and the then defence secretary, John Reid, were sending to Afghanistan's Helmand province was entirely inadequate for its role, and represented gesture strategy. So it has proved. Western defence policy will remain rooted in tokenism until all the European nations, and indeed the US, can field sufficient foot soldiers – who are far more relevant to 'wars among the people' than tanks and stealth bombers – to fulfil policy objectives.

The shortfall is not exclusively the fault of governments. Part of the problem stems from our changing culture. It is becoming progressively more difficult for western societies to recruit infantry. Most British infantry regiments are under establishment, and Scottish units especially so, not only because of Treasury parsimony, but also because recruiting languishes and retention is difficult.

For centuries, armies have largely consisted of young working-class men, often with poor qualifications. They opted for a life of adventure and comradeship, accepting both the duty to kill and the risk of their own deaths. The army was seldom their career of choice, but many prospered in uniform.

Today, however, a lot of parents and schools recoil from seeing young men embrace the warrior ethos. They find repugnant the notion of arming teenagers and dispatching them to fight, whatever the cause. Thanks to the internet, a radio exchange between a female interviewer and an Australian general named Peter Cosgrove has passed into contemporary legend. Cosgrove, as head of the Australian army, described on air a scheme to introduce Australian boy scouts to the exciting life on offer to a soldier by inviting them to bases where they could try climbing, canoeing, archery and rifle-shooting. 'Shooting!' exclaimed the appalled interviewer. 'That's a bit irresponsible, isn't it ?'

'I don't see why,' said the general. 'They'll be properly supervised on the range.' The interviewer was unconvinced: 'Don't you admit that this is a terribly dangerous activity to be teaching children? You're equipping them to become violent killers.' Cosgrove remained unabashed: 'Well, ma'am, you're equipped to be a prostitute, but you're not one, are you?'

A lot of people share the interviewer's instinctive revulsion towards guns, as well as other aspects of soldiering. Some British schools are unwilling to welcome army recruiting teams. The Joseph Rowntree Charitable Trust recently caricatured itself by publishing a report arguing that the army has a duty more frankly to warn recruits in its advertising about the prospect that they may have to kill or be killed.

Overlaid upon such fastidiousness is the problem of many teenagers' lack of fitness for service life. The British army is striving to reduce the high dropout rate in basic training among new entrants who either find discipline unacceptable or cannot contend with the physical demands. Teenagers who have never walked if they could ride, and define enthusiasm for sport by watching it on telly, find assault courses tough going.

The result is that all western nations are struggling to identify enough young men able and willing to carry rifles on battlefields. It is hard to foresee social trends that will make it less so. The armed forces as an institution still command public respect. But this is of limited worth unless it translates into a willingness by the young to sign up and do the business.

It is paradoxical that Tony Blair, who sought to use Britain's armed forces more ambitiously than any modern prime minister, inflicted deep damage by associating them with some unpopular and perhaps unwinnable causes.

Britain's three services are now so small that, if current policies and difficulties continue, it will be almost impossible to reverse the process of decline. Relations between senior officers at the MoD have become rancorous, amid fears and recriminations about budget cuts, real and threatened.

Unless one is an outright pacifist, rejecting military commitment anywhere, in any cause, it is necessary to recognise that the national interest must suffer if the services become tarnished and are penalised for a prime minister's political misjudgments. The old cliche is often trotted out that our armed forces are still world class. In truth, it is no longer valid. However high their quality, they are now too few to fulfil many of the tasks they are assigned. Even if ministers try to delude us otherwise, the public should not be fooled.

MAY 1 2008

# Forget shoes and men – this show nailed our friendships

**LIBBY BROOKS**

I have never really understood why so many people felt personally affronted by *Sex and the City*. The 90s TV hit that charted sex columnist Carrie Bradshaw's navigation of life, love and the latest shoe styles in New York never claimed to be a documentary about contemporary women's lives. Inevitably though, the fictional portrayal of four unfathomably glamorous, sexually experimental and effortlessly successful Manhattan females rendered the series hugely influential, mainly because it was unlike anything else. But just because women are seldom seen on the small screen being hopeful, hilarious and horny all at once is not a good reason to levy the weight of feminist expectation against a single franchise. Still, the much-anticipated release of the *Sex and the City* movie later this month prods those discomforts yet again.

At the risk of collapsing one Bradshaw metaphor into another, I always found the series charming, funny, good-looking and intelligent, rather like the perfect first date. I enjoyed following Carrie and her achingly archetypical friends – Charlotte (Upper East Side princess forced to redefine her sense of perfect when marriage and fertility go wrong); Miranda (fiercely independent lawyer not softened by motherhood); and Samantha (unrepentant fuck machine, latterly breast-cancer survivor). I'm almost afraid to admit it lest it show me up as shallow, but the show did make me ask pertinent questions about my own life and those of my friends – and not solely because we were swithering over Manolo Blahnik designs.

*Sex and the City* was always two parts fantasy shaken with one part delicately skewered reality. So – no – hot, smart women do not only talk about men and shoes, Manhattan isn't always sunny, and newspaper columns aren't generally written, unresearched, in slinky vest tops (though actually, reader, you should see me now).

But this fantastical element was tolerated in exchange for the unprecedented honesty about other areas of women's experience that *Sex and the City* hauled into the mainstream. Most prominently, the series discussed the micro and macro of sexual relationships as they had never been before: when is it all right to fake an orgasm? Ought there to be cleanup etiquette for men giving head? How does maternal ambivalence affect a woman who is already pregnant?

Those gasp-out-loud episodes were embraced by women not only because they'd been there privately, but thanks to the context in which they were discussed. For my money, the enduring appeal of *Sex and the City* has nothing to do with guys or footwear. It's about the uncomfortably accurate presentation of women's relationships with each other. However the critics receive the new film, they ought to bear in mind that, for all the brunch chatter, this show has never been a story about men. *Sex and the City* was always, baseline, about us girls; about how women's friendships can be complicated and bitchy, but also meaningful, supportive and lasting.

I'm a firm believer that all our subsequent interactions are dictated by original familial connections, so it has always fascinated me that Freud didn't bother to create an Oedipus-style template for women's relationships. It's an absence that Shere Hite notes in her latest report on women loving women, alongside the dearth of media representations of what are often the most important relationships in women's lives. Aside from the imported *Desperate Housewives* and the brilliant British-born *Pulling*, it's hard to think of popular art that takes women's friendships seriously.

Perhaps that's because we don't take them seriously ourselves. On the one hand we lionise relationships with other women – it's a given to crow about the super-fantasticness of one's friendships, and we're happy to admit how essential those relationships are in the scheme of our lives. Yet, day to day, we give those connections far less traction than they deserve. When was the last time you sat down with a female friend and asked: 'Where is this relationship going?' Women analyse their interactions with men to the nth degree, while their profound connections with others of their gender go unexamined.

I'm sure it's partly to do with the way women's relationships are set up publicly. From an early age, girls are taught that they are in sexual competition with their peers. Nobody wants to be the loser in the race to couple up, and nobody wants to be deemed a lesbian. Later, women wind up being their own worst enemies, buying into a culture that sets them against one another: the singles v the marrieds, the stay at homes v the working mothers. We are told that we can only understand those who mimic our lifestyle choices. It's interesting that when Hite surveyed she found that, of all barriers to friendship, relationship status was the greatest. Single and partnered women were less likely to be close than those of a different class or race.

*Sex and the City* was seminal because it showed women's friendships according to a panoply of responses: anger, doubt, judgment and envy, as well as love. And it proposed basic needs – flu, a cricked neck, the plus one – as fulfilled by other women. It's not anti-men to acknowledge how females can sustain each other. But it is pro-women to suggest that we cease angsting at each other, especially about shoes.

MAY 3 2008

# Eleven years after it promised a new dawn, Labour's dusk has arrived

## JONATHAN FREEDLAND

On a sunny Friday in May, by the glittering waters of the Thames, Tony Blair famously declared that a 'new dawn' had broken.

Yesterday, exactly 11 years later, and once again on the banks of the Thames, Labour ushered in what will surely be its new dusk. On May 2 1997, the venue was a victory party at the Royal Festival Hall. On May 2 2008 it was a wake at City Hall, witnessing a defeat that seemed to confirm what a day of results had already suggested: that after an era of dominance that has endured since the mid-1990s, Labour is about to enter the twilight.

It threatens to be a slow death, as Labour decays steadily towards defeat in 2010. That, at least, is what plenty in the party fear after a horror show of a performance in local elections across England and Wales.

Labour slumped to third place: that seemed oddly tolerable, given that they had managed no better in 2004, going on to win the general election a year later. But on that occasion Labour had managed at least a 26 per cent share of the vote: this time it was down to 24 per cent, its worst performance in 40 years. And that wipe-out in 1968 was followed two years later by defeat in a general election. Labourites are struggling to believe the same fate does not await them now.

But it was on the stroke of midnight last night that the most dramatic defeat was announced, after 15 hours of counting. Ken Livingstone, a force in London politics for nearly 40 years, shook the hand of Boris Johnson, who had beaten him by 140,000 votes. His voice cracking with emotion, Livingstone told the new mayor: 'Boris, the next few years will be the best years of your life.'

In a generous victory speech, with his wife and children watching in the front row, Johnson praised the outgoing mayor for his 'transparent love of London', courage and 'sheer exuberant nerve'. Perhaps mindful of the uphill task he now faces in winning over ethnic-minority Londoners in particular, Johnson addressed those who had not voted for him: 'I will work flat-out to earn your trust – and to dispel some of the myths about me.' He said he hoped to prove the Tories had changed and closed by declaring: 'Let's get cracking tomorrow – and let's have a drink tonight.'

At least the London contest was close. Elsewhere, Labour took a hiding. As Ed Balls, the children, schools and families secretary, admitted to BBC radio yesterday, this could not be dismissed 'as simply about a mid-term normal set of problems'. This was more than the traditional bloody nose administered by a restless electorate halfway through a parliament. That much was clear from the sheer scale of the punch.

Labour did not just trail the Tories, as they had done in previous council contests. They were 20 points behind. The Tories did not just clear the 40 per cent threshold, they hurdled over it to score 44 per cent, just three points behind the high watermark reached by Tony Blair in local elections in 1995, when New Labour were two years away from a landslide victory.

But this was about more than numbers. Even before the London mayoral result was in, the Conservatives won precisely where they needed to win, toppling Labour in several of its few remaining southern bastions – Southampton brought an unexpected Tory victory – and making inroads in the north. In the nearly three years since David Cameron took over as Conservative leader, one of his most visible weaknesses had been his inability to break through in the north of England. Perhaps it was the toff factor, perhaps it was stubborn distrust of the Tory brand that refused to melt away. But yesterday the Tories took over in bellwether Bury – a northern town with a knack for picking winners – and in North Tyneside as well as making gains in Sunderland and Birmingham. This was the week Cameron broke out of his southern comfort zone.

Why is this happening? Some will say that if Labour does find itself in the same position as John Major's Tories circa 1995, that is not entirely its own fault. There is a pendulum effect in politics and in multiparty democracies governments do eventually lose their grip on power. If that is happening now, in the third term, it is hardly unusual: losing a fourth election is the norm.

It didn't work out that way for Major partly because he was up against an opposition still not deemed credible by the electorate. Yesterday the Tories cleared that hurdle, too: no one in British politics would now describe Cameron or his party as unelectable.

What's more, these are economic hard times. No matter how angry voters were with Blair four years ago, most felt good in their wallets – good enough to re-elect him in 2005. Brown does not have that cushion now.

And something else is at work, too. Yesterday's numbers suggest many, many of those that Labour would think of as its core voters abandoned the party. Angry over the abolition of the 10p tax rate, too many were ready to stay home or even break the habit of a lifetime and vote Conservative. One phone-in show yesterday had ex-Labour supporters queuing up to denounce their party – and its leader – for no longer seeming to know what they are for.

In the capital, the Ken premium put 12 extra points on Labour's national vote share but it was not enough. This result was the revenge of the suburbs, as outer London took on the heart of the metropolis and won. The likes of Bromley and Bexley had long suspected Livingstone was the 'zone 1 mayor' and, in Johnson, they at last found a champion with a chance to win. It was the same pattern that had inflicted such damage on Labour nationally, the suburban 'Blair Conservatives' coming back home. As the LSE's Tony Travers put it, 'Suburban Britain is falling back in love with the Conservative party – and that's a measure of the end of Blairism.'

The mayoral result seemed to herald the end of one of the most remarkable careers in British politics as Livingstone, the man who defied Margaret Thatcher and Tony Blair, succumbed to political mortality. He was the last remaining representative of a brand of leftism that loomed large in the 1970s and is now all but extinct, within the upper reaches of Labour at least.

Now London is about to embark on a different kind of experiment, having apparently anointed Johnson as the most powerful Conservative in Britain. As dusk falls on one era, a new dawn begins.

MAY 7 2008

# Plus ça change: Russia's new president

## LEADER

Dmitri Medvedev's inauguration as Russia's third president today will be carefully choreographed. Vladimir Putin will be the first to walk through the three gilded halls of the Great Kremlin Palace. And he will also be the first to speak in front of 2,000 invited guests. A Kremlin source said the outgoing president will deliver a majestic and political speech. Only then will the incoming president be allowed to say a few words. Like its national symbol, the double-headed eagle, the ceremony will be intended to demonstrate that Russia has two leaders. Nothing could be further from the truth.

Even before Mr Medvedev appoints his old boss as his prime minister, Mr Putin has already ensured that he is unsackable. He has accepted the chairmanship of a party, United Russia, of which he is not even a member. Were the new president, in a wild streak of independence, not to choose Mr Putin as prime minister, he would be shunning the party that controls a constitutional majority, 315 out of 450 seats, in the Duma. There are other indicators that Mr Putin intends to make the premiership the real seat of power. He will take with him many of the Kremlin's key power-brokers, whose job will be to enforce a new system of control over regional governors. The key ministers will report to him, not to the president.

If Russia's domestic policy is firmly in the new premier's grip, its foreign policy is also set on tramlines. One of the last decrees Mr Putin signed as president recognised quasi-state structures in two breakaway provinces of Georgia: South Ossetia and Abkhazia. This stops just short of recognising both regions' claims of independence. Yesterday the Abkhaz foreign minister said Abkhazia was ready to hand over military control to Russia, whose soldiers have been officially acting as peacekeepers. The stage is thus set for another showdown between Georgia and Russia. Little room for manoeuvre there. Mr Medvedev will head eastwards for his first foreign trip, to Kazakhstan and China, and he will make his debut on the international stage at the G8 summit in Japan in July. But what areas of policy will the new president control?

When Mr Medvedev was elected president, Gordon Brown offered him a relationship built on frankness, not rancour. How Mr Medvedev replied has not been made public. Clearly the Foreign Office is pinning its hopes on the theory that the new president is a liberal, keen to break free from his predecessor's authoritarianism. This would not be the first misjudgment Britain has made about Russia. Mr Brown should have sorted out his relationship with Mr Putin first. The new Russian premier shows every sign of outlasting his British counterpart.

# When their number is up

## MARCEL BERLINS

Every French car's number plate has the identity number of the department in which it is registered. Paris is 75, Dordogne 24, etc. Last year, the government announced that the system is to be abolished; from next January number plates will be issued on a national basis, and no longer identify a particular department.

It has taken a little time for opponents to react, but there is now a growing campaign by parliamentarians, of all parties, to try to stop the new scheme. Last week they went as far as writing to the minister of the interior, complaining about the disappearance of this 'mark of belonging to a territory, a native soil, an identity' and calling for the departmental number to be retained.

In an interview, the campaign's leader provided a less romantic reason for his stance: 'When we see a driver who's not from our neck of the woods, we are even more vigilant, because we know that he can get lost and drive dangerously.' That was a slightly tactful way of putting the fact that in the south of France, where I am from, we believe that Parisian drivers, whether lost or not, are bad and reckless. We treat cars from 75 with special circumspection, often followed by fist-waving and invective as they commit their inevitable atrocities. There's a pecking order within Provence too. My department regards drivers from the neighbouring department, 13 – Bouches-du-Rhône, which includes Marseille – with much suspicion.

A senior politician from the north – Pas-de-Calais, 62 – found another reason. When travelling away from their own department, 'we're always looking for other 62s. Think of all the encounters, all the friendships that have been created. There have even been marriages as a result of number plates.'

Sadly, the parliamentary revolt has little chance of making the minister of the interior change her mind, even though the cause is supported by nearly two thirds of the population. The official response is simple. When the new system comes about, there will be a space, to the right of the number plate, for proud motorists to affix the number of their departments, should they wish. That's all very well, but we know that Parisians won't do so, thus enabling them to carry on their dastardly driving, this time under cover of anonymity.

MAY 12 2008

# Obituary: Nuala O'Faolain

**LUKE DODD**

The very pure strain of patriarchy that evolved in post-independence Ireland, where church and state were often indistinguishable, produced a noble tradition of female dissent. The long and illustrious list of women who challenged the status quo – and changed Irish society in the process – had no more eloquent an exponent than Nuala O'Faolain, who has died of cancer aged 68. O'Faolain's formative years coincided with the emergence of the women's movement, and her ability to expose misogyny in all its forms was formidable, forensic and unremitting. However, her feminism stemmed from a fundamental belief in social justice. Unlike most commentators, who maintain a detached, lofty tone, O'Faolain placed herself at the centre of things, a high-risk strategy that worked because of her broad range of erudition, worn lightly, her courage and a truthfulness that sometimes bordered on the self-destructive.

Since the 1980s, O'Faolain has been a household name in Ireland as a broadcaster, journalist and commentator. It was the surprise international success of her candid memoir, *Are You Somebody?* (1996), that brought her to much wider attention and turned her into a full-time writer.

Born in Dublin, O'Faolain was the second eldest of nine children. Her stay-at-home mother turned increasingly to alcohol and reading as a refuge from her 13 pregnancies, and the philandering of her husband, Tomas O'Faolain, the novelist, short-story writer and journalist who, as Terry O'Sullivan, wrote *Dubliners Diary* for the *Dublin Evening Press*. Salvation from a chaotic childhood – she grew up largely in the country around Dublin – followed a familiar path of waywardness, academic brilliance and books. O'Faolain's breadth of reading was astonishing, everything from old English to Proust to popular women's fiction, as was her recall.

After a boarding convent school in County Monaghan, O'Faolain enrolled in the English department at University College Dublin, but dropped out. She completed an undergraduate degree in medieval English at Hull University and a postgraduate degree in 19th-century literature at Oxford University (both on scholarships) before returning to the UCD English department as an academic. As part of Dublin's literary scene of the late 1960s and early 1970s, much of which revolved around pubs and drinking, O'Faolain's circle included Mary Lavin, John McGahern, Patrick Kavanagh, Leland Bardwell, Brian O'Nolan, Louis MacNeice, Seamus Deane and Anthony Cronin.

Although feminism was extremely important to O'Faolain, she readily acknowledged that her convictions were compromised in her dealings with men, to whom she often ceded responsibility for personal happiness. She wrote movingly about this in terms of an unconscious impulse to replicate the disappointment of her mother's life.

Throughout the 1970s, O'Faolain had an enduring but on-off relationship with the art critic and writer Tim Hilton, and she moved to London to be with him. She worked at the BBC as a television producer, first in the access unit, which gave 'ordinary' people the opportunity to make programmes, and then on Open University programming. This involved much travel and included a secondment to Tehran for the planning of an Iranian 'open university' in the last year of the Shah's reign. During this time she also had a relationship with the celebrated American art critic Clement Greenberg.

O'Faolain's relationship to England was complicated – the intellectual milieu both at Oxford and the BBC was exciting but she found the 'relentless English preoccupation with the rungs of class' oppressive, while at the same time acknowledging that it granted outsiders, like her, a certain licence.

At the suggestion of her great friend Seán Mac Réamoinn, O'Faolain attended the Merriman Summer School in County Clare in the mid-1970s, an event that reconnected her with Ireland and its culture. She returned to Dublin in 1977 to Radio Telefis Éireann, where she worked as part of an all-woman production team on programming dealing specifically with women's issues. Her *Plain Tales* – a series of interviews with 'ordinary' women – won Ireland's premier television award, the Jacob's, in 1985.

In 1980, O'Faolain became involved with Nell McCafferty, the feminist, journalist and civil rights activist, a relationship that lasted almost 15 years and which O'Faolain referred to as the single 'most life-giving' relationship of her life. In 1986, she joined the *Irish Times* as a weekly opinion columnist, and that year gained the accolade of journalist of the year. O'Faolain adored her work at the *Irish Times*, which took her all over the island, and she revelled in writing about topics as diverse as abortion, divorce, emigration, Dublin's first gay B&B, the traveller community, sexual mores in 1950s Ireland, the evolution of accents as a function of class, and holidaying.

The publication in 1996 of *Are You Somebody?*, a selection of O'Faolain's *Irish Times* journalism, became a surprise success in Ireland because of its brilliantly honest autobiographical 200-page preface. With a great economy of expression, O'Faolain brought a refreshing insight to the familiar themes of love, rejection, loss, the detrimental effects of alcohol, and the reality of being an unpartnered, middle-aged woman. Within a year, it was No 1 on the *New York Times* bestseller list.

O'Faolain produced three other books, all bestselling – a novel, *My Dream of You* (2001), a sequel to the memoir, *Almost There* (2003), and *The Story of Chicago May* (2005). The latter was awarded the Prix Femina in 2006.

In more recent times, O'Faolain divided her time between Co Clare, Dublin and New York, where she had found happiness (albeit complicated, as she documented in *Almost There*) with a new partner, John Low-Beer. She was given an honorary doctorate by the Open University in 2006. Until she was diagnosed with cancer, she was covering the US presidential election for an Irish Sunday newspaper and responded with great gusto to the dilemma it posed for a feminist – support for Clinton or Obama.

Having lived a very public life, O'Faolain agreed to be interviewed on Irish radio about her diagnosis with terminal cancer and decision to reject chemotherapy. Even in Ireland, where death is readily acknowledged, the interview sparked a remarkable public reaction because of the searing honesty and total lack of sentimentality. At one point in the interview, which was

conducted largely through tears, O'Faolain remarked that one of
the things that saved her from self-pity was that, 'in my time,
which is mostly the 20th century, people have died horribly in
Auschwitz, in Darfur, or are dying of starvation or dying multiply
raped in the Congo or dying horribly like that. I think how
comfortably I am dying, I have friends and family, I am in this
wonderful country, I have money, there is nothing much wrong
with me except I am dying.'

*Nuala O'Faolain, writer and journalist, born March 1 1940;*
*died May 9 2008*


MAY 19 2008

# The last photo of Zhou Yao

## TANIA BRANIGAN

Zhou Yao, aged six, beams at the camera as she poses in a garden.
Next, she is a confident nine-year old, hands on hips, head cocked.
At 14, she is deliberately pensive, with the self-consciousness of a
girl who knows she will soon become a woman.

This photo is the last in her mother's pile. There will be no more.

Yao's casket of ashes stands in her home in Dujiangyan. They
found her body hours after Juyuan middle school collapsed in an
earthquake last Monday. Like others across Sichuan province, her
parents are angry and disbelieving.

Almost 7,000 classrooms across the quake zone were destroyed,
the government acknowledges. Thousands of children were
entombed at their desks. Hundreds are believed to have died in
Juyuan, and at another school across town. Similar numbers were

trapped in the wreckage of seven schools in Mianzhu, the middle school at Beichuan, and a high school in Shifang county.

The toll is staggering, even in a province that has seen so much death. In Beichuan, the town is devastated it seems only a handful of single-storey buildings survive. In Dujiangyan, the distress of parents is magnified by the fact that most buildings – even those directly next to the collapsed schools – still stand.

Passions are so inflamed the government has pledged to investigate claims of shoddy construction, possibly linked to corruption, and to punish severely those responsible. It has even fielded questions of grieving parents online; a remarkable act of openness. 'The tragedy has happened and I have to face up to it. We just want justice,' said Yao's mother, Wang Fengying, her face smeared with tears. Amid exercise and text books, she pulled out a certificate of exam merit.

Competition to enter Juyuan was fierce and Yao had to fight her way in. 'Chinese, maths and English – she got good marks in all of them,' her mother said. 'The school gave them a very good education. But the quality of the buildings was very bad.'

Stacking the schoolbooks, she slumped with grief. 'I've a strong character, but when I see these I feel crushed. I want to burn them but I can't make up my mind to do it,' she said. 'I could overcome any difficulties, but not this one.'

Yao's brother flicked through the pages of a schoolbook listlessly; he helped to dig his little sister out of the rubble. The family is convulsed with grief, her grandmother choking on sobs.

'All the innocent lives were taken by this big disaster. We want an explanation from the school,' said Wang. 'Children are the future of the nation. But the school didn't treasure them. The teacher came here, but the officials haven't even sent their condolences.'

Parents with no history of challenging authority are determined someone must account for their loss. Up the road at the crematorium, a mother sitting by the ashes of her daughter, 11, showed us mobile phone images of the wreckage from Xinjian school. She did not want to give her name, but was eager to talk. 'All the parents are angry. Look, there's no steel in the concrete. We want to fight for justice together, that's why we took these pictures,' she said. 'We've been collecting evidence. The debris was basically sand – not even pieces of concrete.'

She alleged experts had warned local officials three years ago that both destroyed schools were poorly constructed and dangerous – a claim impossible to verify, and that may simply reflect the speed at which rumours rattle around this angry community. But concern at the collapse of so many schools has resonated far beyond the bereaved.

'We cannot afford not to raise uneasy questions about the structural quality of school buildings,' the English-language *China Daily* noted shortly after the quake. The columnist Zhang Jinghua was more pointed in the *Economic Observer*. 'We saw elegant government buildings remain intact while dozens of schools crumbled like houses of sand,' he wrote.

MAY 23 2008

# Hangover, what hangover?

## LUKE HARDING

It was 3am, and the Manchester United players had just arrived back at their Moscow hotel, following their dramatic 6-5 penalty shootout victory over Chelsea. Looking exhausted but exhilarated, the players trooped upstairs to their 10th-floor suites. They got changed.

And then began football's biggest party – a triumphant seven-hour knees-up, involving singing, drinking and Rio Ferdinand serenading fans with an impromptu chant of 'Manchester, la la la'. Some 350 Manchester United guests – players, the manager Sir Alex Ferguson, wives, and hangers on – partied through and beyond the early hours of yesterday.

The team celebrated their Champions League victory in a first floor reception room of the Crowne Plaza hotel. Yesterday the private room was a sea of champagne corks, empty bottles of Veuve Clicquot Ponsardin Brut, and an abandoned stick of magenta Chanel lippy.

After a quick breakfast, the players, some unshaven, most bleary-eyed, but all in team suits, arrived at the airport, the silver trophy – red ribbons still attached – eased into a customised flight case.

Back at the hotel, the clean-up began. 'It was a great party,' Sergei, 18, a waiter, said, after the players had finally checked out and set off back to Manchester at 3pm local time.

'There was a live three-piece band. We had a disco, with a mixture of 80s and modern songs. I was pouring the wine. The players danced and sang. We also laid on a buffet.'

How did they look? 'They were clearly very tired. But they were happy. And there was a lot of dancing.'

Yesterday, workmen were removing the dancefloor where the United players had strutted their stuff. The band had left behind the lyrics to one of their party songs. Given the nerve-jangling nature of United's victory, the words seemed appropriate. They read: 'I don't wanna work today/Maybe I just wanna stay/Just take it easy cause there is no stress.'

Yes, it was, that most traditional of post-match celebrations: a team singalong to French tribal house DJ Laurent Wolf's *No Stress*. It was not entirely clear what Sir Bobby Charlton made of it.

Fans staying in the five-star hotel – just next to the Moscow river, and a short walk from where Boris Yeltsin stood on a tank – said the players were in great spirits. 'We were there when they arrived. They all looked fairly tired but delighted. Rio Ferdinand was limping,' Al Williams, 22, a United fan from Lymm, Cheshire, said.

'We went out to Red Square. When we came back the party was still going on. Rio appeared on the balcony and started clapping and cheering the fans. He was chanting: 'Manchester United are champions. Manchester la la la'. All of the players were wearing their winners' medals.'

A few players – including Darren Fletcher – ventured down to the lobby, to chat with fans. 'Fletcher was there with his dad. He was wearing his medal. His father was as pleased as punch,' Williams said. 'The players weren't drunk. They looked sober but very happy of course,' Claus Bloch, a Danish fan, and a United supporter since 1977, said.

The party went on and on, staff said. While most of the team headed off to bed at 7am, a hard core kept going until 10am.

Team officials suggested that they set off from the hotel later than scheduled because their plane to the UK was delayed. In reality, after finishing the match at 2am local time and partying through the rain-sodden night, nobody was capable of getting up.

The hotel laid on what it called a Uefa Champions League late late breakfast: smoked salmon and caviar and a traditional English fry-up. There was more champagne and vodka. But United's penalty shootout hero, the goalkeeper Edwin van der Sar, proved himself a man of more simple tastes, piling his breakfast plate with a banana and two boxes of Coco Pops – an unlikely breakfast of champions.

'It was just a little party,' said Daniel Welbeck, 17, a member of United's reserve squad, as he wandered somewhat forlornly round the hotel lobby. The coach had apparently left without him for the airport half an hour earlier, whisking away a winking Cristiano Ronaldo, and a mute Wayne Rooney.

Why did he miss the bus? 'I just woke up five minutes ago,' Welbeck confessed. And what were the celebrations like? 'Obviously we were really happy,' he added, before going off in search of a driver.

Hotel staff left yesterday with the task of clearing up said United deserved their victory and knew how to party. 'We removed a whole trolley full of bottles,' Vyacheslav, a hotel employee, said. Next to him, bin liners had been filled to the brim with beer bottles and empty cartons of apple juice. Nearby, workers removed wilting floral decorations, in Manchester United red.

'You Brits drink a lot,' Vyacheslav suggested. 'But we Russians drink more. You should have seen what it was like here after New Year.'

MAY 29 2008

# TV review: *Filth: The Mary Whitehouse Story*

## NANCY BANKS-SMITH

Well, that was an unexpected lollipop. *Filth: The Mary Whitehouse Story* (BBC2) by Amanda Coe was an entertaining account of the bone-splintering contest between a woman from the Midlands and the director general of the BBC.

It opened with Mrs Whitehouse cycling to church past picture-postcard cottages and whitewashed picket fences (oblivious to the occasional wife with a black eye). The background music was a jaunty version of 'Ma's out, Pa's out. Let's talk rude. Pee, po, belly, bum, drawers.' We might have had better luck with that one in the Eurovision Song Contest. She was 50 and looked as if she should be advertising Fairy soap, but she would soon meet the tsunami of the 60s head on. Hugh Carleton Greene was a journalist who had reported the German invasion of Poland to the sleeping Poles and had seen all he ever intended to see of censorship. He was director general of the BBC throughout the 60s, arching over the decade like a great greenhouse. Under his beneficent protection, fresh talent flowered extravagantly: *Till Death*, *Z Cars*, *The Wednesday Play* and *That Was the Week*, which was modelled at his suggestion on pre-Nazi cabarets. They stopped the world. On certain nights the nation swarmed home like bees to the hive and, next day on the bus, buzzed of nothing else. I felt then, and have not felt since, that television really mattered.

He was shouting 'Forward!' and she was crying 'Back!' They never met because he positively refused to see her. She was broccoli and he said the hell with it. He banned the very mention of her name. Mark you, the BBC was like that then. I was told that previews were not a right, they were a privilege. The only sure way to get into TV Centre was to drive very fast past the commissionaires shouting, 'I'm bringing the white mouse!' I have no idea why that worked.

Their closest encounter – not counting her fevered dreams – was in the gallery of the House of Commons when the unfortunately named Sir Barnett Cocks was inveighing against TV filth on her behalf. In her book, *Cleaning Up TV*, Greene is mentioned constantly. In his, *The Third Floor Front*, she is not mentioned at all.

That was a little lordly, admittedly. Greene is shown in settings of positively baronial splendour. Rumbustious, boisterous, slightly salacious and with a wild sense of humour. She is far more tenderly treated, like an aunt with osteoporosis. She greets the sea of nice, tight perms and felt helmets ('Look at the hats! No fuddy duddies here!') at her first big meeting with a cosy 'My goodness me! Look at you all!' Alun Armstrong's performance as her husband was simply something. Tender concern and say-nowt struggled for supremacy under his skin. I hope to live long enough to see Armstrong give a poor performance. That should ensure a telegram from the Queen.

There are titbits I can't resist feeding you, just as Lord Hill, who was a doctor and deft with elderly ladies, fed Mrs Whitehouse coconut cakes. Her reply to a heckle of 'Fascist!': 'I think you'll find Signor Mussolini's methods were slightly more drastic than asking people to leave.' Her fervent 'Thank you, Lord!', with the test card reflected unnervingly in her spectacles when she successfully censors her first programme. And Greene's apologia to Hill, now chairman of the BBC: 'I don't think you realise, the woman wants to censor us, Hill! If she had her say, all we'd show would be Andy bloody Pandy. And she'd stop him climbing into that basket with Looby Lou. Let alone Teddy.' An apologia is not an apology. He never surrendered, but she shot him down with popcorn.

When his plain secretary Miss Venables reads Mrs Whitehouse's latest demand ('In a recent episode Pinky and Perky were constantly unkind, to the point of callousness, to the grown-up in their programme'), Greene lays his big head down on his blotter and groans. Then he places a rude portrait of her in his directorial chair and leaves the building. Asked if he wants a taxi, he says, 'I think I'll walk' but the walk breaks into a frolicking run all the way up Great Portland Street. Just as David Attenborough, controller of BBC2, is said to have shaken off the chains of office and gambolled along Wood Lane shouting, 'Free at last, free at last!'

You may think it odd that the BBC should celebrate this thorn in its side, but the BBC conquers by absorbing and ingesting its enemies. She is no longer a threat. She is now a meal.

I met all the combatants and Julie Walters' Mrs Whitehouse, Hugh Bonneville's Sir Hugh Greene and Ron Cook's Lord Hill are pretty true to life. All the other characters are merely parsley round the plate. Mrs Whitehouse, in my experience, was rather tougher and more down-to-earth than Julie Walters' lovable and vulnerable woman. She was, after all, cut from the same clerical cloth as Mrs Thatcher.

JUNE 4 2008

# Review: *The Lure of the East: British Orientalist Painting*

## JONATHAN JONES

Of all the attempts by Britain's museums to take on the divisive issues of world culture, this is the best, because it is the least platitudinous. It provokes a complex response to a complex history.

There is not a single work by a Muslim artist in this huge display of paintings of the Middle East: it is, on the contrary, a survey of the ways in which 19th- and early 20th-century British artists represented the region. Or rather, many would say, painted an entirely imaginary 'Orient'. At first glance, you might conclude that when a Victorian artist such as William Holman Hunt visited the Middle East, what he saw was indeed predetermined by imperial fantasy. In his painting of a Cairo street scene, a young man playfully tries to pull away a young woman's veil – it is a somewhat shallow view of Islam. And yet spend a little time in this show, and you will find these Victorians surprisingly sensitive travelling companions.

The fascination with medieval Islamic architecture that pervades paintings such as John Frederick Lewis's *The Bezestein Bazaar of El Khan Khalil, Cairo* (1872) makes for superb portrayals of some of the world's great urban spaces. His watercolours are incredibly fine notations of the stucco-work and the tiles, lattices and niches that make Islamic architecture in many ways the most beautiful ever created. It is hard to discern any underlying imperial disdain.

None of these painters is a great artist, and yet the exhibition is full of great art. In Holman Hunt's view of the Sphinx at Giza, he shows us the famous ancient Egyptian sculpture from behind. We do not recognise it we are just looking at a strange geological formation, sculpted perhaps by windblown sand. A familiar view of power relationships in art – the idea that representing the 'other' is necessarily oppressive – becomes unrecognisable here.

# Summer

# A milestone of sorts as Clinton cracks, but doesn't break, the glass ceiling

## SUZANNE GOLDENBERG

For the legions of American women who saw something of themselves in Hillary Clinton's rise – and even more so in her humbling
defeat – it was perhaps the ultimate sadness that she waited until
the very end to fully embrace the transformational nature of her
run for the White House.

For many women, Clinton's farewell address in Washington DC
on Saturday was a moment in feminist history. Gloria Steinem was
there, dressed in black in the sweltering heat, and women carrying their newborn daughters in slings.

But until Saturday, when Clinton bowed out and endorsed
Barack Obama, she seemed to struggle with the idea that her
candidacy was making history. In her 17-month presidential
campaign, toughness and experience mattered as much to Clinton
as breaking the lock of white males on the White House – until she
made that valedictory address.

'When I was asked what it means to be a woman running for
president, I always gave the same answer: that I was proud to be
running as a woman but I was running because I thought I'd be
the best president,' she said. 'But I am a woman, and like millions
of women, I know there are still barriers and biases out there,
often unconscious.'

Clinton spent much of her campaign showing how tough she

was – touting her readiness to answer that 3am phone call as commander-in-chief, threatening to 'obliterate' Iran, refusing to apologise for her vote in favour of the Iraq war, knocking back shots of whiskey in working men's bars. Even her own supporters resorted to male stereotypes to talk up Clinton's qualifications. An Indiana senator, Evan Bayh, who supported Clinton, saluted her 'testicular fortitude'.

'Could a woman really serve as commander-in-chief? Well, I think we answered that one,' Clinton said on Saturday.

For many women who turned out to see Clinton exit the race, that strength and tenacity was crucial to Clinton's appeal. They recognised in Clinton's travails their own struggles in the work-place. 'I've had a really hard time as a woman being a physician and I give her a lot of credit for keeping going,' said Marijane Hynes, 48, an internist from Bethesda, Maryland.

Like many others, she saw Clinton's refusal to quit the race, despite Obama's insurmountable lead, as validation for persever-ing through difficult times. 'You have to be tough in a man's world,' said Hynes.

Clinton's misfortune, though, was that 2008 was an election year when change counted for more than the traditionally male attributes of toughness and experience. And in a contest against a younger, African-American man, race, class and age seemed to count as much as gender. The historic nature of her candidacy was lost amid the excitement over Obama's own quest.

At the polling booth, Clinton's command of the women's vote was shaken by Obama's appeal to young and African-American women, as well as wealthy women.

On television, late-night comics made endless jokes about trouser suits; South Park did an episode about a nuclear weapon hidden in Clinton's vagina. Novelty shops produced Hillary Clinton nutcrackers and toilet bowl scrubbers. Political pundits said Clinton reminded them of their first wives at divorce court, or caused an instinctive reaction to cross their legs.

'She was marginalised a lot. What we see in corporate America, they treated her the same way,' said a 27-year-old lawyer from Philadelphia who took time off from her job to work as an organiser in eight states.

'I think people talk a lot about women being strong, but they don't like to see it – and I think a lot of that went on in this campaign.'

The anger at Clinton's treatment by television pundits and late-night comics was not restricted to Democrats.

As Christine Todd Whitman, a Republican who was the first woman governor of New Jersey, wrote in yesterday's *New York Times*: 'The press presented Barack Obama with his two years in the Senate as an agent of change, not a novice. In contrast, ABC's Charles Gibson asked Clinton if she would 'be in this position' if it weren't for 'her husband'.'

With Clinton's run for the White House now a matter for historians, Americans have begun to ask whether she will inspire more women to enter politics.

The immediate signs are not that promising. A study last month by the Brookings Institution found that the number of American women entering politics has stalled since the 1990s. At present, women make up only 16 per cent of members of Congress. Only nine of America's 50 states have women governors.

But for Martha Bixby, 25, who wore a badge saying 'I can be president' to the rally, maybe Clinton would make it a little easier for future generations of women. 'These kinds of steps for women are only going to create amazing opportunities for all women,' she said. 'I am excited she got so far.'

Or as Clinton admitted in her final moments at the centre of this extraordinary election year, her campaign had failed to

shatter that final glass ceiling. But as she said to a roar of applause:
'It's got about 18 million cracks in it.'

JUNE 10 2008

# Stream the pupils – and stream the teachers too

## PETER WILBY

There was a man on the phone 'with gravitas in his voice', my wife informed me. He sounded, she said, like a headmaster. Martin Stephen, 58, successively head of the Perse school in Cambridge, Manchester grammar and now St Paul's in London, was responding to my request for an interview ('I hear you want to do a hatchet job on me').

He has been a head for more than 20 years and, measured by mentions in the national press, he is the school leader with the second highest profile in the country after Wellington college's Anthony Seldon, the biographer of Tony Blair. He is also apparently the model Jilly Cooper used in her latest novel for a private school head, described as 'a great teacher because he was a great communicator'.

Stephen is a roll-up-the-sleeves, get-out-and-about kind of head. One parent from his time at Manchester grammar recalls that he was always on the sports field on Saturday mornings, chatting to players and spectators. He patrols the school grounds with his pet labrador, to which, with the self-conscious eccentricity that head-teachers often affect, he attaches a school tie.

He is an unashamed elitist – 'one of the saddest things about the past 30 years is how the word 'elite' has changed from a term of admiration to one of derision' – and talking to him is a bit like being in a pub with a man who thinks the country is going to the dogs. You hope he'll stop, or at least give you a chance to request elucidation, but he keeps saying 'and another thing'. He believes in streaming not only children but also teachers (of which more later), doesn't think anything like 50 per cent of the population should go to university, and hates the idea of Oxford and Cambridge admitting comprehensive students with lower grades.

He gets very angry about such things and bursts out with, for example: 'What the hell's wrong with being middle class? When are we going to admit the middle class have got it right?' And: 'It's absolute piffle to say we're looking for potential in 18-year-olds when they've been at school for 13 years.' And: 'Every child in the UK should have an education like the one we give here.' I point out that, if every school had grounds as extensive as St Paul's, there wouldn't be much space left for houses or growing food.

Stephen also gets angry about school league tables which, on several occasions, he has denounced as 'a cancer on the face of education'. He says anger is an important part of his character. 'It is a much underrated emotion. It can produce all sorts of horrible things, but also wonderful things.'

He once had an appalling stammer, and was rejected when he first applied to do a DipEd course because, they said at Leeds University, he'd be a laughing stock in the classroom and could never enter any career that involved public speaking. So he got rid of the stammer, he says, 'by getting angry'. He adds: 'It never leaves you. It's like a rather nasty raven perched on your shoulder. Every time I stand up to speak, I have a fear.'

About a year after he started at St Paul's in 2004, he had a stroke – and got angry again. 'I found myself in a hospital bed, hardly any feeling in my left side, no control over my hands, couldn't talk properly. Got no help from the hospital at all. All they wanted me to do was lie there. For about an hour, I was in complete despair. Then I got angry.'

He still sounds annoyed. The NHS, he says, would have left him to rot, and he had to steal a Zimmer frame to start moving at all. When he got home, he designed his own rehabilitation programme, drawing on the experiences of his father-in-law, who'd also had a stroke. Each day included bouncing and catching a tennis ball 2,000 times, two hours of Victorian copybook handwriting, two hours of reciting poems with a cork between his teeth, and two hours of walking up and down the stripes on the lawn. He also – 'this was the only fun bit' – played computer games, crashing an onscreen jet 4,796 times before he finally landed it.

He's quite riveting about all this – much more so than he is about education – and has written a book, out this month, called *Diary of a Stroke*. I have no idea to what extent his rehab programme is generally applicable but I suspect the book will be an inspiration to many. A chunky extract has already appeared in the *Daily Mail*.

Stephen is no novice as an author. He's written 15 books on English literature and naval history, plus four rather curious historical thrillers. Their hero is Henry Gresham, a sort of 16th- and 17th-century James Bond, who does improbable things with swords and doublets. Most other characters are real historical figures such as James I, Drake and Shakespeare. Stephen gave me *The Conscience of the King* to read. I expected to dislike it because it has a convoluted plot based on silly theories about Shakespeare not writing his own plays, and I don't much care for thrillers anyway. But it's well paced, the 17th-century background is convincingly done and, in the end, I enjoyed it.

It isn't exactly a 'bodice-ripper', as some press accounts promised, though I can report (for St Paul's boys who don't want to linger over the high master's prose) a man fingering his codpiece on page 55, a breast falling out of a gown on page 215 and an aborted rape, quite graphically described, on page 252.

Stephen says writing books was all he ever wanted to do, and he went into teaching by accident. After reading English at Leeds, he intended to get an Oxford or Cambridge PhD and become a don, writing learned tomes about literature. But he fell 'absolutely, totally, stupidly, hopelessly, head-over-heels in love' with a woman in the year below – she is now his wife and also head of a fee-charging school – and didn't dare leave during her final year lest somebody else snap her up.

Rejected by Leeds, he took his DipEd at nearby Sheffield. He still didn't intend to go into teaching, but was advised he should combine it with a part-time PhD, because a university would value proof that he could teach and research at the same time. He did once have a university job lined up, but it fell victim to spending cuts. So, in the end, he wrote his books while teaching and later headmastering. He started the Gresham books, he says, 'because my wife was fed up with losing me every holiday to books that sold only about three copies'.

Apart from a brief spell in remand homes before university – where two boys threatened his life, one with a garden fork, the other with a kitchen knife – and later a visiting lectureship, his entire working life has been in public schools, starting with his old school, Uppingham. That was surprising because he had been 'absolutely miserable' as a boarding pupil there, took up smoking, led a hunger strike against repeated servings of prunes, and nearly got expelled for chatting to village girls. 'The whole system,' he says, 'was alien to my basic instincts.'

His father was a Sheffield GP and chairman of Sheffield Wednesday football club – he later became chairman of the Football Association and sacked Alf Ramsay, England's World Cup-winning manager – and the family lived in a large stone house, around which the council built a housing estate.

'I spent holidays on this estate, and I had a friend who was very, very intelligent but had failed the 11-plus and was clearly going to leave school at 15 for some minor clerical job. I remember going back to school and seeing a charming and delightful member of my year group who was just not very clever. It was clear he would go off and read medicine. I've spent most of my life praying that, if I wake up in casualty, I won't see this guy looking down on me. I thought at the time: this is wrong, wrong.'

Stephen's passionate belief is that independent school places should be allocated strictly on merit. At Manchester grammar, he raised £10m so that 300 out of 1,400 boys were financed by bursaries that paid all or part of their fees. At St Paul's, even more ambitiously, he wants to raise a big enough endowment fund to make admissions completely 'needs-blind' by 2030, so that nobody gets in just because their parents can pay.

Isn't he proposing a more efficient way of creaming off talent from comprehensives? Isn't he aware of research showing the best way to raise standards across the board is to give every school a cross-section of abilities and social backgrounds?

'No, I don't believe it. It irritates me beyond belief when people say middle-class parents will march on bad standards in the maintained sector and change everything. What they'll do is colonise two or three schools. Flinging the nice middle-class child into a comprehensive whose values the parents don't agree with simply wouldn't work.'

Stephen argues bright children should be taught together so 'they egg each other on'. But he doesn't want selection at 11. 'You're hitting children at a massively vulnerable age, when they're very fragile and malleable and plastic. The natural age for transfer to secondary school is 14.'

Even then, he doesn't want conventional selection because, he says, 'you can't ignore the leftwing argument'. He wouldn't stop any children choosing the grammar school at 14. If they wanted to progress, however, they would have to meet the requirements at the end of the first year. If they failed to do so and didn't then leave, they would just stay where they were, with the 14-year-olds. 'Never, ever throw a child out.'

Stephen has several slightly wacky ideas like that. He believes, as I mentioned earlier, in streaming teachers, so that the brightest children are taught by the top graduates in their subjects.

'It's not a question of the best teachers,' he insists. 'It's the most suitable.' Teaching the most able, he argues, should be a specialist career path, like teaching children at the other end of the spectrum.

'Many, many graduates know they can teach their own kind, but can't teach children who will leave at 16. My life at school was ruined by brilliant mathematicians who couldn't understand I was as thick as the main deck of HMS Victory when it came to maths. I was in the bottom set, and my life was saved by a man who came in and ordered us not even to try to understand what he told us. We all fell at his feet, and got the equivalent of a GCSE maths C grade.'

A few years ago, a *Financial Times* profile described Stephen as 'ever so slightly smug'. Inevitably, it made him very angry, but I can't quite clear him of the charge. He explains how St Paul's runs Saturday masterclasses in maths for 30 children from local state schools and, though I'm sure they're a good thing, he can't help sounding a bit patronising. 'We at St Paul's specialise in bright children. We know what switches them on and, more importantly, what switches them off.'

Even when he talks about his stroke, there's a hint of self-satisfaction: 'I am one of only 10 per cent to make a full recovery.'

But, like all journalists, I appreciate a man who uses vivid language and doesn't care too much what he says. The *FT* also called him pompous, but he isn't that. It's just that he's run three of the country's top fee-charging schools, believes absolutely in what they and he do, and offers an articulate, media-savvy defence.

Whereas I, believing the very existence of such schools damages the prospects of more than 90 per cent of our children, would place dynamite under them at once.

JUNE 20 2008

# TV review: *Lost World*

## SAM WOLLASTON

There's something very special about St Kilda. It's partly because of its remoteness. The outermost of the Outer Hebrides, it's a collection of jagged rocks that rise out of a boiling north Atlantic, blasted by wind, spray and screeching seabirds. But its magic also has something to do with the fact that it was inhabited by the most isolated community in Britain. These hardy folk would eat puffins, not muffins, for tea, and lower small boys down cliffs on ropes to catch them. The postal service involved tossing packages into the waves and hoping the currents would take them to somewhere they'd be found and forwarded to whoever they were meant for.

Then, in 1930, the last St Kildans left, evacuated on a Royal Navy warship.

Now Kate '*Springwatch* babe' Humble, Dan 'son of Peter' Snow and Steve 'Look at me in my Speedos' Backshall are going back for a three-part special called Britain's *Lost World* (BBC1). As they approach by boat, they really push the 'Lost World' bit of their little adventure. 'It's like coming to another world,' says Kate, as primitive-looking gannets, silhouetted against the sky, fly overhead. 'It's like mother nature's final frontier,' says Steve. Dan describes it as a 'truly eerie place to arrive at'. There's no mention of the permanently manned MoD radio tracking station there.

Actually, their gung-ho camaraderie, high spirits and jolly japes make it more Enid Blyton than *Jurassic Park*. *Three Go Wild on St Kilda*. All they need is a dog and lashings of ginger beer. They bound off up the slope in their Gore-Tex, pitch their tents, and turn in for the night. 'Dan, you snore like a train,' says Steve, cheerily, in the morning. 'Right, come on chaps.'

'We want to find out what it was like to live here, and why the St Kildans left,' says Kate. Well, why don't you ask them? Or him, because of the two still alive, only one remembers it.

I tried to go to St Kilda earlier this year, but couldn't get there because of a storm. Before not going, though, I did speak on the phone with Norman John Gillies in his home near Ipswich. He was five when, on August 31 1930, he and the other 35 remaining St Kildans finally gave up their harsh existence and left. But he remembers it well – the women looking back from the deck of *HMS Harebell*, waving goodbye as the cliffs of their homeland sank below the horizon for the last time. Norman John, named after his two uncles who drowned when their boat turned over in the swell, remembers living in cottage number 10 on Main Street, in the village on Hirta, the largest island, eating seabirds and going to church. In fact, the death of his own mother (bad weather delayed her getting off the islands during a difficult pregnancy, and she and the baby both died) was instrumental in the decision taken by the remaining St Kildans to leave.

Having only spoken to him by phone, I'm looking forward to seeing him on the telly. But he doesn't appear. Oh no, surely it doesn't mean ... I call again, prepared for the worst. But he's in, and keeping very well, he says. No, they never asked.

That's a shame, I think. But it's probably symptomatic of a lot of television – that it's as much about the presenters as it is about the

THE BEDSIDE GUARDIAN 08

subject, and about trying out rather than finding out. You can't
accuse this lot of not doing their fair share of trying out. Steve, the
most boy-scouty among them, abseils down a cliff, barefoot, to see
what it was like for the St Kildan boys to fetch tea. Kate, who's clearly
terrified of heights, braves precipitous slopes in search of pufflings
– ugly little balls of fluff that will one day become puffins. Then the
boys set off for Boreray, another island in the archipelago, in a little
wooden rowing boat. It's flat calm, but they still manage to sink.
Will this be a terrible repeat of the tragedy that took the lives of
Norman and John, Norman John's two uncles, all those years ago?
No, of course not, because Dan and Steve have two other boats with
them, one of which rescues them while the other films. And when
the weather turns a little less balmy during Steve's solo stay on
Boreray, a coastguard helicopter turns up to winch him off. Back in
1774, a group of three men and eight boys were trapped on Boreray
for nine months when the weather turned bad.

It's stunning, of course. St Kilda is still bewitching and magical,
even with these three cheery and brightly dressed TV people in
the foreground. I'll certainly be tuning in for parts two and three.
I only wish they'd spoken to the one man who really belongs there.

JUNE 23, 2008

# 'I'm waiting for riots in the streets'

## JON HENLEY

It's starting to get nasty out there. In Preston, the *Lancashire Evening
Post* reports, refuse collectors have recently come under a barrage

of abuse from householders furious at 'changes to the way their rubbish is collected'. In some cases, it appears, residents have hurled burst and stinking bin bags, forcing bin men to flee.

In Lynn, west Norfolk, according to the *Lynn News*, long-suffering refuse operatives have been 'verbally and physically abused at least three times in the past month'. Residents angry that overfull wheelie bins are not being emptied have been warned in no uncertain terms to cease attacking bin men or face prosecution.

In normally staid Cannock, meanwhile, the *Birmingham Post* relates that decent, law-abiding family men, unable to cope now the council has switched to fortnightly collections, have been seen stealing into their neighbours' gardens at dead of night and nicking their wheelie bins. 'It's like something out of Mad Max,' says resident Paul Nicholls. 'Every man for himself, scavenging for an extra bin.'

We are in the grip, it would appear, of a national crisis. 'I'm waiting for the riots in the streets,' Doretta Cocks of the Campaign for Weekly Waste Collection, which has grown from nothing to 22,000 highly vocal members in the space of three years, says ominously. 'Though in fact, in some places we've already had them. An awful lot of people are very, very angry.'

The object of all this ire, rather oddly, is household waste: how we collect it, how we dispose of it, how much of it we reuse. The trouble is, we're rubbish at rubbish. Or at least, we were. In 2000, we were bottom of the European league table: only Portugal and Greece dumped more stuff in holes in the ground (the technical term is landfill) than we did. We were recycling barely 5 per cent of what we threw out; the likes of Holland, Germany and Switzerland were at 60 per cent.

Over the past few years, however, stimulated by the prospect of swingeing £180m-a-year EU fines and dire warnings that if we carry on as we are, all of our island's landfill sites will be completely full within the next eight or nine years, we have started to get a bit better. Unfortunately, it's proving to be a painful process.

'I'm afraid change is unpopular,' says Phillip Ward, director of the Waste Resources Action Programme (Wrap – get it?), the government's chief advisory body on the issue. 'We're moving from an easy, familiar system where we just slung everything into a sack and once a week someone came and took it away for us – we neither knew nor cared where – to one where we actually have to do something. Some people will always find that difficult, for whatever reason.'

Judging by the media coverage, to say that some people are finding it difficult may be something of an understatement. The following, for example, is a by no means complete list of the principle rubbish rage incidents reported by the conservative press in recent weeks:

- In Broxbourne, Herts, the local council has begun rationing households to one officially approved, free purple bin bag a week and is charging 28p for each extra one; residents who continue to use black bags face a possible £1,000 fine.
- Mid-Sussex council, for its part, has employed 'snoopers to sift through residents' rubbish' and see exactly how much they throw away. 'It's a gross invasion of privacy,' fumes one opposition councillor.
- In Bolton, Zoe Watmough has been fined £275 for daring to put her rubbish out the day before it was due to be collected.
- Poor Katie Shergold of Warminster, Wiltshire, has been told her bin was too heavy to be emptied because collectors could not move it with two fingers.
- Plucky June Key, 80, who lives in Bolton-by-Bowland, Lancashire, is now supposed to drag her wheelie bin 'half a mile down a steep hill' for collection by the cold, uncaring operatives of

Ribble Valley council. 'I don't know how I'm supposed to manage,' says Key. 'I'm too old.'

- Gareth Corkhill of Whitehaven, Cumbria, has been fined £225 because his bin was too full and its lid raised by four inches (or seven – there is some dispute). It would have been considerably cheaper, Gareth complained, just to 'dump the rubbish in the garden and get done for fly-tipping'.
- And in the ultimate affront to all right-thinking Englishmen, Colin Harrold, a war veteran, was ordered to pay £70 by Scarborough council after he was foolish enough to 'put his rubbish out in the wrong colour bag'.

Why, though, have we suddenly become so inordinately touchy about what happens to our waste? Why is rubbish, of all things, the new hobbyhorse of middle England? In part, suggests Cocks, because one of the marks of a civilised society is its capacity to deal with its waste. In part, too, because refuse collection is just about the one service used by every household in a borough; draconian new collection schemes tend to be seen merely as an attempt to get away with doing less in return for an already exorbitant council tax bill.

In part, also, because we do not take kindly to being told what to do at the best of times – and never by town hall officials. 'We used to be clients,' she observes persuasively, 'and the council was there to provide a service. Now we're the persecuted. We're an easy target, you see. And all we want to do is get rid of our rubbish. It can't be that difficult, can it?'

In fact, though, rubbish has reached the top of our collective agenda principally because boroughs, driven by government targets and financial penalties for failing to meet them, find themselves having to substantially increase the amount this country recycles. Having raised that proportion to 33 per cent in eight years, Britain – along with the rest of the EU – is now looking at a target of recycling 50 per cent of its household waste by 2020. That means sending a lot less to landfill, which means changing people's habits.

Now there are, of course, many ways to change people's habits. You can inform them of the benefits of a new behaviour pattern, and trust that their rapid comprehension and generous goodwill will induce them to cooperate by recycling more of their paper, glass, cans, cardboard, plastic and food and garden waste than they do at present.

Then, when everyone who is willing to cooperate is doing so, you have to address the change-averse, by obliging them to recycle more. One obvious and highly cost-effective way to do this, local authorities argue, is to take steps to constrain the amount of residual, ie non-recyclable, waste that householders produce and that you collect. This is the stage that many English local authorities have now reached. Some of them (see Broxbourne, above) have begun providing smaller or fewer bags for residents' landfill rubbish. Others (nearly half in fact; around 180 authorities at the last count) have moved instead to what is known in the waste trade as AWC, or Alternate Weekly Collection.

As the name suggests, this implies that they now collect recyclables only one week, and non-recyclables only the next. In both cases, a whole lot of new rules are attached to the scheme in order to make sure it works. For householders who don't recycle as much or as sensibly as they might, that unfortunately means being landed, in the worst instances, with an overflowing, malodorous and maggot-infested bin. Plus, if they're really lucky, a fine.

For some people, this is self-evidently a national scandal. 'It's a national scandal,' says Cocks, whose campaign is based on public health concerns and dedicated to eradicating the scourge of AWC. 'In public health terms we're moving back to the middle ages. In this climate we need a weekly collection of all waste otherwise you get maggots, flies, rats, the lot. I've had horror stories: one man had to use a blowtorch to get the maggots off his driveway. This country first introduced weekly refuse collections under the Public Health Act of 1875 precisely to break the breeding cycle of the house fly; now we're getting rid of them. It's beyond absurd.'

For others, it's the only way forward. 'The bin fairy is dead,' proclaims a breezy Paul Bettison, Tory leader of Bracknell Forest borough council and, as chairman of the Local Government Association's environment board, the nation's number one bin baron (or, if you prefer, trash tsar). 'From now on we're all going to have to do a little bit of her work, and that's all there is to it. And in any case, the maggot problem is almost invariably exaggerated.'

Bettison relates, with some relish, the entertaining story of a mystery series of photos of wheelie bins overrun with flies and maggots that appeared in his local newspaper soon after Bracknell Forest first introduced AWC. 'We had a young ranger on the team who had a degree in entymology or some such,' Bettison says, 'and he had a good look at the pictures and he said, 'Those are not the maggots of any fly found in Great Britain.'

'So he investigated further, and he found that they were in fact a breed of maggot particularly favoured by fishermen. So this householder had gone out and bought a load of maggots from the bait shop, and emptied them into his wheelie bin. Just goes to show the lengths some people will go to avoid change. It was just the same when we introduced wheelie bins, mind: I got more hate mail that summer than I've ever had before or since.'

According to Bettison, the key to the problem is good communication, and an understanding that one solution will not fit all circumstances. 'AWC has been shown to boost recycling rates by 30 per cent,' he says. 'It won't work everywhere; it may not be appropriate in areas with a very high proportion of flats, multiple occupancy, that kind of thing. But where it is appropriate you just need to educate people properly. Look, anyone calls us up to complain they can't fit all their rubbish in their non-recyclables bin, we offer to send someone round and empty it onto a tarpaulin in their garden, show them what they could have recycled. They don't have to do it very often.'

But still, some council behaviour has been a tad over the top, wouldn't you say? Not exactly guaranteed to engender the full and willing cooperation of the great British public.

At Wrap, Ward accepts part of the problem is that, as it so often is when rapid change is introduced, 'not always done in the optimum way'. Waste recycling in Britain, he stresses, is still very much a work in progress: 'You have to realise we had no stock of people who knew how to do it. A lot of mistakes have been made along the way.' Nor has it necessarily helped, he acknowledges, that some 300 different local authorities, all independent and all with their own ideas, are in charge.

Nowhere is what Ward calls this 'confusing patchwork of exactly what is collected, when, and in what receptacles' more evident than in one corner of north London. On the boundary between the boroughs of Islington and Hackney, Southgate Road is a fine street: busy, but not excessively so; big handsome houses, not all converted into flats; a couple of decent-looking pubs. And outside every front door, a magnificent display of assorted bins, bags and recycling boxes.

On the Islington side of the road, residents can choose between brown boxes (kitchen waste), green boxes (paper, glass, cans, cardboard, plastic bottles), black bin bags (non-recyclable refuse), and grey sacks (garden waste). That all gets collected on Fridays.

On the Hackney side, there are green boxes (paper, glass, etc), blue boxes (kitchen waste), and black bin bags or dustbins (other refuse), all for collection on Tuesdays. Plus brown wheelie bins (garden waste, alternate Tuesdays). Friends of the Earth last week dubbed Southgate Road 'the most confusing street in the country for waste collection'.

Mark Penbury, one resident, agrees: 'It is a bit of a nightmare,' he says. 'You want to do the right thing, but people inevitably get muddled and put stuff in the wrong bin, or leave it out on the wrong day, then it gets left there and stinks. I think it could be made a bit easier.' Agnes, from Poland, is more forthright: 'It's completely crazy. How do they expect people to do it right? And of course, you make a mistake, you can't argue with them. No way.'

It's the kind of situation that drives Cocks mad. Most people, she believes, now understand that we need to recycle more, for economic as well as environmental reasons (according to Bettison's figures, the UK sends as much rubbish to landfill as the 18 EU countries with the lowest landfill rates combined, and every tonne of waste that gets recycled in future will save local authorities as much as £80 in landfill taxes and fees).

'Most of us are on board,' Cocks says. 'Most of us are prepared to do our bit. But I can't tell you the number of emails I get from people saying they're giving up – they're afraid of being fined, they don't understand the rules, they've been upset once too often, they can't use their back garden because of the swarm of flies round the rubbish bins. It's all too complicated, and too fiercely enforced. People end up driving their rubbish to the tip or the recycling centre themselves – how environmentally friendly is that? They're trying to educate us into change, but they're ending up alienating us.'

The bin baron's riposte is typically robust. 'To those who say they can't do it,' says Bettison, 'I say they have to. The days of easy waste disposal are over. No change is not an option. To those who say it's too complicated, I say it really isn't rocket science. To those who say waste food smells, if you've got a garden, there are ways of reducing kitchen waste to little more than water, at home. It all just takes a bit of extra effort, that's all – and it should even lead to lower council tax bills.'

Across at Wrap, Defra adviser Ward promises that things will get easier. Wrap is about to start a major public consultation process around just what constitutes a good recycling service, with the aim not only of 'really making it work for everyone' but convincing sceptics that materials really are being recycled, not secretly dumped.

'And we need more uniformity,' he says. 'We need to refine further exactly what is collected for recycling, and coalesce around maybe five or six different models. There are too many at present; it is confusing.' But to approach future recycling targets, he warns, 'more motivation, more incentivisation' is going to be needed. We could soon be looking at pay-as-you-throw systems and, once recycling has really taken off, even at once-a-month residual rubbish collections. That, I imagine, really will be fun.

JUNE 28 2008

# Ink-stained finger voters hope will keep them alive

CHRIS McGREAL

The young man who gave his name only as Wilson wanted just one thing from yesterday's presidential election in Zimbabwe: the indelible red ink on his little finger to show he had voted.

'They said they would come to see if we voted,' he said after casting his ballot in a tent in a Harare suburb. 'They know if we went to vote we would have to vote for the president. They were watching.'

Who are 'they'?

'The ones who made us go to the meetings at night. The ones who told us we must be careful to correct our mistake.'

Wilson voted for Robert Mugabe yesterday, against his will but judging that it was the best way to save himself from a beating or worse.

So did many other Zimbabweans, driven to the polls by fear after a bloody and relentless campaign of beatings, abductions and murders against the voters by the ruling Zanu-PF to reverse Mugabe's humiliating defeat at the hands of Morgan Tsvangirai, the Movement for Democratic Change leader who beat him clearly in the first round of voting three months ago but without an outright majority.

The state-run *Herald* newspaper yesterday predicted a 'massive' turnout in support of Mugabe. There were few signs of that in Harare although those who stayed away from the polls in the more upmarket parts of the capital tended to be the homeowners. Their maids and gardeners, subjected to nightly forced political meetings by Zanu-PF, were taking no chances.

The Zanu-PF militia was out early in Chitungwiza, one of the Harare townships where the ruling party unleashed its violent campaign of retribution to 'reorient' people who voted for the opposition last time. They moved from house to house at dawn, singing liberation war songs and banging on doors to warn people to vote.

Near some polling stations in the township, voters were directed to buildings where ruling party activists told them to record the serial numbers of the ballot paper they received at the voting booth and to return with it.

Zanu-PF set up tents close to some polling stations in Harare where people were expected to show their identity cards so their names could be ticked off as having voted.

But some people remained defiant. 'I refuse to vote,' said Blessed Manyonga in Chitungwiza. 'If they ask me I will say I lost my identity card. I will not vote for my own oppression.'

Others said they spoiled their ballot papers. 'I put a question mark next to Robert Mugabe,' said a man who gave his name only as Tendai. 'It's a joke.'

In Harare, one man said he had not voted at all and instead smeared his finger with ink from a ballpoint pen. But in many rural areas people were being driven en masse to the polls and left in no doubt about what they were expected to do.

Opposition officials said some voters reported having their identity numbers written on the back of their ballot papers. In other places they were forced to show how they had marked the ballot before they dropped it in the voting box.

Still others were handed pre-marked ballots by ruling party activists and told to hand back the blank ones they received inside the polling booths to prove they had not voted for the opposition.

Pishai Muchauraya, an opposition MP in Manicaland, said he witnessed a low turnout in Mutare, the province's main city, but had received reports of voters being forced to the polls and intimidated in large numbers in rural areas where the vote swung against Mugabe in March.

'Here in the urban areas people have just stayed at home. They are defiant. In rural areas like Buhera and Makoni people are being forced to go and vote. They say we will check your finger and if you don't vote...' he said. 'They are also expected to say they cannot read and write, and to ask for assistance to vote. People were forced to sleep at Zanu-PF bases and then taken to vote. All that kind of coercion.'

Opposition activists in Mashonaland said whole villages had been warned that if there was anything short of a substantial victory for Mugabe when the count was made at local polling stations, then those who voted there would be collectively punished.

Coastal erosion at Happisburgh, Norfolk, September 2008.
GRAHAM TURNER

Shibboleth by Doris Salcedo, Tate Modern, London, October 2007.
DAVID LEVENE

Gordon and Sarah Brown, Labour party conference, Manchester, September 2008.
CHRISTOPHER THOMOND

David Cameron, Conservative party conference,
Birmingham, September 2008.

But there were those who voted for Mugabe more than will-ingly. 'Why should we vote against our president when he liberated this country?' said Agnes Tapera in Chitungwiza. 'What is Tsvangirai? Did he fight in the liberation war? Why is he so friendly with those white farmers? Why does Britain support him? Tsvangirai is not a president. He runs away every time it gets diffi-cult. Right now he is hiding in that [Dutch] embassy. Mugabe stays and fights. He fought Ian Smith and the British and he is fighting Tsvangirai and he will win.'

It was all in stark contrast to the first round of presidential elec-tions three months ago when Mugabe's opponents briefly believed they might finally remove him from power simply by marking a ballot paper. There was no such illusion yesterday.

Mugabe emerged from voting in Highfield township in Harare proclaiming himself 'very optimistic' and 'upbeat' that yester-day's ballot would reverse his first round defeat. That was one thing Zimbabwe's president for the past 28 years and the opposi-tion agreed on – that there's little doubt Mugabe will be declared the winner.

His Zanu-PF party says it is a popular response to its campaign for '100 per cent empowerment and independence' from British imperialism.

The ruling party chairman, John Nkomo, made a televised appeal to Zimbabweans to support Mugabe by portraying support for the opposition as akin to recolonisation and Tsvangirai as a Downing Street puppet.

'Our statehood and our nationhood are under severe threat. The question before each and every one of us is whether, advertently or inadvertently, we will go down in the annals of history as defend-ers of our motherland or as traitors who unabashedly volunteered for servitude,' he said. 'The ferocity of the anti-Zimbabwe campaign underscores what is at stake – our independence and future as a nation. Evidently this onslaught is being directed from London and Washington.'

Even the Queen – or what the *Herald* called the High Priestess of England – got dragged in for stripping Mugabe of his honorary knighthood this week.

The paper said it was a welcome development ahead of the election which confirmed the need to support 'total independence'.

'No one has ever referred to our president as 'Sir' Robert Mugabe. He is known as 'Comrade' Robert Mugabe and that says it all,' said the *Herald*.

Tsvangirai, who pulled out of the race because of the systematic violence that has virtually wiped out his party's structures on the ground but who remained on the ballot paper, urged his supporters to stay away from the polls. But he said they should vote for Mugabe if that was necessary to save their skins.

'What is happening is not an election,' he said yesterday. 'It is an exercise in mass intimidation with people all over the country being forced to vote. Fortunately, Zimbabweans are attempting to stay away from the polls as they can tell the difference between democracy and a dictatorship desperate for the illusion of legitimacy.'

But Tsvangirai said the vote would strip Mugabe of the last vestiges of legitimacy as president whatever the outcome of the election.' Zimbabweans know that there is nothing legitimate about this election and they know that there will be nothing legitimate about the result. This is a view shared by many African and world leaders,' he said.

'The end of this terrible, violent dictatorship is now assured, the people's victory may have been delayed by this sham election but it will never be denied.'

Many of the voters are not so confident. 'It was our mistake to think we could get rid of Mugabe,' said Wilson. 'He is right when he says only God can get rid of him. I want to ask God if he is on our side.'

All the intimidation may in the end prove academic because ultimately what matters is the numbers on the final returns, and Zimbabwe's state-controlled election commission will decide what they are beyond the reach of prying eyes.

The violence not only scared the voters but drove opposition and independent local election observers away from monitoring the polls. MDC polling agents have been systematically beaten up, thrown into jail, abducted and murdered.

The thousands of independent local observers who oversaw the election three months ago have also been terrorised into staying away, leaving the voting and the count largely unscrutinised by outside witnesses.

Only a few hundred observers from African organisations are monitoring the poll and they were hard-pressed to cover more than 9,000 polling stations. Many of those observers have seen enough to decide that the election was anything but free and fair, and seem ready to say so.

Mugabe plans to attend an African Union summit in Egypt next week as Zimbabwe's newly re-elected president, and he will defy any of the continent's leaders to question his legitimacy.

'When I go to the AU meeting next week, I am going to challenge some leaders to point out when we have had worse elections,' Mugabe told a final election rally on Thursday. 'I would like some African leaders who are making these statements to point at me and we would see if those fingers would be cleaner than mine.'

That is largely irrelevant to the voters, who just wanted to get through the day in one piece. But the end of balloting did not necessarily bring relief. In some parts of Harare, the voters were told to report back to the polling station after dark and to wait for the count to be completed. They were warned that if the numbers were not right, there would be a price to pay.

'I hope everybody did what I did and voted for Mugabe,' said Wilson. 'Otherwise we're all in trouble.'

JULY 7 2008

# Can Laura avoid the path to celebrity wrestling?

## MARTIN KELNER

It is important to manage expectations and the last thing we would want to do is pile any extra pressure on a girl who is only 14 years old but Laura Robson, wow. I mean, LAURA ROBSON!! Phew. ENGLAND'S LAURA ROBSON, Champion of the World or what??? Come on Laura.

That was more or less the tenor of Chris Bailey's and Sam Smith's commentary on BBC TV as England's Laura beat Noppawan Lertcheewakarn in the girls' championship final at Wimbledon on Saturday. 'Unfortunately, the hype around Laura is going to be unstoppable,' said Bailey, as the commentary team ratcheted it up a notch or two.

'I can see her being the new pin-up,' burbled Sam. 'She could be a cover girl for magazines like *Jackie*.' That would indeed be some achievement as *Jackie* went out of business around the time Sam herself was Britain's No1 and subject to similar weight of unfeasible expectations. 'There's the crowd on Henman Hill,' continued the former British No1 and world No55. 'In a few years' time we might be calling it Robson Ridge.'

'We don't want to put too much pressure on her,' one of the commentators said (dear me, no, we are all agreed on that), 'but she looks like a young Ana Ivanovic – same sort of hairstyle, same hair colouring.' (I am not sure who was responsible for this gem, as I was busy managing my expectations at the time).

Other names invoked as Come-on-Laura – as she will henceforth be known – swept to victory included Martina Hingis and Amélie Mauresmo, previous winners of the girls' title and Maria Sharapova, who apparently was lower in the junior rankings when she was the same age as Come-on-Laura.

A name not invoked quite as much was that of Annabel Croft, the last British winner of the title, in 1984, who, by the age of 21, had retired from the game. Croft gave a frank interview on *BBC Breakfast* in which she described tennis as 'a selfish sport' and herself as unable to make the sacrifices needed to continue with her career. 'It's very full-on,' said the former British No 1, *Treasure Hunt* presenter and winner of ITV's *Celebrity Wrestling*. Actually, there are so many former British No 1s floating round the various Wimbledon commentary boxes I sometimes wonder whether becoming British No 1 is little more than a step to a media career.

If it comes down to a choice between spending three years at whatever they call Cardiff Polytechnic these days, watching Jeremy Kyle, eating bad food and begging for work experience at the *Gloucestershire Echo*, and putting some time in on your ground strokes, the tennis might not seem such a sacrifice.

But as Annabel wisely pointed out, what seems like a good idea at 14 may seem less attractive in later teenage years. Girls change, said the former presenter of ITV's *Interceptor*. Prodigious talent or not, Come-on-Laura's further progress remains an open question.

I agree. I may not know much about tennis but consider myself something of an expert on teenage girls, having had two under my tutelage in recent years. I can confirm it is awfully difficult to keep them focused on making the most of talents displayed in early teenage years. It is also very difficult to get them to turn the lights off when they leave a room.

On which topic, there is a ritual attached to the emergence of a precocious talent like Come-on-Laura's, which involves the parents giving interviews stressing that the prodigy is being brought up as 'just a normal kid'.

Laura's mum, Kathy – who will have to get used to being the star of a thousand cutaways – said the family's celebration meal would be in Pizza Hut. Far be it from me to doubt her, but I am sure a family living in prosperous south-west London, with a Shell executive as head of the household, could do better than Pizza Hut (not that I am casting aspersions on Pizza Hut, although their salad bar sometimes seems too heavily reliant on overly chilled green peppers and Thousand Island dressing.) It is just that tennis in Britain, despite encouraging noises from the Lawn Tennis Association, is still mostly played by those who get their pizzas from authentic wood-fired ovens. There is no immediate sign of a British equivalent of the Williams sisters emerging.

The good news is that British tennis is not quite as middle class as Woody Allen perceives it. After the men's doubles on Saturday I made the grave mistake of turning to Woody's film *Match Point* on one of the Sky movie channels. This may be not just Woody Allen's worst film but the worst film ever made.

I was reading in this paper on Saturday about a British film called *Crust* featuring a 7ft boxing shrimp and another, a comedy called *Nine Dead Gay Guys*, both of which attracted considerable investment for tax reasons despite being near-certain flops. Amateurs, I say. *Citizen Kane* compared to *Match Point*, which is as though the great Woody had seen a bunch of Hugh Grant-Working Title movies and decided he liked them, but without all the gritty realism.

Sometimes, though, foreign eyes help show us the truth about ourselves. Pat Cash, on BBC *Five Live* yesterday, congratulated Come-on-Laura but pointed out that many female tennis players turn professional at 16 these days. 'You think she has beaten the best young players in the world but it's far from that,' he said. He also claimed Laura was technically Australian. Spoilsport.

# So, you believe in conspiracy theories, do you?

### CHARLIE BROOKER

I've got a theory – an untested, unprovable theory – that the more interesting your life is at any given point, the less lurid and spectacular your dreams will be. Think of it as a balancing procedure carried out by the brain to stop you getting bored to death.

If your waking life is mundane, it'll inject some thrills into your night-time imaginings to maintain a healthy overall fun quotient. So if you work in a cardboard box factory, and your job is to stare at the side of each box as it passes along a conveyor belt, to ensure they're all uniform and boxy enough – and you do this all day, every day, until your mind grows so dissociated and numb you can scarcely tell where the cardboard ends and your body begins – when your daily routine is THAT dull, chances are you'll spend each night dreaming you're the Emperor of Pluto, wrestling a 6ft green jaguar during a meteor storm in the desert just outside Vegas.

All well and good in the world of dreams. But if you continue to believe you're the Emperor of Pluto after you've woken up, and you go into work and start knocking the boxes around with a homemade sceptre while screaming about your birthright, you're in trouble.

I mention this because recently I've found myself bumping into people – intelligent, level-headed people – who are sincerely prepared to entertain the notion that there might be something in some of the less lurid 9/11 conspiracy theories doing the rounds. They mumble about the 'controlled demolition' of WTC 7 (oft referred to as 'the third tower'), or posit the notion that the Bush administration knew 9/11 was coming and let it happen anyway. I mean, you never know, right? Right? And did I tell you I'm the Emperor of Pluto?

The glaring problem – and it's glaring in 6,000-watt neon, so vivid and intense you can see it from space with your eyes glued shut – is that with any 9/11 conspiracy theory you care to babble can be summed up in one word: paperwork.

Imagine the paperwork. Imagine the level of planning, recruitment, coordination, control, and unbelievable nerve required to pull off a conspiracy of that magnitude. Really picture it in detail. At the very least you're talking about hiring hundreds of civil servants cold-hearted enough to turn a blind eye to the murder of thousands of their fellow countrymen. If you were dealing with faultless, emotionless robots – maybe. But this almighty conspiracy was presumably hatched and executed by fallible humans. And if there's one thing we know about humans, it's that our inherent unreliability will always derail the simplest of schemes.

It's hard enough to successfully operate a video shop with a staff of three, for Christ's sake, let alone slaughter thousands and convince the world someone else was to blame.

That's just one broad objection to all the bullshit theories. But try suggesting it to someone in the midst of a 9/11 fairytale reverie, and they'll pull a face and say, 'Yeah, but ... ' and start banging on about some easily misinterpreted detail that 'makes you think' (when it doesn't) or 'contradicts the official story' (when you misinterpret it). Like nutbag creationists, they fixate on thinly spread, cherry-picked nuggets of 'evidence' and ignore the thundering mass of data pointing the other way.

And when repeatedly pressed on that one, basic, overall point – that a conspiracy this huge would be impossible to pull off – they huff and whine and claim that unless you've sat through every nanosecond of *Loose Change* (the conspiracy flick du jour) and personally refuted every one of its carefully spun 'findings' before their very eyes, using a spirit level and calculator, you have no right to an opinion on the subject.

Oh yeah? So if my four-year-old nephew tells me there's a magic leprechaun in the garden I have to spend a week meticulously peering underneath each individual blade of grass before I can tell him he's wrong, do I?

Look hard enough, and dementedly enough, and you can find 'proof' that Kevin Bacon was responsible for 9/11 – or the 1987 Zeebrugge ferry disaster, come to that. It'd certainly make for a more interesting story, which is precisely why several thousand well-meaning people would go out of their way to believe it. Throughout my 20s I earnestly believed Oliver Stone's account of the JFK assassination. Partly because of the compelling (albeit wildly selective) way the 'evidence' was blended with fiction in his 1991 movie – but mainly because I WANTED to believe it. Believing it made me feel important.

Embrace a conspiracy theory and suddenly you're part of a gang sharing privileged information; your sense of power and dignity rises a smidgen and this troublesome world makes more sense, for a time. You've seen through the matrix! At last you're alive! You ARE the Emperor of Pluto after all!

Except – ahem – you're only deluding yourself, your majesty. Because to believe the 'system' is trying to control you is to believe it considers you worth controlling in the first place. The reality – that 'the man' is scarcely competent enough to control his own bowels, and doesn't give a toss about you anyway – is depressing and emasculating; just another day in the cardboard box factory. And that's no place for an imaginary emperor, now, is it?

JULY 21 2008

# For hard-up voters, it's about local issues – if they vote at all

## AUDREY GILLAN

The computers were broken, but the glass in the monitors remained in one piece and the keyboards' soft clicking left the children delighted as they stabbed at the letters with their fingers. Inside a bin shed on the Easterhouse estate in Glasgow, the seven children were making the best of the remorselessly grey day and the sparseness of playthings in this back court, turning it into their 'office'.

Shouting for one to answer the imaginary phone and another to bring paper and cups of tea, they were oblivious to Margaret Curran, the Labour candidate for Glasgow East, walking past the detritus scattered across the patch of grass – long-dead fridges, the rusting drums of washing machines – for a photocall with an actor from television's Glasgow police series, *Taggart*.

'One of the things that people are getting upset about is the way the East End is being stereotyped during this byelection. People know there are problems and there are issues, I wouldn't deny that, but there's been lots of new development,' the candidate told the TV copper. 'A lot of the housing development has really changed and a lot of the schools, jobs are a lot better – I mean far from perfect – but people are a bit upset about that.'

Minutes before, Curran and the press had gathered outside the bookmaker Ladbrokes before setting off on a walk past some of the human manifestations of what is one of the poorest areas in the country. They skipped by the three junkies, sidestepped a cluster of afternoon drinkers smoking in the doorway of Grieves bar and climbed the slope to Arnisdale Street, where the last of the tenants hang on in buildings long ago marked for demolition, waiting for their new houses to go up on the green patch just across the way.

There are better things round the corner for this constituency, and it is this hope that may win the seat for Labour, and prevent the people here from delivering a blow from which the prime minister might struggle to recover. Parents such as Jason Black have not lost faith. Black, 32, has lived in these flats for 10 years. He and his daughter – busy being the 'office' manager – and his girlfriend and her children are due to relocate at the turn of the year.

'I think Labour has always done better for these parts of Glasgow,' he said. 'They are rebuilding houses for us and demolishing these, which really is the only option for these types of flats. As soon as we get into our new flats, it will be a different standard of living altogether.'

Inside Ladbrokes, Frances, the manager, confirmed that Labour was the bookies' favourite to win the byelection on Thursday. It was called suddenly because of the ill health of David Marshall, the Labour MP in the area for 29 years, who last won the seat with a 13,507 majority. 'Labour are 4-9, SNP 13-8, Conservative 100-1, Liberal Democrats 100-1,' she said.

But the race is close enough, and the government unpopular enough, for the doubts to remain.

The enormous presence of the SNP in the constituency is testament to party members' belief that it may just be theirs for the grabbing. The party has the biggest of the campaign headquarters, renting out three large portable buildings on the grounds of Sherwood garage, which sells performance cars.

Inside, SNP campaigners have gathered from all over the country, the sign-in book has home addresses in London as well as the Highlands, and a handwritten poster offers a room for those helping who don't have a bed for the night in Glasgow. It was suggested that Labour's decision to call the byelection in the middle of the Glasgow fair holiday, when many voters are away, was an attempt to catch the SNP on the hop. If the date was tactical, then it failed, as the nationalist party has flooded the place, with hundreds knocking on doors and canvassing on the telephone.

The SNP candidate is John Mason, 51, a stolid local councillor for the Baillieston ward who speaks of his faith regularly – he is a Baptist. He backs a reduction in abortion limits and is 'extremely unhappy about experiments with babies or research or anything like that', with regard to the human fertilisation and embryology bill – something that may appeal to the 30 per cent of the constituency that is Catholic.

He deflected this issue – which he said was an issue for people of all faiths, not just Catholics – when questioned and said: 'A big plus is that the byelection focuses a lot of attention on the East End of Glasgow and that has got to be good. I admit that there have been a lot of improvements in the East End. But male life expectancy is under 70 and if you look at particular pockets it is not improving and we have had Labour MPs here for 50 years or so.'

He added: 'I am somebody that listens, and somebody that speaks out for people and that's what people want. They are realistic: they don't want the streets to be paved with gold.'

Both candidates have had a direct role in the constituency for a number of years, Mason as a councillor and Curran as a member of the Scottish parliament: she was Labour's fifth choice for the Westminster seat, after four others shied away.

Both concede that the place is still riddled with problems, particularly alcohol and drugs.

According to a profile of the East Glasgow area published by the Glasgow Centre for Population Health this year, life expectancy at birth for men is 68.1 years, five years lower than the Scottish average, while female life expectancy is 76 years. Excessive drinking is the biggest problem. Approximately 1,960 patients are admitted to hospital each year for alcohol-related or attributable causes and there have been 420 deaths due to alcohol over the last five years. There were 800 new cancer cases and 1,400 heart disease patients admitted to hospital last year.

Just under a third of the population are classed as income-deprived. In the last year, 490 serious assaults were recorded, as well as more than 1,600 domestic abuse cases. The rate of low birth-weight babies is 62 per cent above the Scottish average and teenage pregnancies are 42 per cent above. Almost 16,000 people, out of a population of around 124,000, are estimated to be on prescription drugs for depression.

Gerald Spence, a campaigning doctor based at Shettleston health centre for more than 25 years, recently wrote: 'Today, the quality of housing is much improved. Progress has also been made on the health front in terms of identifying heart disease and preventive treatment to reduce the risk of heart attack. The message about the ills of smoking is getting across ... But alcohol is a terrible problem and drug abuse is absolutely ghastly.'

Glasgow East is no longer the centre of heavy industry that it had been for more than 100 years. Sir William Arrol's Dalmarnock ironworks built many railway bridges, including the Forth bridge, while William Beardmore and J&T Boyd made steel forgings then armaments, employing tens of thousands. Now, there is 25 per cent unemployment and the Forge is no longer a byword for the largest steelworks in Europe, but is instead a shopping centre.

Pat Archer, 59, and long-term unemployed, knows that he can count himself in many of the constituency's worrying statistics. The strains of John Denver's *Country Roads* filtered out from the jukebox inside the Cottage Bar as he stood on Shettleston Road with his cigarette.

'Over the past few years my health has deteriorated. I have had a quadruple bypass. I came out of hospital three years ago, I was only out 20 days and I took a stroke, paralysed all down one side. I haven't managed to work since then. It's just the way of life here, I think. Most people my age group like their smoke, their drink and what have you.'

Archer said he would not reveal who he is voting for. But he said: 'I won't be voting for the Labour party because of the high price of fuel, the cost of energy going up. That's all getting passed on to the consumer and the shops. She [his wife] came back from the shops and says "that's £10 worth" in one wee carrier bag ... I still manage my couple of pints, mind you.

'I definitely won't vote Labour and I won't vote Tory. There's just one major party left.'

The Cottage Bar is symbolic, though, of other concerns in the area. CCTV cameras were installed next to the pub because of anti-social behaviour including graffiti, vandalism, disorder and street drinking. They captured loan shark Joseph Gault, 59, passing over cash. He arrived outside the bar at 9am each day, taking his victims' benefit books in exchange for money, for which he charged £3 a week for every £10 lent – equating to an interest rate of 1,560 per cent a year. He was jailed this month for a year.

The media view is that this byelection is a battle between Gordon Brown and Alex Salmond, the SNP leader, and that should Labour lose Glasgow East, it could spell the end for Brown as prime minister. But on the ground, hardly anyone, apart from the politicians, mentions the prime minister's name. The talk is of fuel and food prices, free travel passes and heating allowances for pensioners, health concerns and law and order. For most, the issues are minutely local, in spite of their vote having national significance.

Matthew McConnell said he would vote Labour, but the bottom line was that he would cast his cross for whoever has not threatened to take away his pigeon loft. He keeps his birds in a homemade corrugated iron loft on a patch of grass in Lilybank. Years ago, dozens of these cobbled-together towers stood across the area but now they are diminishing. As the area's slum schemes are turned under the bulldozers and new developments take their place, there is no room for the 6 metre (20ft) coops that many criticise as eyesores.

'I am disabled. I am just through a heart bypass operation and this is something for me to pass the time with,' he said. 'It gives me something to do a couple of days a week and keep an interest in things. They are totemic in the East End because it was a working man's sport. As things deteriorated with work, with the foundries shutting down, the Clyde ironworks and the Forge and things like that, unemployed people took this up as a sport and a pastime.

'I am not a politically motivated person, as long as they don't pull my pigeon loft down. They are building housing here and the pigeon lofts will have to be moved, so they will have to delegate an area for the pigeon fanciers to go, rather than demolish them. It is a dying sport. There might be 30 pigeons fanciers about here and very shortly I don't think there will be many. I have always voted Labour if the truth be known, always, all my life.'

But, said McConnell, 'the SNP might be a great thing for this country, I am not saying that I wouldn't change over. I would consider the SNP next time if they could prove to people that their intentions were good and they were going to do good for the East End of Glasgow and other deprived areas.'

Fellow pigeon fliers were gathered around him, outside a storage container they use as a den. This is where they come to drink and smoke and talk about their birds. Unlike McConnell, most said they would not bother voting. One or two are not even on the voters' roll, for fear the debt collectors will catch up with them.

It was a poor turnout that concerned the government's chief whip, Geoff Hoon, when he turned up canvassing in Mount Vernon, the most affluent residential part of the area. 'It's nice around here, isn't it?' he said.

Round the corner, at a coffee morning in the bowling club, he could have gauged just how poor the turnout might be. The women eating homemade cake did not know who they would vote for, or had decided not to bother.

One said: 'They promise you the sun, the moon and everything until they get in and then nothing comes out of it and you are left high and dry. They tell you pensioners should put in for things, so you put in for things and they come and give you a means test and then turn round and say you don't qualify for it. I really don't know what I am going to do. I might not even bother voting.'

It is the minds of these women that Margaret Curran and John Mason will be desperately trying to change, promising the sun and the moon in the East End of Glasgow.

JULY 30 2008

# Against the odds we can still win, on a platform of change

DAVID MILIBAND

In the aftermath of Labour's third successive defeat at the 1959 election, a famous pamphlet asked the question: 'Must Labour lose?' Today, the temptation is similar fatalism. We must not yield to it. We need to remember that there is little real sense among the public – or even among Tory MPs – of what the Conservatives stand for, or what they would do in power.

The odds are against us, no question. But I still believe we can win the next election. I agree with Jack Straw that we don't need a summer of introspection. The starting point is not debating personalities but winning the argument about our record, our vision for the future and how we achieve it.

When people hear exaggerated claims, either about failure or success, they switch off. That is why politicians across all parties fail to connect. To get our message across, we must be more humble about our shortcomings but more compelling about our achievements.

With hindsight, we should have got on with reforming the NHS sooner. We needed better planning for how to win the peace in Iraq, not just win the war. We should have devolved more power away from Whitehall and Westminster. We needed a clearer drive towards becoming a low-carbon, energy-efficient economy, not just to tackle climate change but to cut energy bills.

But 10 years of rising prosperity, a health service brought back from the brink, and social norms around women's and minority rights transformed, have not come about by accident. After all, the Tories opposed almost all the measures that have made a difference – from the windfall tax on privatised utilities to family-friendly working.

Now what are they offering? The Tories say society is broken. By what measure? Rising crime? No, crime has fallen more in the past 10 years than at any time in the past century. Knife crime and gun crime are serious problems. But since targeting the spike in gun crime, it has been cut by 13 per cent in a year, and we have to do the same with knife crime.

What about the social breakdown that causes crime? More single parents dependent on the state? No, employment has risen sharply for lone parents because the state has funded childcare and made work pay. Falling school standards? No, they are rising. More asylum seekers? No, we said we would reform the system and slash the numbers, and we did.

The Tories overclaim for what they are against because they don't know what they are for. I disagreed with Margaret Thatcher, but at least it was clear what she stood for. She sat uncomfortably within the Tory party because she was a radical, not a conservative. She wanted change and was prepared to take unpopular decisions to achieve it.

The problem with David Cameron is the reverse. His problem is he is a conservative, not a radical. He doesn't share a restlessness for change. He may be likable and sometimes hard to disagree with, but he is empty. He is a politician of the status quo – even a status quo he consistently voted against – not change.

Every member of the Labour party carries with them a simple guiding mission on the membership card: to put power, wealth and opportunity in the hands of the many, not the few. When debating public service reform, tax policies or constitutional changes, we apply those values to the latest challenges.

What is on Cameron's party card? What is his vision for Britain? He doesn't have one. His project is 'decontaminating the Tory party', not changing the country. He is stuck, reconciling himself to New Labour Mk I at just the time when the times demand a radical new phase.

The economic challenge is new. People want protection from a downturn made in Wall Street. The country needs to prepare for an upturn when new service industries – insurance, education, care, creative industries – are growing at home but also among the new Chinese and Indian middle classes. The public service challenge is new, too. The task of government after 1997 was a rescue mission. Now we need the imagination to distribute more power and control to citizens over the education, healthcare and social services they receive. So is the challenge to society – to build a genuine sense of belonging and responsibility on the back of greater protection from outside risks and greater control of local issues.

I really believe that it is only our means, the political creed of the Labour party combining government action and personal freedom, that can achieve the ends the Tories now claim to share.

The modernisation of the Labour party means pursuing traditional goals in a modern way. The Tories claim the reverse. They say they have adopted 'progressive ends' – social justice, better public services and fighting climate change – but they insist on traditional Tory means of charity, deregulation and lower spending to deliver them. It doesn't add up.

If people and business are to take responsibility, you need government to act as a catalyst. High polluting products will not disappear unless government regulates. New nuclear power stations need planning policy to facilitate them. And if we act through the EU, we green the largest single market in the world. In opposition, you can sound green while embracing Euroscepticism. But in government, unless you choose sides, you get found out.

New Labour won three elections by offering real change, not just in policy but in the way we do politics. We must do so again. So let's stop feeling sorry for ourselves, enjoy a break, and then find the confidence to make our case afresh.

*David Miliband is the foreign secretary*

JULY 31 2008

# Miliband's sink or swim challenge to Labour

## LETTERS AND EMAILS

David Miliband's article was the most clearly expressed and concise political commentary I have ever read. In the space of a few column inches he managed to explain what the Labour party stands for, what it has achieved and what it needs to do now to meet current challenges. It also gave a convincing argument why the Labour party can succeed where the Conservatives will not. Why has it taken a potential leadership challenge before the Labour party clearly expresses its vision?

*Gordon Brown, Farnham, Surrey*

JULY 31 2008

# Once again, modern Turkey has hauled itself back from the brink

## SIMON TISDALL

Turkey stepped back from the brink yesterday, having thoroughly frightened itself and its friends. The constitutional court's narrow decision to fine, rather than ban, Recep Tayyip Erdogan and his ruling AKP is a defeat for attempts to manipulate the legal system for political ends. It represents a score-draw in the long-running, unfinished struggle between secular and religious forces. But most of all, it is a vicarious victory for Turkish democracy.

Modern Turkey has a history of half scaring itself to death, only to scrape by. Elected governments have been temporarily forced aside three times since 1960 by the military, acting out its self-appointed role as guardian of Ataturk's elastic legacy. Rumours of another coup swept Ankara last year but the government survived. Only this month 86 ultra-nationalists were charged with subversive plotting.

Turks shocked themselves in 2003, while winning plaudits across Europe and the Arab world, when parliament refused permission for US troops to transit Turkish territory to invade Iraq. Washington's dire retribution was fearfully predicted, even expulsion from Nato. Yet George Bush and Donald Rumsfeld briefly fumed, then got over it.

The catastrophic financial crisis in 2001 looked like another doomsday event. The currency all but collapsed, banks failed, recession took hold. But the slump, and the remedial measures that followed, proved to be a platform for a sustained economic recovery for which the AKP, in power since 2002, can claim some credit. Today Turkey is developing into a booming regional hub.

Yesterday's dramatic denouement fits the pattern of disaster narrowly averted. The stakes were enormous. If Abdurrahman Yalcinkaya, the chief prosecutor, had got his way, a government elected with almost 47 per cent of the vote last year would have been in effect decapitated. A political and constitutional crisis would have ensued, destabilising the country, undermining its economy, emboldening its enemies, and presaging a period of prolonged uncertainty. In short, one of the region's few genuinely democratic systems would have been paralysed and perhaps permanently damaged.

Turkey's increasingly important regional diplomacy would also have been undercut if the ban had gone ahead. Under Erdogan and President Abdullah Gul, Ankara has become an important crossroads between Iran, the Arab Middle East, Israel and the west. Closer to home, hopes of further integration into the EU would have been set back indefinitely.

Most seriously of all, perhaps, a society where secularism and Islam (and other faiths), despite many serious difficulties, have coexisted tolerantly side-by-side in recent years would have been artificially set asunder and turned upon itself. In these polarised times, that's the very opposite of what enlightened leaders are supposedly trying to achieve.

AUGUST 4 2008

# Faith 1, Charity 0

LEADER

There were two texts for the world's Anglican bishops as they prepared to leave Canterbury last night at the end of what was anticipated as a make-or-break Lambeth Conference. The first was about faith the second about inclusivity. Rowan Williams, the Archbishop of Canterbury, dearly hoped that focus on the first would open the way to the second. But for all the talking of the past fortnight, it does not look as if he has had much success in reconciling the two versions of Anglicanism, the evangelical and the liberal, that are straining to breaking point the Communion that links 70 million Anglicans.

Any student of conflict resolution will recognise the problem.

The extremes of both sides are beyond agreement. With good reason: in many parts of Africa, there is a pretence that homosexuality does not exist and to be known as the 'gay church' is a short road to oblivion. In many parts of Europe and America, gay men and women are also subject to violent discrimination and the church naturally believes its role is to reach out to them as to all the oppressed. And many Anglicans (but not all, or schism might already be a reality) also ardently defend inclusivity and believe in a faith of the spirit rather than the biblical fundamentalism of the evangelists, and defend the appointment of women and gay clergy. They feel their autonomy is threatened by domineering conservatives both at home and abroad, while the evangelicals accuse the liberals of a neocolonial disregard for their own autonomy.

The positions are plainly irreconcilable. Some think Rowan Williams was wrong even to try, that he betrayed his own liberal instincts. As the gay bishop Gene Robinson, whose election triggered the crisis, said from his enforced position on the sidelines yesterday, 'bullies always come back for more'.

The archbishop believes time may bring enlightenment, and his job is to stop the confrontationists of both sides forcing a division first. He has some eminent critics – including the Bishop of Winchester and, it is reported, the Bishop of Durham – who feel the avoidance of confrontation this past fortnight has merely set up a worse confrontation in the future. But peacekeeping is an inexact art. The danger of playing it long is that some might walk away from the process. Play it short, and some definitely will. History may say the rift had already opened before the bishops even arrived at Canterbury: after all, 230 of them stayed away. But Dr Williams has probably held off official schism for his tenure in office. His Lambeth Conference – only a decennial event – was not a complete failure. The liberals may feel the price was too high, but sometimes for peacekeepers, a fudge is as good as a success.

AUGUST 6 2008

# Review: *Hamlet*

## MICHAEL BILLINGTON

It's a sign of our star-crazy culture that there has been months of speculation about David Tennant's *Hamlet*. The big news from Stratford is that Gregory Doran's production is one of the most richly textured, best-acted versions of the play we have seen in years. And Tennant, as anyone familiar with his earlier work with the RSC would expect, has no difficulty in making the transition from the BBC's Time Lord to a man who could be bounded in a nutshell and count himself a king of infinite space. He is a fine Hamlet whose virtues, and occasional vices, are inseparable from the production itself.

Doran's production gets off, literally, to a riveting start: the first thing we hear is the sound of hammering and drilling as Denmark's night-working Niebelungen prepare the country for war. And our first glimpse of the chandeliered, mirrored, modern-dress court gives us an instant clue to Hamlet's alienation. Patrick Stewart's superb Claudius insultingly addresses Laertes's problems before those of Hamlet. And, urging Hamlet not to return to university, Stewart has to be publicly reminded that Wittenberg is the place in question. Immediately we sense Claudius's hostile suspicion towards, and cold contempt for, his moody nephew.

Tennant's performance, in short, emerges from a detailed framework. And there is a tremendous shock in seeing how the lean, dark-suited figure of the opening scene dissolves into grief the second he is left alone: instead of rattling off 'O that this too too sullied flesh would melt', Tennant gives the impression that the words have to be wrung from his prostrate frame. Paradoxically, his Hamlet is quickened back to life only by the Ghost; and the overwhelming impression is of a man who, in putting on an 'antic disposition', reveals his true, nervously excitable, mercurial self.

This is a Hamlet of quicksilver intelligence, mimetic vigour and wild humour: one of the funniest I've ever seen. He parodies every-one he talks to, from the prattling Polonius to the verbally ornate Osric. After the play scene, he careers around the court sporting a crown at a tipsy angle. Yet, under the mad capriciousness, Tennant implies a filial rage and impetuous danger: the first half ends with Tennant poised with a dagger over the praying Claudius, crying: 'And now I'll do it'. Newcomers to the play might well believe he will.

Tennant is an active, athletic, immensely engaging Hamlet. If there is any quality I miss, it is the character's philosophical nature, and here he is not helped by the production. Following the First Quarto, Doran places 'To be or not to be' before rather than after the arrival of the players: perfectly logical, except that there is something magnificently wayward about the Folio sequence in which Hamlet, having decided to test Claudius's guilt, launches into an unexpected meditation on human existence.

Unforgivably, Doran also cuts the lines where Hamlet says to Horatio, 'Since no man knows of aught he leaves, what is't to leave betimes? Let be.' Thus Tennant loses some of the most beautiful lines in all literature about acceptance of one's fate.

But this is an exciting performance that in no way overshadows those around it. Stewart's Claudius is a supremely composed, calcu-lating killer: at the end of the play scene, instead of indulging in the usual hysterical panic, he simply strides over to Hamlet and pityingly shakes his head as if to say 'you've blown it now'. Oliver Ford Davies's brilliant Polonius is both a sycophantic politician and a comic pedant who feels the need to define and qualify every word

THE BEDSIDE GUARDIAN 08

he says: a quality he, oddly enough, shares with Hamlet. And I can scarcely remember a better Ophelia than that of Mariah Gale, whose mad-scenes carry a potent sense of danger, and whose skin is as badly scarred by the flowers she has gathered, as her divided mind is by emotional turmoil.

That is typical of a production that bursts with inventive detail. I love the idea that Edward Bennett's Laertes, having lectured Ophelia about her chastity, is shown to have a packet of condoms in his luggage. And the sense that this is a play about, among much else, ruptured families is confirmed when Stewart as the Ghost of Hamlet's father seeks, in the closet scene, tenderly to console Penny Downie's plausibly desolate Gertrude.

Audiences may flock to this production to see the transmogrification of Doctor Who into a wild and witty Hamlet. What they will discover is a rich realisation of the greatest of poetic tragedies.

AUGUST 8 2008

# I can't prove it, but I'm sure that it was the notorious Johnson clan who burgled my uncle's house – twice

## ALEXANDER CHANCELLOR

It was in January last year that a police officer came to my house in Northamptonshire to warn me that I was in danger of having my shotgun licence revoked. This was because I had rashly written that I was so fed up with burglars that I intended to arm myself and lie in wait like Tony Martin for the next intruder.

I wrote this in *G2* knowing full well, as Tony Martin had already discovered to his cost, that one isn't allowed to go around shooting burglars, and I told the officer that I hadn't meant to be taken seriously. He said he had assumed as much, but that his superiors in the Northamptonshire police were not amused and would probably be writing to me. In the event they never did so, and my shotgun is still safely locked up in its metal cupboard, from which – following the conviction this week of five members of the Johnson gang – I have lost all temptation to remove it. For I feel much safer now that the Johnsons are not around.

It now seems more than likely that it was the Johnsons who were responsible for two break-ins at my uncle Robin's house during which most things of any value were removed. That was what the police suspected at the time, and the burglaries certainly had all the hallmarks of a Johnson operation. They had been carefully planned and audaciously carried out.

The burglars must have known that Robin was away wintering in Thailand at the time and that the Inigo Jones pavilion in which he lives would be unoccupied during the Christmas and New Year holidays. It is also the sort of building the Johnsons like to rob – an architectural gem suggesting snootiness and privilege.

Ricky Johnson, 54, the father of the gang, once said in a BBC documentary that 'I feel I have got the fucking right to rob the lords out there', and while Robin is far from being a lord (he bought Stoke Park for £3,500 in 1954), he might well have been seen by the Johnsons as belonging to that hated category.

Anyway, whoever they were, the robbers roared across open parkland in 4x4s, scaled a stone balustrade, smashed a basement window, and ransacked every drawer and cupboard in the house before making off with most of the furniture, silver and china.

This happened three days before Christmas; and living as I do across the lawn from Robin's house and being in charge of it at the time, I had his basement window boarded up the next day – only for the robbers to return a week later and break in again, taking whatever stuff they had missed first time around.

This was more than a little disheartening, and may have been partly responsible for Uncle Robin's subsequent decision (about which I wrote the other day, giving his age wrongly as 88 instead of 86) to settle in Thailand more or less permanently. It must be hard for him to feel the same about a house that has been so comprehensively defiled.

Apart from saying unofficially that they thought it was the Johnsons who had done it, the police didn't appear to hold out any hope of catching the burglars and soon wrote to me saying the crimes were 'unresolved' and that they were closing their investigation.

This led me to write some harsh words about the uselessness of the police and their preference for form filling and 'victim support' over the more difficult task of actually catching criminals, but little did I then know that five police forces were at that time secretly working together to bring the Johnsons to justice. I am happy now to eat my words.

It is, of course, possible that it wasn't the Johnsons but some other gang that ransacked Stoke Park; and the place is not officially listed among the houses they robbed during their 20-year career. But I would be astonished if it turned out not to have been them. Even if the robberies were not as spectacular as the ones at Waddesdon, the Rothschild house (in whose park the Johnsons hid overnight in a camouflaged truck before brazenly driving out with their loot next day), and at Ramsbury Manor, Harry Hyams' home (a window of which they rammed with metal rods attached to the front of a Subaru), they had something of the same dash and ferocity. And whoever robbed Stoke Park was also 'forensically aware', as the judge put it, for they left no fingerprints or other signs of their visit.

It seems likely that the Johnsons carried out many more robberies than have so far been attributed to them, for robbery was their passion. More than for the vast rewards it brought them, they loved it for its own sake, and any day spent without planning or committing a break-in must have seemed an empty one. From their pictures they looked like the kind of staged villains that the British treasure so much – arrogant, ruthless, repulsive, and thoroughly committed and professional. And to protect themselves against the risk of ever feeling any compunction for the havoc and misery they have caused, they claim virtue in a mission to fleece 'the lords out there'. But the most striking thing about the Johnsons is the amount of fear and anxiety just one little gang can cause. They managed to give the impression that the English countryside was swarming with robbers and that no country house was safe.

Now that they are behind bars, everyone will calm down and realise that England is not quite such a crime-infested country as they thought and I, for one, will certainly sleep easier at night.

AUGUST 12 2008

# It's not just war – it's personal

## IAN TRAYNOR

For more than 200 years, tsars, generals and politburos in Russia have controlled Georgia. But for the past 17 years since the collapse of the Soviet empire, the small country on the south side of the Caucasus has gingerly embraced a new experience as an independent state – unstable, immature, corrupt, but hopeful.

Vladimir Putin cannot abide that notion and appears bent on trying to restore a version of the status quo ante. 'Russia has played a positive, stabilising role in the Caucasus for centuries, a guarantor of security, cooperation and progress,' the Russian prime minister said at the weekend. 'This is how it was in the past and this is how it is going to be in future. Let there be no doubt about this.'

By the time his 58th army, his air force, his *spetsnaz* paratroopers, and his Black Sea fleet are finished in Georgia, Putin knows where he wants to be. The Georgians, he said, 'will objectively assess their current leaders' and their 'criminal policies'.

In other words, President Mikheil Saakashvili, wayward darling of the west, will either be much diminished or finished. Saakashvili thinks that's the whole point. 'This is not about South Ossetia, this is not even about Abkhazia,' the Georgian leader said. 'It's all about independence and democracy in Georgia. Putin is personally commanding this operation. The purpose is to depose the democratically elected government of Georgia.'

A former Pentagon official long involved with Georgia agrees: 'The strategic objective is regime change. Putin wants a puppet, a satrap. He is playing an extremely good game.'

Georgia is Putin's second war. The first – also in August – was launched nine years ago in neighbouring Chechnya at the beginning of Putin's rule and entrenched him in power. The current campaign, at the start of President Dmitri Medvedev's term, marks a watershed – it is the first time the Russians have wielded their guns in anger beyond Russia's borders since the Soviet collapse and the end of the cold war.

Putin despised Saakashvili's predecessor, Eduard Shevardnadze, the former Soviet foreign minister and Georgian president, as the man who gave away the Soviet Union. But his contempt for

Saakashvili is much more intense.

Since the American-educated Georgian led the Rose revolution in 2003, Putin has striven mightily to subvert Tbilisi – trade boycotts, embargos on Georgian wine, fruit and mineral water, deporting thousands of Georgians who run Moscow's vegetable markets, cutting transport links over and through the Caucasus, turning off the oil and gas and stopping the post.

It's personal. Saakashvili has been telling western officials and diplomats for months of a looming war and of a foul-mouthed exchange with Putin in April. Last month in Dubrovnik the Georgian leader told senior US state department officials about the war plans and was warned there could be no military solution to the intricate ethnic conflicts of the Caucasus.

Saakashvili blundered. Perhaps he imagined he could pull a fast one in South Ossetia, perhaps he walked straight into a Russian trap. The results would be risible if not so tragic. His crack US-trained troops – a 10th of his army – took the Ossetian town of Tskhinvali and managed to hold it for all of three hours before being hammered by the Russians.

While George Bush watched baseball in Beijing, Putin created facts on the ground. European leaders rushed back from the beaches and villas of August for an 'emergency meeting' in Brussels and John McCain and Barack Obama used Georgia to sling mud at one another.

Saakashvili, who came to power pledging to recover control of Georgia's breakaway regions, has lost South Ossetia and Abkhazia, probably irretrievably, and will be much weakened.

AUGUST 13 2008

# Hare's satire crucifies New Labour

## CHARLOTTE HIGGINS

David Hare anatomised the failure of privatisation in *The Permanent Way* in *Stuff Happens*, he turned a ruthless eye on the double-think and culpable naivety that led to the Iraq war. And in his new play, Hare dramatises his final and bitter disenchantment with New Labour, the *Guardian* can reveal.

*Gethsemane*, which opens at the National Theatre in November, features a group of characters that bear a strong resemblance to the cabinet and confidants of the former prime minister Tony Blair.

A source close to the production said a major character in the play is the party's chief fundraiser, Otto Fallon, a north London Jewish former hairdresser who, as a music producer, has in the past created a number of boy bands. Audiences will perhaps note a likeness to Blair's close friend and former chief fundraiser, Lord Levy, a north London Jewish former accountant who made his fortune managing stars such as Alvin Stardust and Chris Rea, and who founded the label Magnet Records.

The prime minister of the play, named Alex, is a regular kind of guy, in a Tony Blair kind of a way. The home secretary is a woman named Meredith, whose husband, Jack, a wealthy businessman, is described as having a daring portfolio based in many different countries. No great imaginative leap is needed to link the character to Tessa Jowell, culture secretary under Blair, and her husband, David Mills.

During the course of the play, Fallon makes a notably cynical speech, lacking the force of ideas or ideals, in which he describes what New Labour is. We gather together all the most competent people in the country, he says, and call them, for the sake of argument, New Labour.

Fallon rescues the party from a crisis involving the home secretary and her husband, who is embroiled in a number of court cases. In the second act she goes to the prime minister and offers to divorce her husband, if that will make things easier for the government.

The prime minister asks her what her husband thinks. She replies that she hasn't spoken to him yet. The PM says that he fears the government could not survive the spectacle of a home secretary's husband appearing in handcuffs in a foreign country, so she suggests it is put out that her marriage has come to an undignified end with no acrimony on either side.

The situation clearly mirrors that when Jowell announced her intention to separate from Mills in 2006, after Italian prosecutors had been investigating claims that Mills had received a bribe of £344,000 in return for positive testimony on behalf of Silvio Berlusconi in a corruption trial. Jowell was cleared by Blair of breaking the ministers' code of conduct, because she had not known about the money, which Mills claimed came from another client. But some persisted in believing that Jowell had sacrificed her marriage for the sake of political expediency – a line that Hare's play appears to take.

*Gethsemane* is a title that offers itself up to a number of metaphorical interpretations. In the Gospel of Luke, chapter 22, Jesus and his disciples go there to pray after the Last Supper.

The passage reads: 'And when he was at the place, he said unto them, Pray that ye enter not into temptation. And he was withdrawn from them about a stone's cast, and kneeled down, and prayed, saying, Father, if thou be willing, remove this cup from me: nevertheless not my will, but thine, be done. And there appeared an angel unto him from heaven, strengthening him.

'And being in an agony he prayed more earnestly: and his sweat was as it were great drops of blood falling down to the ground.'

The keynote of Gethsemane in the Gospels is anguish and betrayal: this is where the corrupt Judas Iscariot helps the 'chief priests and captains' to capture Jesus.

The National Theatre, though it receives annual state funding of £18m, has never held back from criticising the government. Aside from Hare's earlier plays, under its artistic director, Nicholas Hytner, it has sent out highly charged messages about contemporary politics through new writing, such as David Edgar's *Playing With Fire*, about New Labour's misjudged schemes and initiatives to improve race relations.

It has also done so through pointed productions of the classics, whether Hytner's 2003 production of *Henry V*, which alluded clearly to the Iraq dossier, or Katie Mitchell's recent *The Trojan Women*, which examined the tragedy of 'collateral damage' and the ugly fallout in post-conflict zones.

Though Jowell was a supporter of the National Theatre, and especially its Travelex £10 ticket scheme, when she was culture secretary from 2001-07, she crossed swords with Hytner. He last year attacked her diversion of lottery funds from the arts to the Olympics as characterised by 'a spectacular lack of logic'.

Hare was unavailable yesterday. A spokeswoman from the National Theatre said: 'David has been very clear all along that the play is complete fiction – unlike *Stuff Happens* and *The Permanent Way*, it is not a documentary play. It is fiction: a theatrical and imaginative response to the governing class.'

AUGUST 9 2008

# China makes its point with greatest show

### RICHARD WILLIAMS

From the nation that brought you the 8,000 buried terracotta warriors of Xian in 210BC and the 7,500-mile Long March in 1934, you would anticipate nothing less than a spectacle. The ceremony that opened the 29th Olympic games last night outdid all predecessors in numbers, colour, noise and expense, demonstrating to the world that the new China intends to make its presence felt.

Fireworks – essentially a byproduct of gunpowder, one of several Chinese inventions celebrated during the evening – filled the sky over Beijing, first in the form of a countdown to the ceremony as giant golden footprints traced an airborne path towards the new national stadium. Then an hour-long display replayed Chinese history and gave elaborate expression to the country's national pride.

Around 14,000 performers came and went across the floor of the Bird's Nest stadium, acting out pageants devised by a cadre of designers, choreographers and composers under the supervision of Zhang Yimou, the film director whose works include *Red Sorghum*, *Raise the Red Lantern* and *The House of Flying Daggers*. Among his assistants was Mark Fisher, the British theatre designer who has worked with Pink Floyd, the Rolling Stones and U2.

Now 56, Zhang embodies much of China's recent history. The son of a major in Chiang Kai-shek's nationalist army, he was forced to leave his studies during the Cultural Revolution of 1966 and sent to the country, where he was made to work on a farm and in a cotton mill. Allowed into Beijing once the winds of change had died down, he studied cinematography.

Called on to pull out all the stops, he produced a show to match the scale of its surroundings. Beijing's Olympic facilities are intended to show that China is a modern country built on ancient foundations, and Zhang's show mirrored that. As is the way in China today, Mao Zedong was evident neither in word nor image; the only time you see him is when you pull out a banknote.

Eighty national leaders sat alongside Hu Jintao, president of the People's Republic, and Jacques Rogge, president of the International Olympic Committee: Putin of Russia and Bush of the United States in adjacent seats; Fukuda of Japan and Sarkozy of France. The most notable absentees were Merkel of Germany and Brown of Britain, the latter's decision to stay away underscored by the presence of his predecessor, the man who saddled him with the job of following this in four years' time.

These Olympics are being staged virtually without limits. When darkness had fallen the show began at precisely 8 o'clock with a clap of thunder from 2,008 tightly ranked *fou* drums. These traditional instruments, the shape and size of laundry baskets, were lit from inside, the lights sequenced by computer, and played by robed dancer-drummers flailing illuminated sticks.

The Olympic rings were formed in light and the Chinese flag was carried in by 56 children who handed it to an octet of goose-stepping soldiers before Zhang Yimou and his collaborators gave us elaborate representations of China's scroll paintings, its invention of moveable type and the merchants of the Silk Road. In the most tooth-rottingly sentimental passage, a group of infants sang a little number in praise of the Earth: 'We plant trees, we sow seeds, the land turns green,' they chanted, in the midst of one of the world's most polluted cities.

Then it was time for the entry of the athletes of the 204 participating nations, that quadrennial amalgam of *Jeux Sans Frontieres* and the Eurovision Song Contest. Iraq and Iran came in consecutively and quietly, while Bush waved at his immense contingent of compatriots. The only visible banner was carried by a Senegalese athlete. '*Amitié d'abord, compétition ensuite,*' it read. Friendship first, then let battle commence. There was a decent cheer for the British, their flag carried by the 38-year-old swimmer Mark Foster, about to participate in his fifth Olympics.

Last of all, after a pause to allow the drama to build, came the Chinese, a river of red and yellow flowing around the stadium, each athlete waving a flag. Hu beamed his approval as the 7ft 6in basketball star Yao Ming carried the flag and, a little later, as the Olympic torch was lit on the stadium's rim by the gymnast Li Ning, the last man in the trouble-strewn torch relay that drew protests around the world.

Also beaming at the wonder of it all was the 14-year-old Tom Daley, the object of international interest at the British diving squad's press conference earlier in the day. 'Amazing', he had said, time and again, when invited to give his first impressions.

Last night's show would have done little to diminish his sense of awe.

AUGUST 14 2008

# Amid promise of peace, Georgians live in terror

### LUKE HARDING

The first armoured personnel carrier nudged past the top of the hill. It paused as if getting its bearings, and then set off towards Tbilisi. Behind it, an endless column of Russian military vehicles appeared on a shimmering horizon – trucks, tankers, and a beaten-up Nissan.

The Russian army was on the move. What wasn't clear was where it was going. For the next hour the column continued its sedate progress, past yellow fields and a hazy mountain valley, from Gori towards the Georgian capital, Tbilisi.

Thirty miles from the city, it stopped. A Russian soldier hopped out of his vehicle and began directing traffic. 'We've been told to stay there,' he explained, pointing down a rough dirt track towards the rustic hamlet of Orjosari, just over a mile away.

The soldier said Russia didn't intend to keep going down the main highway connecting Tbilisi to Gori, and the east and west of the country. 'The only reason we've come here is because of a *provokazia* by Mikheil Saakashvili,' he said, accusing Georgia's president of wrongdoing.

In theory the conflict between Russia and Georgia is now over, as European negotiators led by France's president, Nicolas Sarkozy, hammer out a peace deal. In reality, Russia's mighty war machine was trundling insouciantly through Georgia.

Several Russian trucks overshot and missed their turning. One broke down. A soldier got the wheezing vehicle going again. Where was he from? 'Chechnya. We've come here to help,' he said.

For the terrified residents of Gori and surrounding villages, it didn't seem like help. Yesterday morning, as the Russian tanks advanced from their base in South Ossetia they passed through Georgian controlled-villages, telling residents to hang out white flags or be shot.

Behind them, according to people fleeing those villages, came a militia army of Chechen and Ossetian volunteers who had joined up with the regular Russian army. The volunteers embarked on an orgy of looting, burning, murdering and rape, witnesses claimed, adding that the irregulars had carried off young girls and men.

'They killed my neighbour's 15-year-old son. Everyone was fleeing in panic,' Larisa Lazarashvili, 45, said. 'The Russian tanks arrived at our village at 11.20am. We ran away. We left everything – our cattle, our house, and our possessions.'

Achiko Khitarishvili, 39, from Berbuki, added: 'They were killing, burning and stealing. My village isn't in a conflict zone. It's pure Georgia.'

These claims of Russian atrocities were impossible to verify. But the mood of panic was real enough – with villagers fleeing towards Tbilisi by all means possible. One family of eight piled into a tiny white Lada; others fled on tractors.

For much of the day, the Russian troops in Gori were busy destroying Georgia's military infrastructure. Smoke poured from the military supply camp in the village of Uplistsikhe.

Those who fled expressed a feeling of betrayal. They said Russia's president, Dmitry Medvedev, had duped them. 'I believed him when he said there was peace. That's why we stayed in our homes. But it isn't true,' Lamzika Tushmali, 62, said. She added: 'There is no ceasefire.'

At the end of the Russian column, a group of volunteers arrived in a shabby minivan flying a Russian flag. One of them had his face covered with a balaclava; all were heavily armed; their mood was exuberant. What were they doing? 'We've come for a holiday,' one said.

For most of the day there was no sign of the Georgian army. After five days of ferocious bombardment by Russian warplanes, it appears not to exist. With rumours swirling of an imminent Russian attack on Tbilisi, however, Georgia mustered a platoon of 50 soldiers, who took up positions 10 miles down the road from where the Russians appeared to have parked up for the night.

On Georgian radio, meanwhile, military experts were discussing the possibility of a new partisan war against the Russians – suggesting that the government's failure meant that it was time for ordinary Georgians to take the initiative.

It's an idea that may take root. 'I spent two years in the Soviet army. If there is a partisan army I'll be in the first row,' Koba Chkhirodze, 41, said yesterday.

AUGUST 15 2008

# It's WrestleMania: Swede gets his mankini in a knot and throws back bronze medal

MARINA HYDE

My dear, the drama of it all! A podium storm-off, a bronze medal cast in protest to a still sweat-flecked mat, and the suggestion that some Olympic judges may not be the paragons of competent impartiality one might hope. But that's Greco-Roman wrestling:

one turns up expecting to watch various pairs of psychopaths play Twister, and it swiftly descends into accusations of institution-alised corruption and the first medal refusal of the Beijing games.

And so to the Chinese Agricultural University, venue for a sport you are dared to understand the rules of, where yesterday Sweden's 84kg-class wrestler Ara Abrahamian ripped his bronze from his neck the minute it had been hung there, and stalked out, leaving it lying in the centre circle. The medal is now in the hands of wrestling's governing body, Fédération Internationale des Luttes Associées, which is helping the IOC with its inquiries. Abrahamian has declared himself finished with the wrestling game.

A silver medallist in Athens, the Swede had been set on gold, and believes he was denied by erroneous scoring in the semi-final against the Italian Andrea Minguzzi, who went on to take gold. Something to do with those controversial reverse clinch calls we've all been hearing so much about, perhaps, or some unautho-rised mankini-tugging during the bit where one of them gets down on all fours like a dog and the other one has to try and flip him over like a beetle. Your correspondent couldn't be more on top of the rules, naturally, but the Swedish wrestling coach Leo Myllari was good enough to provide the following technical summary of the complaint: 'It's all politics. They're all corrupt.'

'They' being the judges, who had been borne down upon by Abrahamian after he fought back for bronze in the repechage. The Swede – who in compliance with unwritten Greco-Roman wrestling law looks Russian – marched toward them, shouting furiously, before swatting away an official urging restraint and punching a metal barrier. He and his coach are considering taking the whole business to the court of arbitration for sport. Minguzzi, a police-man, declined to open his own investigation, accusing Abrahamian of spoiling the medal ceremony. 'In sports,' he declared tartly, 'it is appropriate to show sportsmanship and accept the results.'

Frankly, it felt wrong to attempt to defuse the tension by saying something along the lines of: 'So come on Andrea – do you want The Undertaker next? Could you just stare menacingly into a TV camera and yelp "I want you, Undertaker, you can't hide from me!"'

And yet, given Abrahamian's obvious gift for theatrics, and that promised career change, perhaps it will be the Swede who will entice the call from WWE overlord Vince McMahon. And those calls do come. The path from Olympic wrestling to the gilded cages and nuanced storylines of the WWE has been trodden, which some might argue does few favours to a sport which can struggle to be taken seriously. Still, why not just celebrate the success stories like Kurt Angle, who won gold in the 100kg freestyle wrestling at Atlanta and went on to become a WWE superstar (WWF, as it was)? He even beat The Rock at No Mercy in 2000, and though The Rock would eventually return from that and take the championship at No Way Out in February of the next year, it should remind us all that there can be second acts in wrestling lives.

One who resisted the call, though, was the two-time Olympic medallist Rulon Gardner, who has been commenting for NBC this week, and underscoring Greco-Roman's reputation as a sport so fiendishly esoteric even former champions get in a muddle about the rules. 'Even Rulon gets confused when he's commentating sometimes,' explained Danny Macy, a wrestling fan who has travelled to Beijing from Oregon. 'They're always changing the rules to bring in new fans, but they're just driving people away.'

Whatever the rules are at the minute, the Beijing announcer rattled through them yesterday in the same high-speed mumble as the advert voiceover which warns that a medication can-cause-dizziness-numbness-palpitations-fevers-and-in-some-cases-death. Given much more airtime were the soft rock classics by Van Halen and Starship, interspersed with constant reminders that 'YOU are at the China Agricultural University!' And here come the big-eared farm boys. That's nonsense, actually: not all the competitors worked their way up from the notoriously competitive cattle-wrestling leagues. Indeed, a 37-year-old Canadian with his own city law firm had wrestled earlier in the day. Unfortunately, Ari Taub lost in his first bout, and will be going home to Calgary, probably to listen to a lot of people think they're the first person to joke that these days, he's just wrestling with his case files. Overall, though – and despite several favourites going out perplexingly early – it was Russia's event, as they gained three golds and a silver, with the Cuban Mijain Lopez triumphing in the 120kg class.

All of which would have wrapped up this Olympiad's Greco-Roman news, had it not been for Abrahamian's protest. Where it will all end now we cannot say. But a bronze medal has hit the mat, and we must officially class this story as developing.

AUGUST 18 2008

# Just how fast will Bolt go when he really puts his mind to it?

## MICHAEL PHILIPS

Usain Bolt broke the world record with such phenomenal brilliance at the Bird's Nest Stadium that he even had time to turn his head and smile at the photo-finish camera. No one at these games could remember a 100m race where they have seen such a picture.

Normally, the snapshot is a blur of profiles crossing the line, but that was before the boy from north-west Jamaica won an argument with his coach, Glen Mills, who let him run the 100m instead of the 400m as a way of training for the 200m. Mills is the guiding force behind this young man, who turns 22 on Thursday.

Mills knows his every move. He spots mistakes that the sprinter himself does not know he has made. He sets the daily schedules, the diet, the preparation, the races. He runs the show. But even he was stumped about how Bolt took the world record. His time of 9.69sec was achieved as he slowed down with 20 metres left.

It is an area of the race that normally is crucial. At last summer's world championships in Osaka, Tyson Gay was just hitting top gear at that point after storming past Asafa Powell to take the title. It is probably why Mills is so perplexed about what his sprinter will do next.

'Who knows how fast he can go?' said Mills. 'Obviously from the race, he can go faster than the 9.69. He was having fun in the last 20m, celebrating and breaking the world record. That's awesome. You can read into it ... he can probably go under 9.60, but I am not good at predictions. I just love to see things unfold.'

Watching the 6ft 5in frame of Bolt unfold at the start of the 100m race is something to behold. He is the tallest man to hold the world record, breaking his own mark of 9.72 with this remarkable run. He ran wearing golden spikes, with the laces on the left foot flapping about in the wind, and he is defying all the other rules of the 100m.

Ask any sprinter and they will declare that the first 30 metres of a race is the most important, to keep the head facing downwards and power into the drive motion to develop speed. Bolt is virtually out of that stage by 20 metres. His long legs eat up so much ground that by halfway there is no chance of catching him. When Powell, his fellow Jamaican whose world record of 9.74 he broke in May, beat him in Stockholm last month, he did so because Bolt had a poor start.

It is the only way. By 50 metres, it becomes a procession, a freak show if nothing else, because this quiet, respectful Jamaican is the most remarkable runner to have tried the distance. As Bolt was conducting his leg-slapping celebratory routine well before the end, his rivals had their cheeks puffed and were straining every sinew.

'I could see him slowing down and I was still pumping to the line,' said Richard Thompson, of Trinidad and Tobago, who was second in 9.89. 'He's a phenomenal athlete and I don't think there's any way anyone could have beaten him.

'A lot of people are of the belief that you have to be short, strong and stocky to be a great sprinter and Usain Bolt has defied that. He has shown that he's a 6ft 5in sprinter and can run well and break world records. He has great starts and it's the beginning of something else.'

Walter Dix, of the US, who was third with 9.91, said: 'I am definitely not going to say he's the epitome of the sprinter, because there's too many different kinds of sprinters that I've admired over the years. But the way he drives and his pattern, the way it goes together, his amazing first 40 metres ... I give it to him.'

If you listen to his father, Wellesley, it is nothing to do with training. It is all about the vegetables grown locally to where Bolt was born. 'It is the Trelawny yam,' said his dad. Not that Bolt was engaging in such a diet. Fast man, fast food. 'I never had breakfast,' said the Jamaican as he recalled the start of his greatest day. 'I woke up around 11, I watched television and then I had some [chicken] nuggets for lunch. I went back to my room, I slept for two hours, I went back for some more nuggets and came to the track.'

For dinner, he had the world record. Bolt is the first Jamaican and only the second sprinter from the Caribbean to win the Olympic title. Hasely Crawford, from Trinidad and Tobago, triumphed at Montreal in 1976 and this run here obliterated the Olympic record of 9.84, a world record when the Canadian

Donovan Bailey won gold in Atlanta 12 years ago. 'I am just pleased I made my country proud,' said Bolt, whose next stop after Beijing will be Zurich on Friday week for the Weltklasse grand prix. Clever man, that promoter. He signed Bolt up before the games. In the space of 9.69sec here on Saturday, his box-office value grew tenfold.

AUGUST 19 2008

# Baffled by Beijing?: Britain's brilliant Olympic weekend has provoked intriguing questions

## STEPHEN MOSS, KIRA COCHRANE AND SIMON BURNTON

*Q: Why are we so good at sailing, rowing and cycling, but useless at track and field?*
The Australians like to joke that we Brits are good at sitting-down sports. Unfortunately, they're right. The 3,000m steeplechase, the pole vault, weightlifting, not a hope. But give us a seat on a bike, in a boat or on a horse and we're potential world-beaters.

Part of the reason may be our innate laziness – the weather in the UK is bad and we spend most of our time indoors watching TV or playing online Scrabble – but the real key is the number of countries that participate in each sport. In three-day eventing, at which we are traditionally strong (and where we usually manage to find a member of the royal family able to compete), there are just 75 competitors. In athletics there are 2,000. To succeed in eventing you would need a fantastic horse, probably worth £250,000 or more, and the means to transport it to Beijing; in athletics you need a strong pair of lungs. Ethiopia, Morocco and Kenya are very good at athletics, but they are absolute crap at three-day eventing.

The key to winning medals at the Olympics is to think small. Don't target sports that everyone can be good at – athletics, boxing, football. Go for technologically complicated and expensive sports that hardly anyone can afford, such as yachting. Or, better still, sports that are both mind-blowingly dull and need expensive facilities, such as cycling and rowing. Britain should press for formula one motor racing to be included in 2012. Then let's see Jamaica find someone to rival Lewis Hamilton and his McLaren. *SM*

*Q: How does Chris Hoy find trousers to fit him when he's not cycling?*
With great difficulty, we presume. Look at those thighs. They're incredible. If ever a pair of legs deserved their own postcode ...

Someone who works at the British Cycling Federation (not in an official capacity) says, gamely: 'I'm sure that buying trousers is a problem that the sprinters have, because they do have very well-developed legs, to put it mildly, and I'm sure some of the slimmer-line styles wouldn't fit them.

'The two guys who really stand out as being likely to have trouser problems are Chris and Jamie Staff. I would imagine Jamie Staff has major trouser problems. They've both got a very, very well-developed muscle mass.' Yes, yes, but what do they wear? 'I see Chris and Jamie around the office, and they wear quite normal jeans and things like that – I just think that they would probably struggle with some of the fashion-type trousers. If you see the legs close to they are incredibly impressive. I'm sure that a tailor would be extremely shocked.' *KC*

*Q: What is yngling and how do you pronounce it?*
Yngling is a type of keelboat, and easily the silliest of the 23 vari-
eties of keelboat currently accredited by the International Sailing
Federation, most of which sound like cast members of the
Gladiators – Tempest, Lightning, Dragon, Melges 24. OK, the last
one doesn't sound like a Gladiator. Its Norwegian inventor
designed it for his son in 1967 and named it Yngling, Norwegian
for young man. This is its second appearance in the Olympics,
where it is raced only by women – the men's keelboat is the more
gladiatorial Star. A spokeswoman from the Norwegian embassy
says the word 'is slightly old-fashioned now' but confirms that it
is pronounced 'erngling', with the initial Y sounding like a
German U with an umlaut. 'It's not really a word we use a lot,' says
a colleague. *SB*

AUGUST 23 2008

# The Great British Games

### RICHARD WILLIAMS

It was the row that could have defined Britain's Beijing experience. When Tom Daley, the 14-year-old face of Team GB, fell out
with his diving partner, Blake Aldridge, on the third day of competition, the spat might have become a symbol of a divided and
underperforming squad. Instead the incident quickly drowned
beneath a wave of success that appears likely to roll on long after
the athletes and their medals are safely home.

For some, the key moment came when Mansfield's own
Rebecca Adlington sliced through the water to win the first

women's gold medal in the swimming pool for Britain since 1968 before firming up her candidacy for the BBC's Sports Personality of the Year award – she is currently the 6-4 favourite – by doing it again. For others it was a graceful young man on the pommel horse competing successfully against the might of China, Russia and the United States: the bronze medal won by Louis Smith may not have glittered like the gold that fell elsewhere upon the British team but it was the first Olympic reward for an individual British male gymnast in a century and a source of astonishment to everyone except those in the know about what goes on at Paul Hall's Huntingdon gym club.

Here were British athletes not feeling sorry for themselves or crumbling under the weight of national expectations and their opponents' aura or slinking home after performances that failed to approach personal bests achieved in less pressurised circumstances. The announcement that the fancied boxer Frankie Gavin had failed to meet his weight limit, made on the eve of the opening ceremony, turned out to be no more of a cue for general panic than the little difficulty between the unsynchronised divers.

It was when Nicole Cooke emerged through the rain and mist, picking off the four riders ahead of her as she powered to the finish of the women's road race in the shadow of the Great Wall of China, that the tide began to flow. A reassuring sight after a slightly uncertain start elsewhere, Britain's first medal of the Games came as a result of years of sheer bloody hard work in a discipline lacking much in the way of glamour.

Cycling has popular appeal now, all right. Cooke showed us the pattern and others followed in her wheeltracks: a group of outstanding individuals supported by capable management. Through the intelligent application of substantial resources, a British team was dominating a sport taken seriously by other big countries. Dave Brailsford, the team director, became the man everybody wanted to talk to, the man with a formula for success that blended ruthlessness with humanity.

The Laoshan velodrome became a place of pilgrimage. Everybody came to watch. Tony Blair, Bernie Ecclestone, the Princess Royal and the Queen of Spain were all there on the night Chris Hoy won his third gold medal of the Games. So was Sir Clive Woodward, who praised the team's attention to detail and noted with pleasure how good they looked in their blue outfits, to be worn in strict daily alternation with red and white, just as he had specified for the whole of Team GB.

Adlington was the next to feed Britain's Olympic flame and suddenly the legacy of the swimming team's much maligned former coach Bill Sweetenham was beginning to flower. Plenty of swimmers had good reason to resent the Australian's bluntness but now it could be appreciated how, during his relatively short time in charge, he banished the culture of the comfort zone and the easy excuse.

At almost every venue, from the Bird's Nest to the Qingdao sailing centre, there was a sense of something spreading. The mentality was changing. Athletes were turning up for their events with a reinforced core of determination. Like failure, success is a fast-acting virus. Across the disciplines they drew confidence from each other's feats. Those who might once have been happy just to turn up were now hunting for medals. Those who might have been content with silver or bronze were risking everything in pursuit of gold. Nobody wanted to be left out.

Four years down the line, London 2012 was already providing extra impetus for veterans keen to stress that they have no intention of being excluded from a party in their own home and younger ones aware that this is the biggest stage they will ever have. The extension of their focus from one games to two seemed to intensify their motivation. Journalists from all over the world were approaching their British counterparts, asking what on earth was going on.

All this put a large question mark against the under-performing runners and jumpers, who started with a couple of high-profile disasters. Reaction to Paula Radcliffe's failure ranged from praise for her decision to complete the marathon with an injured leg to criticism for a self-indulgent readiness to deprive a fully fit athlete of a place in Beijing, and Kelly Sotherton had to settle for fourth place in a Carolina Kluft-less heptathlon despite posting a couple of personal bests. Although Christine Ohuruogu gave us the Kelly Holmes moment, the track and field team showed itself to be the last repository of the old make-do-and-mend mentality, ready for a takeover by someone with the strategic vision, organisational rigour and deeply ingrained man-management skills of Brailsford and his team.

If the Bird's Nest was mostly a low-achievement zone for Britain, the gymnasium was probably the last place most of us would have gone looking for British medals, at least when the men were performing. But as Smith and his team-mate Daniel Keatings, who made it to the final of the all-around competition, went toe to toe with the superpowers, it was possible to see British sport developing in unexpected ways over the next four years.

This was a fortnight in which paradigm-shifting became a British Olympic speciality, and the attitude of some of the silver and bronze winners underlined the change of mood. For every athlete justifiably delighted with bronze, including the hurdler Natasha Danvers and the windsurfer Bryony Shaw, there were others, such as the triple jumper Phillips Idowu and the women's quad sculls crew, deeply unimpressed with the glitter of silver. Yesterday, too, there was one who opted for gold or nothing. Nothing was what Shanaze Reade got but it is not what she takes home.

AUGUST 25 2008

# The torch is passed, from Beijing epic to London bus queue

## MARINA HYDE

At times during this ceremony it felt as if London would have to prise the Olympic torch from China's cold, dead hands. Come to that, at no point in either the opening or the closing ceremonies would it have seemed particularly surprising if the floor of the stadium had opened and a vast superweapon had risen up, reminding all present that the Bird's Nest is basically the Death Star with a better percussion section.

The closing ceremony offered Beijing another chance to make Cirque du Soleil look like a barn dance. Your outgoing Olympic host city last night reiterated that they have more excellent drummers than other countries have people. They paraded more orthodonti-cally screened children. They gave their euphorically shell-shocked audience a flavour of the kind of entertainment that might be on offer were Ernst Blofeld to retain the services of Busby Berkeley.

For a certain little city waiting in the wings, though, the clos-ing ceremony provided something else – a chance to respond to China's deliciously understated 16-day world domination infomer-cial. The IOC manual will tell you that this brief section of the closing ceremony is a handover of the sacred flame to its next custodian. But what these eight minutes really do is allow London to clamber inside the Olympic host simulator and twiddle a few knobs. Let's see what this baby can do!

London's Olympiad began with the IOC's chairman, Jacques Rogge, taking the flag from the mayor of Beijing and handing it to his opposite number, Boris Johnson. This was to symbolise that at least Londoners can vote, even if the choice is a bit duff. Apologies, having examined the notes, it turns out that this is another piece of IOC protocol without which the Olympic games would descend into a semi-lawless world of shameless politicking and corporate entertainment.

Anyway, Boris took the flag; it tangled, he failed to stifle his giggles, and he waved it six times, in a performance the critics are already calling his finest work since describing the opening ceremony substitution of the less photogenic Chinese girl as 'the switcheroo'.

Enter the bus. After the cinematic drama of Beijing's opening and closing ceremonies, the Waldorf and Statlers of Her Majesty's Press had been waiting for London's straight-to-video offering. It wasn't a complete turkey, but it's probably fair to say 2012 has yet to give the world its *House of Flying Daggers*.

Eight minutes isn't long, though, and the double-decker had to navigate its way round the edge of the stadium to a bus-stop queue of snazzily dressed folk with umbrellas. Apparently this was intended to symbolise 'the British preoccupation with the weather', which seemed less than enticing. Come to London! It'll tip down.

There was no room on the bus, which would have made this a cinema verite look at capital life had the bus not begun turning into a hedge, like a particularly benign Transformer. The it tipped out a little girl, chosen by *Blue Peter* viewers (if you can believe that these days).

And then it was on to the main attraction: Leona Lewis, the winner of one of our fine reality television shows, rising out of the bus on a podium, accompanied by none other than Led Zeppelin's Jimmy Page. One look at Page and you could be in no doubt that this was the moment he had been waiting on for his entire career.

Not the moment he performs at an Olympic closing ceremony – but the moment they cut straight to his solo.

Could London do without having to succumb to its fifth 'swinging London' rebrand since 1995? There wasn't time to dwell on it, because everyone knew the bus was saving its most precious cargo till last. And suddenly he was there, and in an unbranded tracksuit, of all things. Behold, world, our Beckham! Look on his works, ye mighty, and despair! This guy the crowd did recognise, and they gave him the biggest reception of Britain's segment by far. One free kick into the crowd later, and London shunted themselves off, umbrellas twirling rather wanly.

China's riposte? A total of 396 performers harnessed on to a vast tower structure, who contorted themselves into ever more complex and precarious formations before 16 vast ribbons were drawn skywards, and a deafening, firework-accompanied anthem began, sending the stadium into screaming rapture. Realistically, the memory of the bus had receded a bit.

Traditionally, though, these eight-minute segments are always dodgy. Yesterday your correspondent watched every one of the eight-minute handovers, all the way back to Seoul. They were all rubbish. So know this: our rubbish can more than hold its own with the rest of the world's rubbish. In fact, after the cloying nonsense of Beijing's 'one world, one dream', perhaps that's just the defiantly British slogan that 2012 needs.

AUGUST 29 2008

# Clinton dazzles while Biden stirs

## JONATHAN FREEDLAND

After two days that had often seemed more about healing their party than winning the November election, day three of the Democratic convention finally did everything it needed to do. To quote a dazzling speech by the undoubted star of the evening's proceedings, Bill Clinton, the Democrats 'hit it out of the park'.

The excitement began early with the formal roll-call vote, when, one by one, state delegations announce which candidate they are backing for the party's presidential nomination. Usually a unanimous, ceremonial event, this time it had been the object of fierce negotiation between the Clinton and Obama camps, as they sought to devise a way that would allow supporters of Hillary Clinton the 'catharsis' or a vote for their candidate without projecting an image of party disunity.

In the end, party managers needn't have worried. About halfway through the alphabetical roll-call – once they had reached N for New York – Hillary Clinton herself swept into the hall, stood with her state delegation and took the microphone. 'In the spirit of unity, with the goal of victory,' she said, 'let's declare together in one voice, right here and right now, that Barack Obama is our candidate and he will be our president.'

The formal vote was abandoned and at 4.47pm Obama became the first African-American to be nominated by a major party – by a thunderous roar of acclamation.

Yes, it was stage-managed but it set the tone perfectly for what was to follow. A series of speeches that finally laid to rest the disunity storyline that had dominated the first half of the convention – and which, at last, took the fight to John McCain.

The most important was the one delivered by the former president. Bill Clinton went further than his wife had the night before in endorsing Obama. He did not just remind diehard Hillaryites of their obligation to back the party leader. He gave a detailed, specific character reference for Obama, spelling out the qualities that make him qualified to be president – from his understanding of the great questions of the age to his 'intelligence and curiosity'.

He also did what Hillary had failed to do, addressing the Republican charge that Obama is too inexperienced for the Oval Office. In perhaps his most important sentence, he declared: 'Barack Obama is ready to be president of the United States.'

He even seemed to anoint the young senator as his political heir, noting that back in 1992, 'the Republicans said I was too young and too inexperienced to be commander-in-chief. Sound familiar?'

No less valuably, Clinton also framed the election ahead, saying the next president would have to rebuild prosperity at home and restore America's standing in the world, both badly damaged by the Bush years. In both those areas Obama was in the right, while McCain, for all his maverick stances on some issues, was still bound up with the 'extreme philosophy' of Bush Republicanism.

It was an almost impossibly hard act to follow for the official star of the evening, the vice-presidential nominee, Joe Biden. But he delivered a stirring performance, too, strong on emotion as he described his humble beginnings, clearly seeking to connect with the many Americans experiencing economic anxiety. He also tore into his fellow Senate veteran John McCain, even daring to challenge the relevance of his much-vaunted military record. 'These times require more than a good soldier; they require a wise leader,' he said.

Finally, Obama himself – absent from the convention until that moment – appeared on stage, the climax of a day in which, at last, his party had stopped looking inward and had started looked forward, towards November 4.

AUGUST 30 2008

# Barack Obama: American promise

## LEADER

In a 24-hour rolling news cycle nothing lasts for long. Yesterday afternoon there was an almost audible screeching of gears as the blogocracy abandoned its post-Obama analysis mid-sentence and 'Sarah Palin' became the hottest search terms on Google. John McCain's choice of the obscure Alaskan governor as running mate caused enough shock and awe to wash the Denver convention off the airwaves. Which is a shame. For, in years to come – and especially if he becomes the first black president of the United States – the 2008 Democratic convention will rightly be remembered as Barack Obama's moment in history and for the climactic political theatre of his open-air acceptance speech on Thursday evening. What may not be so often recalled was the sometimes ruthless hard politics that went into Obama's success in Denver this week. It helped turn a convention that threatened up to the last minute to be unmanageable into a successful launchpad for the Democratic assault on the White House on November 4.

First things, however, must be said first. The Democrats made bold, optimistic and wonderful history in Denver this week. No one with any sense of either America's past or of the long march for human justice can fail to be inspired by the sight of an American political party nominating a black man to lead a country with such a long, shameful and bloody history of racial division. That it should happen on the anniversary of the great speech in which Martin Luther King dreamed of the day in which his children would be judged, not by the colour of their skin, but by the content of their character, was magnificently fitting. Whether the majority of American voters in enough states will have enough confidence in Obama's campaign for change to elect him as their president remains to be seen. But it is the political question of the next 67 days.

Mr Obama will not get elected just because he is an orator. His speech in Denver marked a recognition that elections are won on the basis of policy pledges and by framing the contest in a clear and sometimes confrontational way. In his acceptance speech, which will have been the first time that many voters have listened to him, Mr Obama framed the election as a classic contest between aspiration – the 'American promise' – and fear. He offered a substantial menu of domestic spending promises on health, education and the environment, along with individual and small business tax cuts, though there was less detail about how he will pay for them. And he went on the offensive against Mr McCain on foreign and security policy, seeking to tie his opponent to the Bush years and hinting that he will make Mr McCain's age and temperament into campaign issues.

All this shows that Mr Obama is a clear-eyed, not a dewy-eyed, campaigner. He managed the potentially divisive convention with great firmness, recognising that the supporters of Hillary Clinton must have their moments but never allowing them to indulge themselves. The Clintons, especially Bill Clinton, responded impeccably. But it was all done on Mr Obama's unflinching terms, and he was notably less conciliatory to his opponents in his speech than they were to him in theirs.

Now, though, another fight begins, this time against opponents who will stop at nothing to exploit his weaknesses, which exist. Sarah Palin is a daring choice by McCain. She is a young, fresh, outside-the-Beltway conservative with great appeal to the Republican grassroots. She is also massively inexperienced, at a stroke neutralising the very same charge against Obama. How, with an elderly potential president, Americans will judge governor Palin on the heartbeat test may prove critical in the months ahead. The times call for fresh vision and toughness. Mr Obama will need plenty of both if his dream is to become the reality for which we hope.

AUGUST 30 2008

# Storm warning

## DECCA AITKENHEAD

When Tony Blair's first cabinet met in 1997, anyone trying to guess which faces would still be there a decade later would probably not have picked out Alistair Darling's. Back then, the chief secretary to the treasury already felt like part of the political furniture. But for a veteran, he seemed a strangely anonymous figure – opaque to the point of unknown.

A blaze of glitzier New Labour stars have since fallen, yet Darling survived, accumulating five ministerial posts on a stainless ascent to the exchequer last year. His career had been distinguished by an almost freakish absence of failure. He has never lost an election, he joined the front bench after just 12 months in parliament, and 20 years later he has never left. Only two other members of that first cabinet, Gordon Brown and Jack Straw, are still in government with Darling today.

Yet he remains something of an enigma. What is the occupant of Number 11 really like? Few outside his inner circle would claim to know. 'For most of my political life,' Darling admits, 'I've kept out of doing this kind of interview. You have to be quite careful – unless you're one of those people who's happy to give everything of themselves. And I, for one, am not.'

In sunnier economic times, a chancellor might have been allowed the luxury of privacy. But people want to know if he is the man who can steer us out of trouble. After a stormy year of 10p tax rows, lost disks, the collapse of the housing market, rising prices and recession fears, rumours of his demotion are rumbling through Westminster. Darling gives no impression of believing them. But the mood is so febrile, it's even possible he won't be chancellor by the time this interview appears.

The last time we met, on a *Question Time* panel 10 years ago, he had been rigid with nerves – a rod of anxiety in a suit – so I was wondering how we'd get through two days together on a remote Scottish island. The croft on Lewis in the Outer Hebrides where we're heading belongs to Darling, his mother and his sisters, and has been a family retreat all his life. It is the place where, he says, he is happiest. When he greets us at the gate looking tanned and rumpled, a bowl of homemade soup in one hand, the other pointing to eagles overhead, I scarcely recognise him.

We are welcomed like old friends by his wife, Maggie, a gregarious Scottish former journalist who cooks and makes tea and supper while Darling lights a fire. His dry, deadpan humour lends itself to his ironic take on the grumpy old man, which he plays with gruff good nature. Wendy Alexander, the former Scottish Labour leader, is 'not likable at all'; Cherie Blair's memoirs were 'awful', and as for the Dome – 'well, thank God I didn't have to go there on Millennium night'. He can't abide this modern practice of kissing – people lurching at each other's faces – 'when they've never even met!'

He reminds me of childhood friends' fathers who seemed fearsome until we got old enough to realise they were being funny. His press adviser, Catherine, another Scottish former journalist, teases him about his limited wardrobe and reluctance to spend money. He doesn't like having his picture taken either, grumbling, 'It's like being at a wedding' – but allows the photographer to take all the time he wants without once objecting.

On the beach, the photographer asks him to look out to sea. He obediently gazes west across the Atlantic, murmuring, 'I am looking at the sub-prime market.' Even when he gets soaked by a wave on the beach, he doesn't complain. 'Oh no, you didn't have your collar all scruffed up like that for the pictures, did you?' Maggie exclaims when we get back to the house. 'But that's just what I look like,' he says.

'Now Alistair,' Catherine tells him firmly when eventually we sit down for the interview, 'tell her everything. Make sure you tell her everything.'

When his old friend handed over the keys to Number 11, Darling didn't expect the job to be easy. 'Becoming chancellor is completely different from any other appointment. Completely different. Even when times are easy, it's important, because you're dealing with money, and money affects how everything works. When times are far from easy, it's even more difficult. And we knew the economy was going to slow down.' But he hadn't the faintest inkling of the financial crisis about to unfold before him. 'No, no one did. No one had any idea.'

He can clearly recall the day last summer when alarm bells first began to sound. The chancellor was on holiday with his wife and their two teenage children in Majorca. 'I remember I picked up the *FT* in the supermarket, as you do, and it had the European central bank starting to put money into the economy. I phoned the office to ask why they were doing quite so much. It didn't surprise me that money was going in – there was concern going around – but it was the sheer scale of it. I said, what about our institutions? This was when Northern Rock started to figure.'

When news broke of the first run on a British bank in more than a century, Darling was back in Edinburgh. 'I received a phone call and went straight down to London. From where I never returned. That was the last time I saw Edinburgh.'

Even then, the gravity of the credit crunch was still not fully clear. 'No one knew how serious it was yet.' Then he received the second catastrophic phone call of last summer, from his private secretary – and this time the head of Her Majesty's Revenue & Customs was also on the line, with news of a major blunder.

'I just thought,' Darling says, 'this is a disaster. This is terrible. I said, We have to search the place from top to bottom. One of them said, We'll start Monday. I said, No, we start today. I phoned Gordon up. I said, We appear to have lost two disks containing the personal details of just about every family in the country. We knew it was bad.' What did Brown say? 'He said it was bad.'

Darling's life, in his wife's words, has been 'a crisis a week' ever since. The economic times we are facing 'are arguably the worst they've been in 60 years', he says bluntly. 'And I think it's going to be more profound and long-lasting than people thought.'

In Edinburgh, Darling used to enjoy what would pass in Westminster for a healthy hinterland. He loves Leonard Cohen, and lists *Midnight Express*, *Annie Hall* and *Local Hero* as his favourite films. 'There's got to be a life outside politics. It was nice to go to the pictures and go for a nice meal afterwards. One of the great pleasures was getting to Edinburgh and going out for a meal with friends who don't do politics.'

But he has not been to the cinema in more than a year. His wife has moved down to Downing Street, and when they went for a meal with another couple recently, and tried to order a second bottle of wine, 'the waiter came over and said "too much wine". In a loud voice. So we stuck to the one bottle for the entire meal.' Another meal out with his press adviser was reported in the *News of the World* as a decadent affront to struggling families. 'It's just the way things are,' he says, matter-of-factly. 'It's understandable.'

I wonder what it must be like for someone whose career had been hitherto blameless to find himself publicly upbraided by wine waiters. 'Well, I think most people understand perfectly well that most of the problems they face are international. However, that doesn't help sell their house. I was at a filling station recently, and a chap said, "I know it's to do with oil prices – but what are you going to do about it?" People think, Well, surely you can do something, you are responsible – so of course it reflects on me.'

Is it painful to be blamed so personally?

'No, there's nothing more pathetic than people feeling sorry for themselves. So you get on with it, you just have to deal with it. There's lots of people who'd like to do my job. And no doubt,' he adds, half under his breath, 'actively trying to do it.'

Ministers are seldom willing to discuss their own job prospects, so when I raise the rumours of an imminent reshuffle, I expect a formula along the lines of 'that's up to the prime minister'. But Darling can be surprisingly direct, and shakes his head impatiently.

'Frankly, if you had a reshuffle just now, I think the public would say, Who are they anyway? You name me a reshuffle that ever made a difference to a government, actually.' Brown, he points out, had to make ministerial changes in January, follow-ing Peter Hain's resignation. 'And you can't be chopping and changing people that often. I mean, undoubtedly at some stage before the end of the parliament he will want to do a reshuffle, but I'm not expecting one imminently. I do not think there will be a reshuffle.'

Does he expect Labour to hang on to its seat at the forthcoming byelection? 'Well, we'll give it our best shot. But we've got our work cut out. This coming 12 months will be the most difficult 12 months the Labour party has had in a generation, quite frankly. Both the general economic situation, and in terms of the politics. In the space of 10 months we've gone from a position where people generally felt we were doing OK to where we're certainly not doing OK. We've got to rediscover that zeal which won three elections, and that is a huge problem for us at the moment. People are pissed off with us.

'We really have to make our minds up; are we ready to try and persuade this country to support us for another term? Because the next 12 months are critical. It's still there to play for. But we've got a hell of a lot to do. We patently have not been able to get across what we are for, and what we are about.'

Can Brown communicate it? 'Yes, I do think he can. I do think he will.' Then why hasn't he? 'Er, well,' Darling falters. 'Well, it's always difficult, you know. You can always say, what could you have done better, and all the rest of it. But Gordon, in September, up to party conference, has got the opportunity to do that. And he will do that. It's absolutely imperative.'

Darling is one of Brown's closest and oldest political friends. When his daughter phones during dinner, she is babysitting for the prime minister; his wife is friends with Sarah Brown. The orchestra of criticism has been upsetting – 'We're grown-ups, but no one likes to read nasty things about their friends' – and he flatly refuses to blame Brown for anything. There will not, he insists, be a leadership challenge.

For Brown to repay his friend's loyalty by sacking him would be brutal – even Shakespearean. But then, politics can be like that. Darling is one of the most experienced politicians in the country. And yet, more than once, I find myself wondering how much of a political animal he really is.

Darling was born in 1953, the eldest of four in a middle-class family that was neither tribal, nor intellectual, nor even Labour. Both his grandfathers had been Liberals, his great-uncle a Tory MP in Edinburgh, and his father, a civil engineer, voted Conservative.

'We were an ordinary family. We talked about events, but we didn't sit around the table having intense discussions about what Marx thought.' Not like the Milibands, then? 'No,' he agrees quickly. 'Very different people. But we had a very clear sense of what was right and what was wrong. My father always thought Conservatism was about helping people less fortunate than you. My mother was very clear about what you did and didn't do, she was very clear about saying thank you and being courteous.'

He was educated at Loretto, a rather traditional boarding school in Scotland. There was no teenage radicalism, and he would have been astonished, he says, if he'd known his future lay in poli-tics. Studying law at Aberdeen, he stood for election in the student union, but not for a party. 'I was just quite interested in getting things done.' His manifesto favoured 'strictly bread-and-butter issues, things like food prices in the student refectory'. When he joined the Labour party in 1977, he never expected to be more than a member. 'I was enjoying becoming a lawyer.' He'd simply realised, he explains, that 'if you want to make any changes, there's only one way you can do it, and that's by getting into a position where you can influence things. And the obvious thing to do seemed to be to join a party.' Why Labour?

'Just ... I suppose, overall, I thought the Tories were unfair. They were only for one side, and not for everyone. The Labour party just seemed to reflect my outlook on life – you know, that we were better working together – fairness, helping everyone to get on, rather than just a few. The Labour government in 1977 was in a terrible mess, and I was getting fed up looking at all these things on the television, and thinking, God, surely we can do better than that. I wanted to do things. But I was never really interested in the theory of achieving things, just the practicality of doing things.'

One might say this has been Darling's great strength. The pragmatic clarity made him a highly effective minister, and probably explains why he was one of the few to maintain close relations with both Brown and Blair throughout their internecine rivalry. But it may well also be his weakness – for at times he seems almost too straightforward, even high-minded, for the low cunning of political warfare.

Earlier this month, on the *Today* programme, the chancellor chose not to deny a newspaper report of a proposal under consideration for a holiday for stamp duty. Property sales promptly seized up as buyers held off to wait for his decision, and furious estate agents accused him of destroying what was left of the market. 'The news story didn't come from us,' he protests, 'we weren't the ones who leaked it. It had already appeared in other newspapers before, and at any other time I would just have ignored it. But understandably, I was asked about it.' The option of lying and denying it didn't seem to occur to him – but then nor, he admits, had the consequences for the property market of his words.

If that was a schoolboy error, you might have thought Darling would want to put it right as quickly as he could, by issuing a definitive statement. 'When I've got something to say about housing,' he retorts stiffly, 'then I need to deal with a whole range of things.' If I was trying to sell my house right now, I would wish he'd hurry up. 'Yes, all right, but if you're going to announce anything in the housing market, you don't do it in the middle of

August. It's just a silly time to do it.' Does he feel no sense of urgency? 'I'll do it when I'm ready to do it.'

When voters are complaining that Labour seems indifferent to their problems, such an own goal seems mystifying. Other ministers are currently exhorting Labour to 'show' the voters it cares – and Darling rightly scoffs at this line. 'I get very exasperated when people say we need to show people we are concerned. It's just the wrong approach. I think there's not a man, woman or child in this country who doesn't understand the problems people are facing. People are not particularly interested in public demonstrations of your 'understanding'. You just need to get on with it.' Why he doesn't apply his own advice to stamp duty, and get on with it, is a mystery.

It is also a gift to the opposition. George Osborne has grown adept at pouncing on such opportunities – yet when I ask Darling why his shadow would make a bad chancellor, he pauses before replying, 'I wouldn't personalise it. My criticism is not of him as an individual.' But, I exclaim, Osborne is after your job! And he doesn't seem to mind personalising the fight.

'Why I think the Tories are bad is different from why I think Osborne would be a bad chancellor,' Darling goes on. 'I think my criticisms are of the Tory party rather than him.' But his criticisms are oddly contradictory, for one minute he says, 'the Tories haven't really changed. They may have packaged things differently, but fundamentally I think they are still very much focused on helping a few people, and not very bothered about most people.' But then he says,: 'There are times when I listen to Cameron and I'm not sure what he does believe in. I don't say that in any nasty sense. I just don't have any sense of what, if he was prime minister, he would want to do.'

When you are trailing by more than 20 points in the polls, it's probably time to start fighting dirty. Yet Darling continues, 'I think you're right, George Osborne is a politician, and he's made an enormous amount of promises, but it's not clear how he would pay for them. Osborne knows what he's doing in terms of playing the political field. That's why I say he's a very good politician, because he takes his moment. But what's his long-term view of where the country needs to go? What is his vision for the future? What sort of country does he see Britain becoming in the next 20 to 30 years? I just don't know.'

In the current climate, I'm not sure voters give a stuff about abstract visions for a generation away. But Darling does share most people's daily concerns – probably more than Osborne, the son of a titled millionaire, ever could. He does the family shopping in Tesco, and when I test him on the price of groceries he is spot-on. 'Half a dozen eggs? That would be £1.20. I know they have cheaper ones, I saw them. But the ones my wife specifically wanted were £1.20.'

If Darling lacks the pugnacity of a devious old Labour bruiser, he also struggles to compensate for it with a new Labour instinct for spin. 'Throughout my life,' he agrees, 'I much prefer to be doing things than shouting about them.' Of course, he adds, 'part of politics is you do need to shout. Politics is the art of communication. If you can't communicate, then it doesn't matter if you're truly brilliant as a technocrat. There are lots of people who are very good, but they just can't communicate it.' He doesn't say so, but I suspect this is a lesson he has learned most forcibly since Brown took charge.

What did he think, I ask, when he saw the photographs of the Browns and the Camerons on their holidays. 'Well, it was the same reaction I used to have with the Blairs – thank God I don't have to do that.' Didn't he notice any presentational issues?

'Well, they're just different people.' he says. 'I mean, it was probably an accurate representation of both of them. I didn't ...

Honestly, I just couldn't get excited about those pictures one way or the other. I mean, of course they're both posed. Cameron was as posed as they come!' But the trick, I suggest, is appearing relaxed even when posing. 'Well, to me it looked posed,' he retorts. 'But I'm not going to be hypocritical about it when I've spent 15 minutes on a beach being photographed in a very unnatural posture.'

Maybe, he reflects, 'that's why I'm not a great politician. You know, I'm not very good at looking at pictures and subjecting them to the equivalent of textual analysis.'

The funny thing is, on paper, Darling should be the perfect politician. He is exactly what the public always says it wants: decent, straightforward, unostentatious. The ideological intensity of Brown unnerves voters, and they didn't trust Blair's showmanship – but if Darling has vanity it seems invested entirely in doing the job well. He doesn't call himself a socialist – 'There's nothing wrong with the term, it's just not one I use' – and feels uncomfortable with political labels. Class envy is a mystery to him; he sees no point in raising taxes for the super rich, because, he says, it wouldn't raise much revenue. 'I'm not offended if someone earns large sums of money. Is it fair or not? It's just a fact of life.' Asked to define his politics, he offers, 'Pragmatic. I passionately believe in living in a fair country, and treating people properly, with proper respect and fairness.' Until the past year, Darling has never really had to fight. 'For 10 years,' he acknowledges, 'as a minister, by and large I had a charmed life. I was sorting out problems rather than being landed with them.' For the first time he is now facing an effective opposition – and the possibility of failure. The intriguing question will be whether he can survive, without the old political fuel of ideology or ego to drive him.

SEPTEMBER 3 2008

# This may help Brown.
# It will not help home buyers

## LARRY ELLIOTT

Last week, the Nationwide Building Society released its monthly snapshot of the housing market. The lender said that at the end of July the average price of a home in the UK stood at £169,316. By the end of August, it had fallen to £164,654 – a drop of £4,662.

Yesterday, Alistair Darling announced that there would be a 12-month holiday on the payment of the 1 per cent stamp duty on all property sales up to £175,000, a maximum saving of £1,750.

Treasury sources insisted that the measure was not aimed at shoring up a collapsing property market, which is just as well, as any potential homebuyer equipped with basic numeracy – or even a calculator – can see that the potential saving from waiting until the market has bottomed out will swamp any benefit from the non-payment of stamp duty. Darling's argument is that the stamp duty announcement is aimed at helping people who have no choice but to move and are having trouble getting on the housing ladder. If that is the case, the package will have a worthwhile but tiny impact. The same applies to the sensible measures designed to limit repossessions. But as a mechanism for putting air back into a deflating property bubble, the package is a complete dud.

Ed Stansfield, property economist at Capital Economics, said that despite the government's measures he saw no imminent end to the housing correction: 'Our view is that we will not see a recovery in the housing market until prices have fallen back to a level which is widely perceived to represent fair value. Only then will lenders, homebuyers and housebuilders be able to act with confidence, allowing transactions to recover and prices to stabilise.'

The Treasury knows from experience that Stansfield is right. The stamp duty holiday of the early 1990s only created a bunching effect as the deadline for the end of the holiday neared, followed by weaker activity thereafter.

What's more, the government's spin that the £600m earmarked for non-payment of stamp duty over the next 12 months is designed to meet 'current challenges in the housing market' is a joke. Even after the 70 per cent drop in demand for home loans over the past year, there were 33,000 new mortgages granted in July, worth a total of £4.3bn. As Darling knows full well, £600m – which is all the government can afford – is chickenfeed when set against the overall size of the property market.'

Diana Choyleva, an economist with Lombard Street Research, said: 'Little room for fiscal manoeuvre has limited the support the state can offer. But this is the good news. Part of the solution to the UK's excess debt problem is a fall in house prices. The sooner the housing market adjustment takes place the faster the economy will emerge from its slump. The state should not let off the hook either the irresponsible households or the reckless banks.'

Many Treasury economists would privately agree with this assessment. The best possible assistance for first-time buyers would be a fall in house prices to a level where those trying to get on the ladder can do so without incurring excessive amounts of debt.

This package, however, will not be judged in Whitehall by whether it puts a floor under the property market, which it will not. It will be judged against its primary purpose – providing Gordon Brown with breathing space while he fights for his political life.

SEPTEMBER 6 2008

# Who came out on top in the convention battle?

## MICHAEL TOMASKY

So, they're over. Party conventions may look fun on television, and sometimes they are, but it's nice to get home. Which party won the battle of the conventions? The scoring system is simple.

Conventions last four nights (by design at least, but more on this below). Each party gets one point for a successful night, half a point for a reasonably successful night, and a zero for a dud. So let's have a look.

*Democrats, night one:* The marquee speakers here were Ted Kennedy, the great liberal lion making what, God willing, was not his final public appearance in the wake of his cancer diagnosis, and Michelle Obama, the wife of the candidate. Kennedy's appearance was deeply moving for the delegates, and Michelle's talk was poised and folksy. On the downside, no theme was established. Half a point.

*Republicans, night one:* There was no night one. Hurricane Gustav intervened. Some wanted the GOP to forge ahead anyway, but US cable networks were wall-to-wall with hurricane footage and interviews, so it just would have looked strange. Acts of God aren't covered by insurance policies, so as we say in America, them's the breaks. No points.

*Democrats, night two:* Hillary Clinton was the featured player here. She delivered what most of the experts on television deemed a great speech but what I thought was merely a good one. Pro-Hillary and anti-Obama sentiment lingered in Denver into the next day. She did her job, but I say just half a point.

*Republicans, night two:* Fred Thompson and Joe Lieberman were the speakers. It was conspicuous that an entire party with thousands of elected officials across America could find, to feature on this important night, only a man who is now out of work both as an actor and a politician (he ran a dreadful presidential campaign) and a former Democrat whose speeches are well known to be the next best thing to Mogadon. I've been to bingo games that were more exciting. Still, it's possible that Lieberman reached some independents, so half a point.

*Democrats, night three:* Here we had Bill Clinton and Joe Biden. The former president gave one of the finest speeches I've ever heard him give. The general consensus was that he did not only what was demanded – show delegates and viewers that he was fully behind the candidates – but went well beyond the bare minimum.

Biden could have blown his chance in the spotlight – he has a well-earned talky reputation – but was energetic and mostly on target. One point.

*Republicans, night three:* Finally, the GOP woke up. Rudy Giuliani did what he does best – attack the infidels, foreign and domestic – and then Sarah Palin delivered her zingerfest.

Early signs were that her bombast was not a hit with independent voters, but she certainly electrified the hall. One point.

*Democrats, night four:* Obama's Invesco Field speech before 84,000 avoided all the cult-of-personality pitfalls the pundits warned against. And he managed to be specific and clear on his plans.

For me, 'we need a president who puts Barney Smith before Smith Barney' remains the best single line from either convention. One point.

*Republicans, night four:* Sigh. John McCain. His speech was dreadful. I mean, irresponsibly bad. Rhetorical malpractice, given the prominence of the forum and the opportunity it presented. But hey, he's the nominee. Give him half a point for getting through it without making any mistakes.

Total: Democrats 3, Republicans 2.

We can't really know until the middle of next week, when polls will appear telling us whether the GOP got its bounce. But I think most observers would agree that the Democrats won this skirmish. However, conventions are just the end of the middle phase. They still have many promises to keep, and miles to go before they sleep.

SEPTEMBER 6 2008

# Unseating Gordon Brown
# may be Labour's last chance

**POLLY TOYNBEE**

The smell of death around this government is so overpowering it seems to have anaesthetised them all. One bungle follows another and yet those about to die sit silently by. So is that it – the great September relaunch, the great economic recovery plan?

The problem is not lack of substance but absurdly grandiose expectations, raised mostly by briefings from No10 suggesting that there were magic answers. The ineptitude of Brown's Downing Street worsens by the week. The shrinking band of those he trusts are now his old rottweilers, who shred what's left of their leader's reputation. This week when they mauled Alistair Darling for telling an obvious truth (his actual words much exaggerated in the reporting), they attacked one of Brown's few truly loyal friends and a decent man. This is the sign of an inner cabal out of control.

Brown apparently denies he orders these attacks on others, but fails to sack those who carry them out.

The latest disaster is Downing Street's mishandling of a windfall tax on energy companies. The idea was allowed to run until the last moment, suggesting £1bn of unearned profits might be taken to ease the pain of the poorest. Downing Street started the talk of issuing energy vouchers to the needy, and only days ago denied the idea was dead. When Compass, the left-of-centre pressure group, gathered a great popular petition in support of it, endorsed by 122 MPs, several parliamentary private secretaries and, privately, many ministers, it looked like pushing at an open door. After all, Brown himself was the architect of that £5bn windfall on the utilities.

So it was a needless shock when the prime minister told the Scottish CBI that windfalls were 'short-term gimmicks and giveaways'. Instead, the energy companies will next week spend a lot less than that £1bn on lagging lofts and insulating windows. Of course energy saving is essential – but it will get few of the vulnerable through this winter. As talks continue, the government now negotiates like a highwayman without a gun. What's to negotiate?

It was not the left, but the Conservative-run Local Government Association that exposed the big six energy companies for giving shareholders a 20 per cent dividend increase. Now there will be a stormy Labour conference as Compass and the unions prepare an emergency motion. The winter death figures will be watched by Brown's enemies: fairly or not, any extra old-and-cold deaths will be laid at his door.

All this was so avoidable. In both the housing and fuel plans, no clear principle was spelled out. Brown should have said the government will not, and cannot, stop house prices falling. The stamp duty holiday is a bad mistake – all too characteristic of the prime minister. It's an expensive way to entice first-time buyers into negative equity, as all predictions are of steeper falls in house price. That money – maybe £600m – would be much better spent letting councils buy homes to keep a roof over the heads of families whose own homes have been repossessed – and buying cheap properties for social housing.

But again, Brown yearns for that 'tax cut' headline. Again he cuts a good tax on property as he did in income tax, while letting unfair purchase taxes hit the poorest hardest. A windfall tax was a chance not only to relieve the hard-pressed, but to signal some recompense for a decade of wealth trickling upwards.

Charles Clarke's call for Brown's head was met by resounding silence this week, making it look less a clarion call than a lonely trumpeting of the Last Post. But it may come to be seen as the opening assassination salvo. The danger is it will be a painfully slow-motion stabbing, too late to make much difference.

A cabinet of minnows and spineless backbenchers include many – perhaps most – who want Brown gone, but lack the nerve to act. They wait for someone else, for Brown to walk away or for a proverbial bus to save them from the task. First they put it off in July: wait until after the summer, many said. Now it's wait until the party conference – as if that 'speech of a lifetime' could make a scrap of difference at this stage. Then it will be 'Don't rock the boat before the Glenrothes byelection'. Will that deliver the electric shock to end the inertia that neither Crewe nor Glasgow East could? Or will they put it off until after Christmas, or catastrophic May elections? Some say a recession is no time for internal wrangling; but the longer they leave it, the longer the leadership question hangs over them. It will not go away.

Soon Cameron's lead will be gold-plated, his succession virtually inevitable. Another year effectively unchallenged by Labour, his contradictions and vacuities unridiculed and unexposed, will gift him an almost unopposed victory. Already at conferences the lobby groups and voluntary organisations hang on every word of shadow ministers, yawning through mere ministers on their way out. Already power, money, glamour, foreign interest and attention flock to Cameron in a political tide whose undertow knocks Labour off its feet with every wave.

Stoking up fear of some fictitious Blairite coup is the Brown camp's trump card. They spook the unions with warnings that privatisers, tax-cutters and wealth-worshippers will take over if Brown is unseated. Personal rivalries – as between David Miliband and Ed Balls – are falsely dressed up as second-generation Brown/ Blair battles. But this is all costume drama, wearing the political clothes of yesterday. The imaginary Blair/Brown ideological distinction has now been exposed as the sham it always was. Brown used to let it be known he opposed university fees, war, ID cards, Trident, foundation hospitals and a host of other things he now supports. The 10p tax band abolition to bribe the better off was a wickedness entirely of his own devising. Letting rip the disastrous house price boom was him, as was letting top earnings soar unchecked while reckless banks had 'light-touch regulation' and public sector workers were pinned to below-inflation pay. The sad truth is that he opposed Blair, not Blair policies.

So why would unions save his skin now? As the TUC gathers this weekend, they should consider that whoever was to stand as leader, they could win an election in the Labour party only with a radical new agenda. Unseating a prime minister is very high risk – but a dying party should be ready to take dangerous medicine if that's the last chance left.

SEPTEMBER 8 2008

# Muddy end to season in which some thrived but others went to the wall

PAUL LEWIS

Thirty thousand revellers brought Britain's music festival season to a fitting end yesterday, stomping through a carpet of mud on the Isle of Wight in fancy dress. Exhibiting a loose interpretation of the theme '30,000 freaks under the sea', an assortment of pirates, sharks, nurses, rubber dinghies, jellyfish, Teletubbies and giant eggs jiggled until the early hours at Bestival, the last big outdoor festival of the summer.

'It's the most fun you can have, anywhere, at any point,' said Yousef Zaher, 33, a trout in a waistcoat. 'Mud makes it harder to get around but it makes people disarmed. It's like Disneyland for adults.'

Wearing just a nappy stuffed with a rabbit, Johnny Stevens, 25, agreed. 'Fancy dress allows people to be themselves,' he said, giving a thumbs up.

The determination to have fun persisted despite downpours and sludge. 'I'm just going to not sleep,' said teacup lookalike Gemma Wilkins, 19, after a pond appeared in her tent. 'I've got the rest of the year for that.'

Organisers scrambled to lay sheeting around stages and straw on walkways. But most visitors treated the weather as just a nuisance. 'This is what they're all about, festivals,' said Ellie Williams, 19, a seaweed monster. 'This is the last party of the summer, and I'm having it.'

Within hours of the festival starting, some were disappointed and trickled out. 'Dancing in the rain just isn't fun, is it?' said Charles Ridings, 24.

The mixed verdict is appropriate for a festival season that has seen triumph and catastrophe in equal measure. There were a record 450 festivals, with pundits predicting at the start that the new independent 'boutique' events would overtake the traditional festivals. In the end it was the smaller events that struggled in the economic downturn.

'Overall, for the big festivals it has been a very successful year,' said Vince Power, founder of the festival promoter Mean Fiddler, now Festival Republic. 'Everyone with a piece of land had decided they wanted to do a festival this year. These people may have beautiful sites but the music is the main ingredient for any festival.'

Bestival, a winner, sold out in record time with a 'heritage' lineup including My Bloody Valentine, Gary Numan, Sugar Hill Gang, Human League, Amy Winehouse and Grace Jones.

Glastonbury had to sell tickets on the high street to sell out its 135,000 places but, basking in sunshine and a headline performance from the rapper Jay-Z that conquered rock traditionalists' scepticism, in the end it was judged to have been the best event in recent years.

Reading and Leeds, V Festival and T in the Park sold out, helped by big-name acts such as Metallica, Arctic Monkeys, REM, the Verve and Kaiser Chiefs.

By contrast, dozens of lesser-known events were cancelled after poor ticket sales. One of the first to go, in April, was Wax: On Live, in Leeds, whose organiser blamed the 'credit crunch that has the UK in the grip of an economic stranglehold'. Then Wild in the Country, at Knebworth, Hertfordshire, was abandoned, along with Blissfields in Hampshire. Sunrise Festival, in Yeovil was called off after heavy rain, and the plug was pulled on the Isle of Skye Music festival. Tennents Vital, in Belfast, also went to the wall.

By this weekend 38 British music festivals had cancelled, according to efestivals.com. Many more were forced to downsize and close camping grounds.

Even Power, the 'Godfather of Gigs', felt the pinch, failing to sell out his comedy-based event at The Hop Farm, in Kent.

Bestival's founder, Robert Gorham – the radio DJ Rob da Bank – said: 'It's been the most soap opera-like year for festivals. I feel sorry for people who had to pull their events, but it's really a volatile game.' In June, as many festival organisers complained that corporate promoters had got a stranglehold on the market, Gorham set up the Association of Independent Festivals, a non-profit trade body to support smaller events.

The view at Bestival yesterday was that the spirit of small, independent festivals should be kept alive. 'You've got to love these kinds of parties,' said Greg Bell, 30, a fork. 'I can't wait for next year.'